AF608229

THE MARRIAGE CONTRACT AND THE PROCREATION OF OFFSPRING

THE CATHOLIC UNIVERSITY OF AMERICA
CANON LAW STUDIES
No. 226

THE MARRIAGE CONTRACT AND THE PROCREATION OF OFFSPRING

By

REV. N. ORVILLE GRIESE, S.T.D., J.C.L.
Priest of the Diocese of Green Bay

A DISSERTATION

Submitted to the Faculty of the School of Canon Law of the Catholic University of America in Partial Fulfillment of the Requirements for the Degree of Doctor of Canon Law

THE CATHOLIC UNIVERSITY OF AMERICA PRESS
WASHINGTON, D. C.
1946

Nihil Obstat:

JOANNIS ROGG SCHMIDT, A.B., J.C.D.,
Censor Deputatus.

Washingtonii, D. C., die 8 Novembris, 1946.

Imprimatur:

✠ STANISLAUS VINCENTIUS BONA, D.D.,
Episcopus Sinus Viridis.

Sinus Viridis, die 8 Novembris, 1946.

Printed by
THE PAULIST PRESS
401 WEST 59TH STREET
NEW YORK 19, N. Y.
51

RESPECTFULLY DEDICATED

TO

HIS EXCELLENCY

THE MOST REVEREND STANISLAUS V. BONA, D.D.

BISHOP OF GREEN BAY

TABLE OF CONTENTS

CHAPTER II

SECTION II

PROOFS OF THE EXCLUSION OF THE BOON OF OFFSPRING

CHAPTER III

FOREWORD

It is the purpose of this study to determine precisely what sort of opposition to the procreation and the education of offspring on the part of the contracting parties results in the invalidity of the marriage contract, and to investigate the type of proof which suffices to establish certainty in the external forum of the invalidity of the marriage contract in such cases. It is essential to recall that the marriage contract may be invalid on one of three scores: the lack of the proper canonical form; the presence of a diriment impediment; defectiveness in the all-important element of matrimonial consent. Obviously, if opposition to the procreation and the education of offspring affects the validity of the marriage contract at all, it is on the score of defective matrimonial consent.

Matrimonial consent may be defective because of a deficiency in the operation of either of man's faculties, the intellect or the will. There is a defect in the operation of the intellect if there is a lack of knowledge in regard to the essential object of matrimonial consent,[1] or if there is an error in regard to the identity of the person with whom marriage is contracted.[2] There is a defect in the operation of the will if the consent to the marriage contract is not free,[3] or if the consent is simulated,[4] or if the giving of consent is made dependent upon a future condition which is contrary to the very essence of marriage.[5] The present study is concerned particularly with the two latter types of defective consent, i. e. simulated consent and the type of conditional consent mentioned above.

[1] *Codex Iuris Canonici Pii X Pontificis Maximi iussu digestus, Benedicti Papae XV auctoritate promulgatus* (Romae: Typis Polyglottis Vaticanis, 1917. Reimpressio, 1933), canon 1082.

[2] Canon 1083.

[3] Canon 1087.

[4] Canon 1086, § 2.

[5] Canon 1092, 2°.

Simulated Consent

The fundamental principle involved here is that a marriage contract can not come into being without the consent of the contracting parties.[6] Unless the internal consent of the parties is in conformity with the consent as manifested externally, the consent is not true but simulated. If such deception means that one of the parties, by a positive act of the will, excludes or rejects marriage itself, it is a case of total simulation. If, however, such deception means that one of the parties, by a positive act of the will, excludes not the marriage contract as such, but something which pertains to the very essence of marriage, it is a case of partial simulation.[7] Since the present discussion concerns the invalidating effect of opposition to the procreation of offspring inasmuch as the procreation of offspring pertains

[6] "Matrimonium facit partium consensus inter personas iure habiles legitime manifestatus; qui nulla humana potestate suppleri valet."—Canon 1081, § 1.

[7] This distinction between total and partial simulation is a matter of common teaching among the authors today. Cf. Gasparri (1852-1934), *Tractatus Canonicus de Matrimonio* (editio nova ad mentem Codicis I. C., 2 vols., Romae: Typis Polyglottis Vaticanis, 1932), II, n. 814 (cited hereafter as *De Matrimonio*); Cappello, *Tractatus Canonico-Moralis de Sacramentis* (3 vols. in 6, Romae: Marietti, 1932-1939), III (*De Matrimonio*, 4. ed., 1939), n. 593, 4 (cited hereafter as *De Sacramentis*, III); Payen, *De Matrimonio in Missionibus ac Potissimum in Sinis, Tractatus et Casus* (3 vols., Zi-ka-wei: in typographia T'ou-sè-wè, 1929), II, n. 1669 (cited hereafter as *De Matrimonio*); Sipos, *Enchiridion Iuris Canonici* (editio altera, Pécs, Hungary: Ex Typographia "Haladás R. T.," 1931), § 131, II; Ayrinhac (1867-1930)—Lydon, *Marriage Legislation in the New Code of Canon Law* (new, revised edition, New York: Benziger Brothers, 1943), n. 204 (cited hereafter as *Marriage Legislation*). As evidence that the same distinction is upheld in the decisions of the Sacred Roman Rota, cf. *Sacrae Romanae Rotae Decisiones seu Sententiae quae iuxta Legem Propriam et Constitutionem "Sapienti Consilio" Pii PP. X prodierunt, cura eiusdem S. Tribunalis editae* (23 vols. —, Romae, 1912—) cited hereafter by indicating the date when the decision was given, the name of the *ponens* and the source as follows: *S.R.R., Nullitatis Matrimonii,* 10 iun. 1922, coram Rm̃o P. D. Ioanne Prior, Decano, dec. XVIII, n. 3—*Decisiones,* XIV (1922), 181; 5 iul. 1923, coram R.P.D. Francisco Parrillo, dec. XVI, n. 2 f.—*Decisiones,* XV (1923), 143; 5 dec. 1927, coram R.P.D. Francisco Parrillo, dec. LV, n. 4—*Decisiones,* XIX (1927), 499 f.; 25 febr. 1929, coram R.P.D. Ubaldo Mannucci, dec. XV, n. 2—*Decisiones,* XXI (1929), 133 f.; 10 febr. 1931, coram R.P.D. Arcturo Wynen, dec. VII, n. 2—*Decisiones,* XXIII (1931), 47 f.

to the essence of marriage, it revolves primarily about the question of partially simulated consent.

The reason why partial as well as total simulation invalidates the marriage contract follows from the very nature of a contract. Just as it is impossible to conceive of a man without a body and a rational soul, so it is impossible to conceive of a contract as existing without its essential obligations.[8] These obligations arise necessarily from consent to all that constitutes the essential object of marriage: the mutual giving and accepting of a perpetual and exclusive right over the body for the performance of acts which are suitable of themselves for the procreation of offspring.[9]

Conditional Consent

Since the most manifest indication of opposition to one or the other of the essential elements of marriage usually takes the form of an express condition which retains its force at the time of the external expression of the consent (and sometimes is agreed upon by both parties), it is clear that a complete discussion of the invalidating effect of opposition to the procreation and the education of offspring must include an analysis of certain types of conditions. It is entirely beyond the scope of this study, however, to attempt an elaborate analysis of these conditions as such. They will be discussed in the present study only in so far as their presence indicates simulated consent. In other words, the discussion will be restricted to future conditions which are contrary to the essence of marriage.[10]

The subject under discussion does not warrant a preliminary presentation of the development of canonical legislation, and this for the simple reason that the legislation as enacted both in canon 1092, 2° on future conditions which are contrary to the essence of marriage, and in canon 1086, § 2 on simulated consent, has entered the Code of Canon Law in substantially the same form that it had when it was

[8] S.R.R., *Nullitatis Matrimonii*, 21 ian. 1911, coram R.P.D. Seraphino Many, dec. III, n. 2: ". . . contractus enim concipi nequit sine eius obligationibus substantialibus, sicut ne homo sine corpore et anima rationali, et ideo, qui vult contractum, vult eius obligationes substantiales."—*Decisiones, III* (1911), 16.

[9] Canon 1081, § 2.

[10] Canon 1092, 2°.

established by two great pontiffs, centuries ago. The canon on future conditions which are contrary to the essence of marriage is based on a similar norm which was included in the decretals of Gregory IX (1227-1241).[11] The canon on simulated consent is based, in principle, upon the decretal *Tua Nos* of Innocent III (1198-1216), which was issued in the year 1212.[12]

Order of Procedure

As a preparation for the discussion of the practical problem of proving in the external forum the invalidity of a marriage on the score of the exclusion of the procreation of offspring (Section Two), several chapters will be devoted to a presentation of preliminary concepts and principles (Section One). The first chapter of this preliminary section will be entitled: "The Procreation of Offspring and the Essence of Marriage." The second chapter will bear the title: "Types of Opposition to the Boon of Offspring."

[11] C. 7, X, *de conditionibus appositis in desponsatione vel in aliis contractibus,* IV, 5—Potthast (1824-1898), *Regesta Pontificum Romanorum inde ab anno post Christum natum MCXCVIII ad annum MCCCIV* (2 vols., Berolini, 1874-1875), n. 9664 (cited hereafter as Potthast).

[12] This document was incorporated in the *Compilatio quarta* (Friedberg, *Quinque Compilationes Antiquae,* Lipsiae, 1882), c. 1., *de sponsalibus et matrimonio,* IV, 1, and later found its way into the Gregorian Decretals, c. 26, *de sponsalibus et matrimonio,* IV, 1—Potthast, n. 4379.

Section One

Preliminary Concepts and Principles

CHAPTER I

THE PROCREATION OF OFFSPRING AND THE ESSENCE OF MARRIAGE

SINCE the time of St. Augustine (354-430), theologians and canonists frequently have summarized the doctrine on Christian marriage simply by referring to the three blessings or boons of marriage (*tria bona matrimonii*). Since the teaching of St. Augustine in regard to the three boons of marriage has occupied such an important place in Christian thought and theology, it will be well to view the essence of marriage in the light of that teaching. The first article of the present chapter will be devoted to a brief explanation of the origin and meaning of St. Augustine's teaching. The relation between the three boons of marriage and the essence of marriage will be discussed in the second article. The controverted question of the validity of a marriage which is contracted with a condition of perpetual abstinence from the use of the marriage right, will be discussed in Article 3. The chapter will close with a discussion of the invalidating effect of opposition to the boon of offspring (Article 4).

ARTICLE I. THE THREE BOONS OF MARRIAGE

Many of the heresies during the early days of the Church included vicious attacks upon the dignity of marriage.[1] According to

[1] Cf. Denzinger—Bannwart—Umberg, *Enchiridion Symbolorum Definitionum et Declarationum de Rebus Fidei et Morum* (21.-23. ed., Friburgi Brisgoviae: Herder, 1937), nn. 36, 241, 367 and 430 (cited hereafter as Denzinger), wherein the dignity and decency of marriage are vindicated against the attacks of groups such as the Manicheans, Priscillians, Marcionites, Encratites, etc.

those heretical views, marriage was to be condemned because of the three banes associated with it, i. e., marriage was (a) a perpetual servitude, (b) characterized by a surrender to strong, human passions, and (c) carried with it the heavy burden of pleasing another, and of begetting, rearing and providing for offspring. The best defense against these ever-recurrent errors was found to be the teaching of St. Augustine in regard to the three boons of marriage.[2]

As Sanchez (1550-1610) pointed out, this Augustinian doctrine emphasizes that there is no need to seek extrinsic reasons in order to justify marriage; rather, there are three boons which are associated with marriage intrinsically, so as to make it a noble and dignified contract, and more than compensate for whatever banes may be alleged against it.[3] Two are united in marriage not as in servitude, but by a love which is like unto the love between Christ and His Church (boon of sacramental stability—*bonum sacramenti*); offspring are brought into the world, but as a loving service to God (boon of offspring—*bonum prolis*); man and wife surrender to human passion, but only between themselves and not with another (boon of conjugal fidelity—*bonum fidei*).[4]

This Augustinian teaching in regard to the three boons of mar-

[2] Cf. especially *De Bono Coniugali*, cap. XXIV, n. 32—*Corpus Scriptorum Ecclesiasticorum Latinorum* (68 vols., Vindobonae, 1866—), XLI, 227 (cited hereafter as *CSEL*); also *De Genesi ad Litteram*, lib. IX, cap. 7— *CSEL*, XXVIII, 275 ff.

[3] "Haec autem bona non adveniunt matrimonio ab extrinseco, sed sunt de matrimonii ratione, quare non indiget eis, quasi quibusdam extrinsecis ad illud honestandum: sed quasi causantibus in ipso intrinsece honestatem: . . . ex se, et ab intrinseco habet unde excusentur, et compensentur detrimenta, quae affert, . . ."—*Disputationum de Sancto Matrimonii Sacramento Tomi Tres* (Antverpiae, 1626), lib. II, disp. XXIX, n. 5 (cited hereafter as *De Matrimonio*). Cf. also Salmanticenses, *Cursus Theologiae Moralis* (6 vols., Venetiis, 1714), lib. I, cap. III, n. 21.

[4] Cf. Sanchez, *ibid.*, n. 4; Salmanticenses, *loc. cit.;* St. Thomas Aquinas (1226-1274), *Summa Theologica* (6 vols., Taurini: Marietti, 1937), *Suppl.*, III, q. 49, articles 1 and 2; Laymann (1574-1635), *Theologia Moralis* (5 vols., Venetiis, 1630), lib. V, tr. X, pars. 4, *introductio;* Vlaming (+1935), *Praelectiones Iuris Matrimonii* (3. ed., 2 vols., Bussum in Hollandia, 1919-1921), I, n. 21; Merkelbach, *Summa Theologiae Moralis* (editio altera aucta et emendata, 3 vols., Parisiis: Typis Desclée de Brouwer et Soc., 1936), III, n. 795.

riage was mentioned in the Decree to the Armenians in 1439.[5] It was likewise mentioned and explained in the Roman Catechism.[6] In his encyclical letter on Christian marriage, Pius XI referred to this same doctrine as a "splendid summary of the whole doctrine of Christian marriage," and explained the teaching in the very words of St. Augustine:

> Quae vero quantaque sint haec veri matrimonii bona divinitus data dum exponere aggredimur, Venerabiles Fratres, illius Nobis praeclarissimi Ecclesiae Doctoris verba occurrunt, quem non ita pridem, Nostris Encyclicis Litteris *Ad salutem* pleno ab eius obitu saeculo XV datis, celebravimus: "Haec omnia—inquit S. Augustinus—bona sunt, propter quae nuptiae bonae sunt: PROLES, FIDES, SACRAMENTUM." Quae tria capita qua ratione luculentissimam totius de christiano connubio doctrinae summam continere iure dicantur, ipse Sanctus Doctor diserte declarat, cum ait: "*In fide* attenditur ne praeter vinculum coniugale cum altero vel altera concumbatur; *in prole,* ut amanter suscipiatur, benigne nutriatur, religiose educetur; *in sacramento* autem, ut coniugium non separetur, et dimissus aut dimissa, nec causa prolis, alteri coniungatur. Haec est tamquam regula nuptiarum, qua vel naturae decoratur fecunditas vel incontinentiae regitur pravitas." [7]

As evidence that this teaching of St. Augustine was accepted among the early canonists, it may be mentioned that Gratian (+ before 1158) upheld the marriage of the Blessed Virgin Mary and St. Joseph as a true marriage in all respects because all three of the boons of marriage—offspring (the Child Jesus), conjugal fidelity (no adultery) and sacramental stability (no divorce) were enjoyed

[5] Decretum pro Armenis (Bulla *Exultate Deo,* 22 nov. 1439): "Assignatur autem triplex bonum matrimonii. Primum est proles suscipienda et educanda ad cultum Dei. Secundum est fides, quam unus coniugum alteri servare debet. Tertium indivisibilitas matrimonii, propter hoc quod significat indivisibilem coniunctionem Christi et Ecclesiae."—Denzinger, n. 702.

[6] *Catechismus Romanus ex Decreto Concilii Tridentini ad Parochos Pii V. Pontificis Maximi iussu editus* (4. ed., 4 vols., Ratisbonae, Romae, Neo Eboraci et Cincinnati: Sumptibus et typis Friderici Pustet, 1907), pars II, cap. VIII, quaestio XXI.

[7] Ex litt. encycl. *Casti Connubii,* 31 dec. 1930—*Acta Apostolicae Sedis, Commentarium Officiale* (Romae, 1909—), XXII (1930), 543 (cited hereafter as *AAS*).

in that holy union.[8] Gregory IX (1227-1241) listed three conditions as contrary to the essence of marriage, each of which was contrary to one of the three boons or blessings of marriage:

> Si conditiones contra substantiam coniugii inserantur, puta si alter dicat alteri: "contraho tecum, si generationem prolis evites," vel: "donec inveniam aliam honore vel facultatibus digniorem," aut: "si pro quaestu adulterandam te tradas," matrimonialis contractus, quantumcunque sit favorabilis, caret effectu; . . .[9]

If such conditions are introduced into the marriage contract itself, the very essence of marriage is affected, and the contract is invalid.[10]

Article II. The Three Boons of Marriage and the Essence of Marriage

The word essence is understood here as the logical essence of marriage, i. e., that without which marriage could not exist. The

[8] "Omne . . . nuptiarum bonum impletum est in illis parentibus Christi, fides, sacramentum, proles. Prolem cognoscimus ipsum Dominum, fidem: quia nullum adulterium; sacramentum: quia nullum divortium; . . ."—C. 10, C. XXVII, q. 2. The glossator of this text mentions (s. v. *omne*) that one author, Gandolphus (c. 1170), deduced that there were but two boons of marriage, conjugal fidelity and offspring: "quia sacramentum matrimonii nihil aliud est quam matrimonium." Freisen (1853-1932) presents ample exidence, however, that Gandolphus was in error on this point. Cf. *Geschichte des Canonischen Eherechts bis zum Verfall der Glassenliteratur* (2. ed., Paderborn: Ferdinand Schöningh, 1893), 36 f. St. Thomas vigorously corrected this false view relative to the boon of sacramental stability in his *Summa Theologica, Suppl.*, III, q. 49, art. 2 ad 7. Gratian referred to the three boons or blessings of marriage also in c. 6, C. XXXII, q. 2.

[9] C. 7, X, *de conditionibus appositis in desponsatione vel in aliis contractibus*, IV, 5—Potthast, n. 9664. The glossator of this text states clearly that these conditions refer to the boon of offspring (s. v. *si generationem*, etc.), the boon of sacramental stability (s. v. *donec inveniam aliam*), and the boon of conjugal fidelity (s. v. *aut si pro quaestu*) respectively.

[10] "Per illas tres conditiones extinguuntur illa tria bona, quae in quolibet matrimonio necessario requiruntur, aliter non erit matrimonium, . . ."—*Ibid., glossa ordinaria*, s. v. *contra substantiam coniugii*. Cf. also Ioannes Andreae (1272-1348), *Commentaria in Quinque Decretalium Libros* (Venetiis, 1581), in c. 7, IV, 5, n. 1 f. (cited hereafter as *Commentaria*).

essence of marriage, as indicated in the Code of Canon Law, consists in the mutual giving and accepting of a "perpetual and exclusive right over the body for the performance of acts suitable of themselves for the procreation of offspring." [11] The reference to the "procreation of offspring" in canon 1081, § 2, points to the primary end of marriage as stated in canon 1013, § 1.[12] Inasmuch as the same canon refers to the perpetuity and exclusiveness of the "right over the body," it indicates the essential properties of marriage as mentioned in canon 1013, § 2.[13]

If one or both of the parties withhold consent in regard to any of the elements mentioned in canon 1081, § 2, their consent is not a true matrimonial consent, and a valid marriage cannot exist.[14] It is only when the right over the body is given and accepted "for the exercise of acts suitable of themselves for the procreation of offspring," and as a perpetual and exclusive right, that a valid marriage bond arises, perpetual and exclusive, with "equal rights and duties concerning the acts proper to conjugal life." [15]

[11] "Matrimonium facit partium consensus . . ."—Canon 1081, § 1. "Consensus matrimonialis est actus voluntatis quo utraque pars tradit et acceptat ius in corpus, perpetuum et exclusivum, in ordine ad actus per se aptos ad prolis generationem."—Canon 1081, § 2.

[12] "Matrimonii finis primarius est procreatio atque educatio prolis: . . ."

[13] "Essentiales matrimonii proprietates sunt unitas ac indissolubilitas, quae in matrimonio christiano peculiarem obtinent firmitatem ratione sacramenti."

[14] " . . . substantia matrimonii consistit in consensu ad societatem coniugalem, sub quo tacite includitur ad perpetuam societatem, ad fidem mutuo sibi servandam, prolemque suscipiendam, quae sunt tria bona matrimonii . . ." —Sanchez, *De Matrimonio*, lib. V, disp. IX, n. 3. "Consensus, tam apud infideles quam apud fideles, debet esse ***matrimonialis***, id est qui debet ferri in obiectum contractus necnon in eius proprietates et obligationes essentiales; . . ." —Vromant, *Ius Missionariorum* (7 vols., Louvain: Museum Lessianum, 1931), V (*De Matrimonio*), n. 174 (cited hereafter as *De Matrimonio*). Cf. also Lehmkuhl (1834-1918), *Theologia Moralis* (6. ed., 2 vols., Friburgi Brisgoviae: Herder, 1890), II, n. 679; Ayrinhac-Lydon, *Marriage Legislation*, n. 230.

[15] "Ex valido matrimonio enascitur inter coniuges vinculum natura sua perpetuum et exclusivum; . . ."—Canon 1110. "Utrique coniugi ab ipso matrimonii initio aequum ius et officium est quod attinet ad actus proprios coniugalis vitae."—Canon 1111. These two canons refer to marriage considered as the bond which results from the marriage contract, or, as the authors say, *matrimonium in facto esse*. Canon 1081, § 2 refers to marriage considered as a

The canons cited above indicate that there is a definite connection between the elements which constitute the essence of marriage and the three boons of marriage. The references to the "acts suitable of themselves for the procreation of offspring" (canon 1081, § 2) and to the "acts proper to conjugal life" (canon 1111) point to the blessing of offspring. The references to the essential properties of marriage (canon 1013, § 2) and to the perpetuity and exclusiveness of the marriage right (canon 1081, § 2) and of the marriage bond (canon 1110) point to the boons of sacramental stability and conjugal fidelity respectively.

In order to understand the sense in which the three boons of marriage pertain to the essence of marriage, however, it must be noted that the boon of sacramental stability (indissolubility) is enjoyed at the moment that the contracting parties exchange matrimonial consent, whereas the boon of offspring and the boon of conjugal fidelity depend for their enjoyment upon the use of the marriage right. In the case of the latter two boons or blessings of marriage, therefore, a distinction can be made between the giving and accepting of the marriage right with regard to offspring and conjugal fidelity, and the actual enjoyment of those boons in married life through the use of the marriage right.

All three of the boons of marriage pertain to the essence of marriage in the sense that true matrimonial consent necessarily includes consent to give and to accept all of the essential rights and obligations of marriage. If, however, the contracting parties, by a positive act of the will, exclude the marriage right or reject the corresponding essential obligation with regard to any one of the three boons of marriage, the consent is vitiated and a valid marriage can not exist. The mere fact that the contracting parties do not intend to avail

contract, or *matrimonium in fieri.* As indicated by the title of this study, the present discussion concerns the essence of marriage considered as a contract. For a review of the distinction between marriage considered as a bond, and as a contract, cf. De Smet (1868-1927), *Tractatus Theologico-Canonicum de Sponsalibus et Matrimonio* (4. ed., Brugis: Beyaert, 1927), nn. 74 ff. and 206 ff. (cited hereafter as *De Sponsalibus et Matrimonio*); Wernz-Vidal, *Ius Canonicum* (7 vols. in 9, Romae: Apud Aedes Universitatis Gregorianae, 1923-1938), V (*Ius Matrimoniale,* 2. ed., 1928), n. 21; Cappello, *De Matrimonio,* III, n. 2; Merklebach, *Summa Theologiae Moralis,* III, nn. 772 ff.

themselves of the boon of offspring or the boon of conjugal fidelity in their married life, however, does not in itself indicate that they intend to exclude the marriage right or to reject the corresponding essential obligation with regard to the boon of offspring or the boon of conjugal fidelity. For the enjoyment of these two boons of marriage depends upon the use of the marriage right, and the *use* (or abuse) of the marriage right does not pertain to the essence of marriage.[16] Since the boon of sacramental stability is enjoyed at the moment of matrimonial consent, independently of the use of the marriage right, it always pertains to the essence of marriage. Marriage cannot exist without being a stable and perpetual union. Offspring and conjugal fidelity pertain to the essence of marriage not inasmuch as they are boons to be enjoyed through the use of the marriage right, but in the sense that the exclusion of the marriage right in regard to the procreation of offspring or conjugal fidelity affects the validity of the marriage contract.

This distinction, as applied to the boons of offspring and conjugal fidelity, is based on the distinction between the marriage *right* and the *use* of the marriage right. In actual cases, however, the contracting parties usually do not refuse to *accept* the marriage right in

[16] ". . . fides et proles possunt dupliciter considerari: uno modo in seipsis, et sic pertinent ad usum matrimonii, per quem et proles producitur, et pactio coniugalis servatur. Sed indivisibilitas, quam sacramentum importat, pertinet ad ipsum matrimonium secundum se, quia ex hoc ipso quod per pactionem coniugalem sui potestatem sibi invicem in perpetuum coniuges tradunt, sequitur quod separari non possunt: et inde est quod matrimonium nunquam invenitur sine inseparabilitate; invenitur autem sine fide et prole, quia *esse* rei non dependet ab usu suo . . . Alio modo possunt considerari fides et proles secundum quod sunt in suis principiis, ut pro prole accipiatur intentio prolis, et pro fide debitum servandi fidem, sine quibus etiam matrimonium esse non potest, quia haec in matrimonio ex ipsa pactione coniugali causantur; ita quod si aliquid contrarium his exprimeretur in consensu, qui matrimonium facit, non esset verum matrimonium; . . ."—St. Thomas, *Summa Theologica, Suppl.*, q. 49, art. 3, *in corp.* Pope Pius XI cites the concluding lines of the passage from the *Summa Theologica* of St. Thomas quoted above in his encyclical letter, *Casti Connubii*, of Dec. 31, 1930—*AAS*, XXII (1930), 542. For other references to the distinction advanced by St. Thomas in the passage quoted above, cf. Sanchez, *De Matrimonio*, lib. II, disp. XXIX, n. 12; Wernz-Vidal, *Ius Matrimoniale*, n. 28, *sub fine; Cappello, De Sacramentis*, III, n. 601, 2.

regard to offspring and conjugal fidelity, but rather refuse to *give* the marriage right and accept the corresponding obligation in regard of these boons or blessings of marriage.[17] This explains why authors frequently express the same view as expressed in the paragraph above my making a distinction between the *accepting of the obligation and the fulfillment of the obligation.*[18] These distinctions between the marriage right and the use of the right, and between the obligation which corresponds to the marriage right and the fulfillment of that obligation are employed frequently in the decisions of the Sacred Roman Rota.[19]

[17] S.R.R., *Nullitatis Matrimonii,* 25 iun. 1931, coram R.P.D. Francisco Morano, dec. XXX, n. 3: ". . . cum traditio iuris potius molesta sit quam acceptatio, communior est casus in quo excluditur sola iuris traditio, seu obligationis susceptio."—*Decisiones,* XXIII (1931), 260.

[18] "Id tamen observandum est, aliud esse sentiendum de tribus matrimonii bonis quoad obligationem, et aliud quoad executionem: nam quoad obligationem, omnia illa sunt de matrimonii essentia: . . ."—Sanchez, *De Matrimonio,* lib. II, disp. XXIX, n. 12; cf. also *ibid.,* lib. V, disp. IX, n. 6. Other authors express the same distinction by referring to the intention of assuming the obligation (*animus sese obligandi*) and the intention of fulfilling the obligation (*animus obligationes implendi*). Cf. Payen, *De Matrimonio,* II, n. 1669 ff.; Wernz-Vidal, *Ius Matrimoniale,* n. 406 ff.; Chelodi (1880-1922), *Ius Matrimoniale iuxta Codicem Iuris Canonici* (3. ed., Tridenti: Libr. Edit. Tridentum, 1921), n. 115 ff. (cited hereafter as *Ius Matrimoniale*); Cappello, *De Sacramentis,* III, n. 593 ff.

[19] S.R.R., *Nullitatis Matrimonii,* 23 iun, 1931, coram R.P.D. Francisco Morano, dec. XXX, n. 4: "Quod attinet autem ad exclusionem prolis vel actus coniugalis, magni momenti est distinguere ius ab exercitio iuris, obligationem ab exsecutione obligationis. Ius profecto non tollitur per hoc quod quis ius ipsum non exerceat vel eo abutatur; item obligatio non tollitur per hoc quod quis obligationem violet."—*Decisiones,* XXIII (1931), 260; 5 iun. 1926, coram R.P.D. Iosepho Florczak, dec. XXIV, n. 4: "Quando agitur de conditione contra bonum prolis, sedulo distinguendum est inter ius coëundi et eius usum, seu inter assumptionem obligationis et huius obligationis exsecutionem. Si ius ad rectum usum matrimonii (obligatio ipsa) fuit ex animo contrahentium omnino exclusum, nuptiae sunt invalidae." *Decisiones,* XVIII (1926), 192. Cf. also S.R.R. *Nullitatis Matrimonii,* 10 iun. 1922, coram Rm̃o P.D. Ioanne Prior, Decano, dec. XVIII, n. 4—*Decisiones,* XIV (1922), 182; 5 iul. 1923, coram R.P.D. Francisco Parillo, dec. XVI, n. 4—*Decisiones,* XV (1923), 143 f.; 7 iun. 1927, coram R.P.D. Iosepho Florczak, dec. XXVI, n. 2—*Decisiones,* XIX (1927), 208 f.; 9 iul. 1927, coram Rm̃o P.D. Maximo Massimi, Decano, dec. XXXV,

It is important to note, however, that sometimes the boons of offspring and conjugal fidelity are referred to in their essential aspect, i.e. to emphasize that if the marriage right or the corresponding obligation is excluded in regard to the procreation of offspring or in regard to the observance of conjugal fidelity, the marriage is invalid.[20] In one passage of his encyclical letter on Christian marriage in particular, Pius XI refers to the boons of marriage in such a manner:

> Nam Angelicus Doctor de fide et prole disserens, "haec, inquit, in matrimonio ex ipsa pactione coniugali causantur, ita quod si aliquid contrarium his exprimeretur in consensu qui matrimonium facit, non esset verum matrimonium."[21]

At other times, the boon of offspring and the boon of conjugal fidelity are referred to strictly as blessings, the benefits of which are to be enjoyed in married life through the use of the marriage right.[22] Considered in this latter sense, the boon of offspring and the boon of conjugal fidelity do not pertain to the essence of marriage.

A. The Three Boons of Marriage and the Essential Elements of Marriage

The relation between the three boons of marriage and the essence of marriage, therefore, is to be found in the relation between offspring, conjugal fidelity and sacramental stability on the one hand, and the

n. 3—*Decisiones,* XIX (1927), 300; 7 ian. 1929, coram R.P.D. Francisco Parrillo, dec. II, n. 3 ff.—*Decisiones,* XXI (1929), 13 ff.; 14 ian. 1930, coram Rmo P.D. Maximo Massimi, Decano, dec. IV, n. 3—*Decisiones,* XXII (1930), 46 f.; 21 iul. 1930, coram R.P.D. Iulio Grazioli, dec. XXXVIII, n. 2—*Decisiones,* XXII (1930), 423; 10 febr. 1931, coram R.P.D. Arcturo Wynen, dec. VII, n. 7 —*Decisiones,* XXIII (1931), 48; 16 iul. 1931, coram R.P.D. Francisco Guglielmi, dec. XXXV, n. 3—*Decisiones,* XXIII (1931), 293.

[20] Cf. c. 7, X, *de conditionibus appositis in desponsatione vel in aliis contractibus,* IV, 5—Potthast, n. 9664; Wernz-Vidal, *Ius Matrimoniale,* n. 28; Cappello, *De Sacramentis,* III, n. 15.

[21] Ex litt. encycl. *Casti Connubii,* 31 dec. 1930—*AAS,* XXII (1930), 542. The quotation is from the *Summa Theologica* of St. Thomas as quoted earlier in this study (p. 10).

[22] Cf. the text of St. Augustine as cited by Gratian, c. 10, C. XXVII, q. 2; litt. encycl. *Casti Connubii,* 31 dec. 1930—*AAS,* XXII (1930), 543; Merkelbach, *Summa Theologiae Moralis,* III, n. 793.

essential object and the essential properties of marriage on the other. The reason why a valid marriage can not exist if the marriage right is excluded in regard to the "acts suitable of themselves for the procreation of offspring" (canon 1081, § 2) follows from the very nature of marriage and conjugal union.[23] The reason why a marriage is invalid if the perpetuity or exclusiveness of the marriage right is excluded follows from the fact that unity and indissolubility are essential properties of marriage. It would be beyond the scope of the present study to investigate the extent to which the unity and indissolubility of marriage are based on the natural law. It is sufficient to note that Christ restored marriage to its original unity and indissolubility,[24] and that the Code of Canon Law mentions unity and indissolubility as essential properties of marriage.[25] In the present order of the divine economy, marriage cannot exist without unity and indissolubility.

Even in the present order, however, marriage is not indissoluble absolutely. The Church retains the authority from Christ Himself to dissolve the marriage bond in certain circumstances.[26] It is only

[23] ". . . quod ius in corpus determinatur addendo: in ordine ad . . . quatenus non agatur de dominio in mutuum corpus in ordine ad laborem vel aliud quid praestandum, sed in ordine ad actus de se aptos ad generationem."—De Smet, *De Sponsalibus et Matrimonio*, n. 75.

[24] As to the unity of marriage, cf. Matth. XIX, 9; Mark, X, 11 ff.; Luke, XVI, 18; Denzinger, n. 972. Christ restored the indissolubility of marriage and gave a divine interpretation to the text of Gen. II, 24 when He said: "Propter hoc dimittet homo patrem et matrem, et adhaerebit uxori suae, et erunt duo in carne una. Itaque iam non sunt duo, sed una caro. Quod ergo Deus coniunxit, homo non separet." Matth. XIX, 5 ff. Cf. also Matth., V, 32; Mark, X, 11; Luke, XVI, 18; I Corinthians, VII, 10 f.; Romans, VII, 2 f., and Denzinger, nn. 1765-1767.

[25] Canon 1013, § 2.

[26] Cf. canon 1119. "Ecclesia, ex una parte, dissolvendo descriptum matrimonium [i.e. ratified, non-consummated marriage] non exercet . . . potestatem quasi propriam, sed quasi *ministerialem et instrumentalem*, quatenus nempe ea utatur nomine et auctoritate Dei, cui soli competit sive mediate sive immediate, dispensare in iure naturae secundario. Ex alia parte Ecclesia *veram* exercet *potestatem*, ac *auctoritative* relaxat vinculum matrimonii non consummati, ex virtute auctoritatis divinae ipsi, intra certos limites, ministerialiter concreditae . . ."—De Smet, *De Sponsalibus et Matrimonio*, n. 329. Cf. also Cappello,

when the marriage has been consummated that the union between two baptized persons becomes indissoluble absolutely.[27] In his encyclical letter on Christian marriage, Pius XI gave the reason for this absolute indissolubility of marriage as follows:

> Huius autem divinae voluntatis intimam rationem si reverenter investigare velimus, Venerabiles Fratres, facile eam inveniemus in mystica christiani connubii significatione, quae in consummato inter fideles matrimonio plene perfecteque habetur. Teste enim Apostolo, in sua (quam ab initio innuimus) ad Ephesios epistola, christianorum connubium perfectissimam illam refert coniunctionem, quae Christum inter et Ecclesiam intercedit: "Sacramentum hoc magnum est, ego autem dico, in Christo et in Ecclesia": quae quidem coniunctio, quamdiu Christus vivet et Ecclesia per ipsum, nulla profecto separatione unquam dissolvi poterit. Quod etiam Sanctus Augustinus diserte docet his verbis: "Hoc enim custoditur in Christo et Ecclesia, ut vivens cum vivente in aeternum nullo divortio separetur . . ."[28]

B. The Three Boons of Marriage and the Ends of Marriage

If offspring and conjugal fidelity are considered not inasmuch as the marriage right in regard to the procreation of offspring and the observance of conjugal fidelity is contained in the marriage contract itself, but in themselves, as blessings to be enjoyed in married life through the use of the marriage right, they may be compared to the ends of marriage. The ends of marriage are also boons or blessings which marriage is calculated to produce: the procreation and education of offspring, mutual help and the relief of concupiscence.[29] It is easy to perceive the relation between the boon of offspring and the primary end of marriage. The boon of conjugal fidelity may be associated with the secondary ends of marriage.[30] Likewise the

De Sacramentis, III, n. 755, 2; Wernz-Vidal, *Ius Matrimoniale*, n. 624 and note 39; Gasparri, *De Matrimonio*, II, nn. 1122 ff.

[27] Canon 1118.

[28] Ex litt. encycl. *Casti Connubii*, 31 dec. 1930—*AAS*, XXII (1930), 552.

[29] "Matrimonii finis primarius est procreatio atque educatio prolis; secundarius mutuum adiutorium et remedium concupiscentiae."—Canon 1013, § 1.

[30] The boon of conjugal fidelity embraces both a positive and a negative aspect: ". . . non tantum esse bonum fidei essentiale quoad obligationem red-

boon of sacramental stability (indissolubility), if considered as a contributing factor to security in marital life, is associated particularly with the secondary end of marriage which is known as mutual help: ". . . indissolubility when realized in practice amounts to something more than a mere quality of a juridical bond. When it is actuated it becomes life in common. It is merely another way of looking at mutual help." [81] It is only when the marriage right has been given and accepted for the exercise of acts suitable of themselves for the procreation of offspring, and as a perpetual and exclusive right, that both the boons or blessings of marriage (considered in the sense explained above) and the ends of marriage can be realized fully in the manner intended by the Author of Nature.

Just as the boon of offspring and the boon of conjugal fidelity, considered in themselves, do not pertain to the essence of marriage, so the ends of marriage, considered as boons or blessings which marriage is calculated to produce, do not constitute the essence of

dendi sibi ipsis debitum, sed etiam quoad obligationem servandi fidem, non tradendo alteri corpus: . . ."—Sanchez, *De Matrimonio,* lib. II, disp. XXIX, n. 12. Cf. also litt. encycl. *Casti Connubii,* 31 dec. 1930—*AAS,* XXII (1930), 546; Wernz-Vidal, *Ius Matrimoniale,* n. 28; Cappello, *De Sacramentis,* III, n. 15; Noldin-Schmitt, *Summa Theologiae Moralis* (26. ed., 3 vols., Oeniponte—Lipsiae: sumptibus et typis Feliciani Rauch, 1940), III, n. 505; Vermeersch, *What is Marriage? A Catechism according to the Encyclical "Casti Connubii" of Pope Pius XI* (New York: The America Press, 1932), nn. 45 ff. and 51 ff. The relation between conjugal fidelity considered in its positive aspect (granting the use of the marriage right one to another) and the secondary end of marriage which is known as the relief of concupiscence is apparent. Considered particularly in its negative aspect (i.e. whereby conjugal union with others is excluded), conjugal fidelity is associated also with the secondary end of marriage which is known as mutual help and with the element of conjugal love: "*Bonum fidelitatis,* quo coniuges imprimis obtinent mutuum et exclusivum *ius* in corpus, ut vinculo matrimonii perdurante absque adulterio neque novum matrimonium attentare neque cum alia persona rem habere possint. Praeterea illud importat, ut coniuges sese mutuo sancto amore prosequantur sibique mutuum praestent *adiutorium* et *solamen,* in quo reperitur *secundus* finis matrimonii."—Wernz-Vidal, *loc. cit.*

[81] Ford, *The Validity of Virginal Marriage.* A Doctoral Dissertation presented in the Theological Faculty of the Pontifical Gregorian University (Worcester, Mass.: Harrigan Press, 1938), p. 39.

marriage.[32] Formerly, some authors distinguished between the intrinsic *essential* ends and the intrinsic *accidental* ends of marriage.[33] What these authors listed as the intrinsic essential ends of marriage correspond to the essential object and the essential property of indissolubility as mentioned in the Code of Canon Law.[34] Conceived in such a manner, the "intrinsic essential" ends of marriage undoubtedly are to be classed among the elements which constitute the very essence of marriage. Although some modern authors still retain this terminology,[35] it must be admitted that such a terminology is not in accordance with the concepts of the ends of marriage as mentioned in the Code of Canon Law, and leads to a confusion between the ends of marriage and the essence of marriage.[36]

[32] Zeiger, "Nova matrimonii definitio?": ". . . procreatio et educatio prolis est *finis operis primarius* matrimonii. Finis est; non essentia, sed bonum extra rationem essentialem positum, quod ope matrimonii appeti et obtineri potest."—*Periodica de re Canonica, Morali, Liturgica* (Brugis et Romae, Vols. I-VIII, 1905-1919; Vols. IX-XV, 1920-1927; Vol. XVI [1927]—), XX (1931), 56*. Cf. also Claeys Bouuaert-Simenon, *Manuale Iuris Canonici* (3 vols., Vol. II, *De Sacramentis,* Gandae et Leodii, 1931), II, n. 217, 2.

[33] Cf. St. Alphonsus de Liguori (1696-1787), *Theologia Moralis* (11 ed., Gaudé, 4 vols., Romae, 1905-1912), lib. VI, n. 882; Konings, *Theologia Moralis, Novissimi Ecclesiae Doctoris S. Alphonsi, in Compendium Redacta, et Usui Venerabilis Cleri Americani Accomodata* (4. ed., 2 vols., Neo-Eboraci: Benziger Fratres, 1880), II, n. 1548, quaer. 6°.

[34] "Fines intrinsici essentiales sunt duo; traditio mutua cum obligatione reddendi debitum, et vinculum indissolubile; fines intrinsici accidentales pariter sunt duo, procreatio prolis et remedium concupiscentiae."—St. Alphonsus de Ligouri, *loc cit.* Cf. also Konings, *loc. cit.*

[35] Lavaud, *Le Monde Moderne et le Mariage* (Paris: Desclée de Brouwer, 1935), p. 22; Raus, *Institutiones Canonicae iuxta Novum Codicem Iuris pro Scholis vel ad Usum Privatum Synthetice Redactae* (altera editio aucta atque emendata, Lugduni-Parisiis: Typis Emmanuelis Vitte, 1931), n. 268 (cited hereafter as *Institutiones Canonicae*).

[36] "Eiusmodi locutio, . . . relinquenda omnino est, ad normam cit. can. 1013, § 1. Etenim mutua traditio cum obligatione reddendi debitum, et vinculum indissolubile non sunt *fines* matrimonii, cum eiusdem potius essentiam constituant; procreatio prolis et remedium concupiscentiae nullatenus fines *accidentales* sunt, si finis *operis* seu ipsius matrimonii spectetur. Qua de re nulla esse potest dubitatio."—Cappello, *De Sacramentis,* III, n. 9.

Article 3. The Marriage Right and Perpetual Virginity

It can be that the boon of offspring is not enjoyed in married life for one of three reasons: that the husband or wife is sterile, or that the parties abstain from the use of the marriage right, or that they abuse the marriage right in such a manner as to prevent the conception of children. There will be ample opportunity throughout this study to emphasize the fact that an intention to abuse the marriage right does not in itself indicate an exclusion of the marriage right itself in regard to the blessing of offspring. Just as a person may obligate himself by an oath, even though he is determined never to carry out the obligation, so the parties of a marriage contract may assume all of the essential obligations of such a contract, even though they are determined not to fulfill these obligations.[37] Likewise the fact that one or both of the parties are sterile does not imply the exclusion of the marriage right itself. Much could be said, however, in regard to the question of total abstinence from the use of the marriage right. Since this question will not be involved directly in the remaining chapters of this study, it may be well to discuss it briefly here.

For centuries theologians and canonists argued the question whether the marriage right itself could be given if the parties entered an agreement never to use the marriage right. In other words, is the perpetual exclusion of the *use* of the marriage right, if reduced to a mutual pact, incompatible with the giving of the marriage right? Benedict XIV (1740-1758) and a host of other eminent authors maintained that such an agreement would invalidate the marriage, inasmuch as it precludes the giving of a true right over the body.[38]

[37] Cf. S.R.R., *Nullitatis Matrimonii,* 7 ian. 1929, coram R.P.D. Francisco Parrillo, dec. II, n. 3—*Decisiones,* XXI (1929), 13.

[38] "Matrimonii substantiae non repugnat non uti, sed uti non posse."—*De Synodo Dioecesana* (2 vols., Ex Typographia Sacrae Congregationis de Propaganda Fide, Romae, 1806), lib. XIII, cap. 22, n. 11. Ford, who made an extensive study of this point in his thesis, *The Validity of Virginal Marriage,* lists more than 50 authors who share the opinion of Benedict XIV. He mentions among them: Aichner (1816-1911), Billot (1846-1931), Blat, Cappello, Chelodi (1880-1922), D'Annibale (1815-1892), Gonzales-Tellez (+ after 1673), Laymann (1574-1635), Payen, Pitonius (+ 1729), Pirhing (1606-1679), Sanchez

St. Thomas' view on the subject is not clear.[39] An equally impressive list of authors can be cited in support of the opposite opinion, i.e., that such an agreement would not invalidate the marriage.[40] The opinion of this latter group is based on the distinction between the radical right and the proximate right over the body.[41] They argue that an agreement to abstain from the use of the marriage right forever amounts merely to an exclusion of the *proximate* right over the body, whereas only the *radical* right over the body pertains to the essence of marriage.[42]

A. *An Appraisal of the Two Opposite Opinions*

Although the distinction between the radical right and the proximate right may appear to be arbitrary and unnecessary,[43] the

(1550-1610), Santi (1830-1885), Soto (1494-1560) and Vlaming (+ 1935).—*Op. cit.*, pp. 137 ff.

39 Cf. *Summa Theologica, Suppl.*, III, q. 48, art. 1, and 3, where he apparently shares the view referred to above. In other passages of his Summa Theologica, however (e.g. III, q. 29, art. 2) he speaks of the marriage of the Blessed Virgin Mary in such a way, that one could conclude that a marriage would be possible even with a condition of perpetual virginity. Cf. also Ford, *op. cit.*, p. 139.

40 Ford mentions over 75 authors in support of this opinion, e.g.: Aertnys (1828-1915), Damen, Ballerini (1805-1881), Palmieri (1829-1909), Billuart (1685-1757), Bonacina (1585-1631), De Luca (+ 904), Ferreres (1861-1936), Gasparri (1852-1934), Lehmkuhl (1834-1918), St. Alphonsus de Liguori (1696-1787), Noldin (1838-1922), Schmitt, Merklebach, Vasquez (1551-1604), Vermeersch (1858-1936). *Ibid.*, pp. 135 ff. Ford upholds this same view. *Ibid.*, p. 134.

41 Cf. Böckhn (1690-1752), *Commentarium in Ius Canonicum Universum* Salisburgi, 1776), lib. IV, tit. V, c. 7, nn. 33 ff. and n. 56 (cited hereafter as *Commentarium*); Schmier (1680-1728), *Iurisprudentia Canonico-Civilis* (3 vols., Salisburgi, 1716), lib. IV, nn. 122 and 130 ff. (cited hereafter as *Iurisprudentia*); Gasparri, *De Matrimonio,* II, n. 903; Timlin, *Conditional Matrimonial Consent,* The Catholic University of America Canon Law Studies, n. 89 (Washington, D. C.: The Catholic University of America, 1934) pp. 314 ff.

42 Gasparri, *loc. cit.;* Schmier, *loc. cit.*

43 S.R.R., *Nullitatis Matrimonii,* 14 mart. 1924, coram R.P.D. Raphaele Chimenti, dec. XIV, n. 2: "Cum rigorose standum sit dispositis praefati canonis [i.e. 1086, § 2], patres censuerunt recedendum esse a formula *'ius radicale'* quam appellata sententia opposuit *'usui,'* quia arbitraria videtur, cum Codex

opinion which favors the validity of a marriage with an agreement of perpetual abstinence from the use of the marriage right appears to be preferable. It is admitted that one can separate the marriage right from its use without affecting the validity of the marriage. Objectively considered, the fact that the parties introduce such an agreement into their marriage contract as a matter of obligation does not indicate necessarily that the marriage right itself is excluded.

Those who hold the opposite opinion say that the marriage right consists in the fact that the contracting parties are entitled to use that right, and that if the parties obligate themselves by a mutual agreement never to use that right, the right itself is reduced to nothing.[44] Gasparri answers such an objection by pointing out that even if the right never can be used, the right nevertheless is acquired. This is evidenced by the fact that the marriage right is excluded in regard to a third person, so that if one of the parties concedes intimacies to a third person, he or she is guilty of adultery. If, despite the agreement, one of the parties forces the other to grant the use of the marriage right, there would be no question of adultery. Furthermore, the parties could rescind their agreement, so that the use of the marriage right would be lawful between them.[45]

Furthermore, it is admitted that marriage between two who

dicat sufficere ad nullitatem matrimonii ut excludatur *ius*. Est quoque confusionis conciliatrix cum per eam ius ad coniugalem actum dividi videatur in ignota genera."—*Decisiones*, XVI (1924), 108.

[44] Chelodi says, for example: ". . . quando ius in ipso usu consistit, hoc per pactum sublato, nec ius intelligitur, prout non intelligitur ius servitutis, puta transeundi per fundum alienum, si dominus *iure* potest transitum impedire."—*Ius Matrimoniale*, n. 125. Cf. also Sanchez, *De Matrimonio*, lib. V, disp. X, n. 2; Schmalzgrueber (1663-1735, *Ius Ecclesiasticum Universum* (5 vols. in 12, Romae, 1843-1845), lib. IV, tit. V, n. 121; Cappello, *De Sacramentis*, III n. 636.

[45] "Neque dicas hoc ius esse inutile et iners, si coniux eodem nunquam uti potest; . . . In primis hoc iure ceteri omnes excluduntur; hinc copula cum tertia persona est adulterium. Insuper conventio mutua mutuo consensu auferri potest, et consequenter usus matrimonii licitus evadit. Tandem vir, vi metuve mulierem ad copulam adigens, fornicationem non committit, sed solum contra fidem datam peccat, quod est minus grave. Atque ita solvitur argumentum fundamentale oppositum."—*De Matrimonio*, II, 903. Cf. also Lehmkuhl, *Theologia Moralis*, II, n. 690; Wernz-Vidal, *Ius Matrimoniale*, n. 521 and note 46.

are bound by the vow of virginity is not invalid [46] unless, of course, the parties intend to withhold the giving of the marriage right itself.[47] If the marriage right can be given in such cases despite the assumed, permanent obligation never to use the right, it seems logical to conclude that the same applies if the parties, when contracting marriage, entered a pact or agreement never to use the marriage right.[48] In both cases, the parties do not repudiate the right or corresponding obligation but merely obligate *themselves* never to use the marriage right.[49]

B. *The Attitude of the Holy See*

Because of the controversy in regard to the possibility of transferring the marriage *right* if the *use* of the same is excluded *forever*, authors agree that, until the Holy See declares otherwise, marriages which involve such an agreement are to be considered as valid in the external forum.[50] A recent decision of the Sacred Roman Rota states

[46] Cf., for example, S.C.C. *Salernitana, Matrimonii,* 24 mart. 1871: "... ita sponsi voto castitatis obstricti veram potestatem habent ad generationem ordinatam, licet propter votum emissum haec potestas non sit libera, expedita et proxima: quod sane non impedit, quominus verum inter ipsos adsit matrimonium, . . ."—*Thesaurus Resolutionum Sacrae Congregationis Concilii* (167 vols., Romae, 1718-1908), CXXX (1871), 363 (cited hereafter as *Thesaurus*).

[47] As in one noted decision in 1724: S.C.C. *Ulixbonen Occidentalis, Matrimonii,* 8 iul. 1724—*Thesaurus,* III (1724-1726), 39 ff.; *Codicis Iuris Canonici Fontes cura Emi Petri Card. Gasparri editi* (9 vols., Romae [postea civitate Vaticana]: Typis Polyglottis Vaticanis, 1923-1939), V, n. 3278 (cited hereafter as *Fontes*). See also a review of the same case by Benedict XIV in *De Synodo Dioecesana,* lib. XIII, cap. 22, n. 10 ff.

[48] "Sicut autem non est contradictio accipere ius iam in ipsa acceptione impeditum quoad usum, ut evenit quando duo voto castitatis ligati contrahunt matrimonium; ita non est contradictio tradere ius quoad usum impeditum ex consensu alterius partis in tale impedimentum."—Wernz-Vidal, *Ius Matrimoniale,* n. 521, note (46), *in fine.* Cf. also S.R.R. *Romana, Nullitatis Matrimonii et Dispensationis Super Rato,* 22 ian. 1944, coram R.P.D. Arcturo Wynen, n. 25—*AAS,* XXXVI (1944), 189 f.

[49] ". . . coniuges non obligantur ad copulam nisi in quantum altera pars petat, quae iuri petendi renuntiare potest se obligando ad non petendum, . . ."—Wernz-Vidal, *Ius Matrimoniale,* n. 521 (p. 614).

[50] Cf. Gasparri, *De Matrimonio,* II, n. 904; Cappello, *De Sacramentis,* III, n. 636.

that a marriage could not be declared invalid in such cases.[51] In 1907, the Sacred Congregation of the Council was confronted with a case in which the young man had been persuaded to sign a promise never to consummate the marriage.[52] The decision was not a declaration of nullity on the score of the exclusion of the essence of marriage, but an eventual dispensation from a ratified, non-consummated marriage.[53]

C. The Marriage of the Blessed Virgin Mary and St. Joseph

It is believed that the Blessed Virgin Mary dedicated her life to God by a vow of perpetual virginity.[54] This gave rise to the question of how the Blessed Virgin, bound to God by such a vow, could have entered a true marriage without jeopardizing the observance of her vow. Those who maintain that the marriage right can be transferred even though the parties agree to abstain from the *use* of the marriage right forever, answer simply that the Mother of Christ safeguarded her vow by entering an agreement with St. Joseph never to use the marriage right.[55] Those who maintain that the exclusion of the use of the marriage right forever would preclude the giving of the right itself, advance various arguments to vindicate

[51] S.R.R., *Romana, Nullitatis Matrimonii et Dispensationis Super Rato,* 22 ian. 1944, coram R.P.D. Arcturo Wynen, n. 25—*AAS,* XXXVI (1944), 190.

[52] S.C.C. *Elboren., Matrimonii,* 27 iul. 1907—*Thesaurus,* CLXVI (1907), 390 ff.

[53] Cf. *Acta Sanctae Sedis* (41 vols., Romae, 1865-1908), XL (1907), 494 ff. Cf. also Chelodi, *Ius Matrimoniale,* n. 125, note 3; Cappello, *De Sacramentis,* III, n. 631, 2. A recent case, which involved an agreement to exclude cohabitation and the use of the marriage right (because the girl suffered from a communicable disease) also resulted in a petition for a dispensation from a ratified, non-consummated marriage."—S.R.R. *Romana, Nullitatis Matrimonii et Dispensationis Super Rato,* 22 ian. 1944, coram R.P.D. Arcturo Wynen—*AAS,* XXXVI (1944), 179 ff.

[54] Cf. Benedictus XIV, *De Synodo Dioecesana,* lib. XIII, cap. 22, n. 13; Cappello, *De Sacramentis,* III, n. 637, 2.

[55] Cf. Schmier, *Iurisprudentia,* lib. IV, nn. 119-122; Böckhn, *Commentarium,* lib. IV, tit. V, n. 40. In a case decided by the Sacred Roman Rota in 1929, the parties claimed to have entered a so-called Josephetic marriage. Cf. *infra.* Chapter V, case n. 15.

the validity of this holy union of the Blessed Virgin Mary and St. Joseph. One prevalent argument, mentioned by Benedict XIV, is that Mary knew by divine revelation that St. Joseph likewise had made a vow of perpetual virginity.[56] These same authors, however, find greater difficulty in vindicating the validity and lawfulness of the marriages of other pious persons who were bound by vows of perpetual virginity and yet entered the married state. St. Pulcheria (399-453), for example, was bound by a vow of perpetual virginity, but nevertheless married the Emperor Marcian (450-457). The usual argument is that St. Pulcheria was so certain of the virtue and holiness of the Emperor Marcian, that she knew that he also would observe a vow of perpetual virginity in married life.[57]

Article 4. The Invalidating Effect of Opposition to the Boon of Offspring

In order to establish that a condition which is expressive of opposition to the boon of offspring actually is contrary to the essence of marriage in a given case, two things must be considered: whether the condition is one of those which, if introduced into the marriage contract itself, is incompatible with the giving of the marriage right with reference to the procreation of offspring, and whether the condition, as such, actually was introduced into the marriage contract itself so as to become an essential part of the contract. The practical problem of establishing that such a condition was introduced into the marriage contract itself will be discussed and illustrated in the second section of this study (Chapters III, IV and V). The purpose of the present article is to formulate a complete answer to the following question: what conditions which are expressive of opposition to the boon of offspring, are incompatible with the very essence of

[56] *De Synodo Dioecesana*, lib. XIII, cap. 22, n. 13. Cf. also Cappello, *De Sacramentis*, n. 637, 2.

[57] Cf. Cappello, *ibid.*, n. 636, 3°. Bachofen [Augustine] states that there are no documents to prove that St. Pulcheria had made an absolute vow of virginity.—*A Commentary on the New Code of Canon Law* (8 vols., St. Louis: B. Herder Book Co., 1931), V (4. ed., 1929), 258 (cited hereafter as *A Commentary*).

marriage if they are introduced into the marriage contract itself as an essential part of the contract? [58]

The mere statement that only conditions which indicate an exclusion of the marriage right itself with reference to the boon of offspring invalidate a marriage, does not constitute a complete answer to the question stated above. In order to formulate a complete answer to that question, it is essential to obtain a clear concept of what is meant by the expression, *boon of offspring*. Is the expression to be understood in the sense that only opposition to the conception of offspring, if introduced into the marriage contract, indicates an exclusion of the marriage right, or is it to be understood in the sense that opposition to the birth, rearing or education of the offspring conceived also indicates an exclusion of the marriage right? The answer to this question will furnish a concept of what may be called the essential aspect of the boon of offspring.

If one of the contracting parties excludes the boon of offspring in its essential aspect, that boon of marriage is excluded in a *direct* manner. It is to be noted, however, that the boon of offspring may be excluded also in an *indirect* manner, e. g. if one of the contracting parties excludes the marriage right altogether or refuses to accept the corresponding essential obligation. Although there is no objective indication in such cases that the contracting parties are opposed to the boon of offspring in particular, the very fact that they are opposed to granting the marriage right as such indicates that the marriage right is excluded with reference to all three of the boons of marriage. After the question of the direct exclusion of the boon of offspring has been discussed, a few words will be said about the indirect exclusion of the boon of offspring.

A. The Direct Exclusion of the Boon of Offspring

It is important to distinguish between conditions which are in themselves (*per se*) incompatible with the giving of the marriage

[58] It must be remembered that Gregory IX stated: "Si conditiones contra substantiam coniugii *inserantur* (italics ours) . . . matrimonialis contractus, . . . caret effectu; . . ."—C. 7, X, *de conditionibus appositis in desponsatione vel in aliis contractibus,* IV, 5—Potthast, n. 9664. That is, the marriage is invalid if such conditions are *inserted* into the marriage contract itself.

right, if introduced into the marriage contract itself, and conditions which are not in themselves incompatible with the giving of the marriage right if introduced into the marriage contract itself, but which may incidentally (*per accidens*) indicate an exclusion of the marriage right itself in the given circumstances of an individual case.

It seems that the only conditions which are in themselves incompatible with the giving of the marriage right in regard to the procreation of offspring (if introduced into the marriage contract) are those which indicate positive opposition to the *conception* of offspring. Such conditions are incompatible with the giving of the "right over the body for the performance of acts suitable of themselves for the procreation of offspring." (canon 1081, § 2). The other conditions which frequently are mentioned as contrary to the boon of offspring, if introduced into the marriage contract itself, do not indicate necessarily an exclusion of the "right over the body for the performance of acts suitable of themselves for the procreation of offspring." The fact that such an indication frequently may be present due to the given circumstances of an individual case is quite another matter. To this class belong especially those conditions which involve a positive intention to procure the abortion of the offspring, or to kill the offspring begotten of the marriage union or to abandon them completely. In order to substantiate the assertion stated above, the various conditions which usually are mentioned as contrary to the boon of offspring will be divided into two categories—those which concern the physical welfare of the offspring, and those which concern the moral welfare of the offspring—and each category of conditions will be discussed separately.

(1) The Physical Welfare of the Offspring

As indicated above, canon 1081, § 2, which states the essential object of matrimonial consent, indicates merely that the marriage right must not be excluded in regard to the "performance of acts suitable of themselves for the procreation of offspring." If the parties intend positively not to use their marriage right in a natural manner or if they intend positively to do something to impede the natural effect of conjugal union, and a stipulation to that effect is introduced into the marriage contract itself, it is clear that they intend to exclude the marriage right in regard to the performance of the acts which are suitable of themselves for the procreation of offspring. It seems logical to say that the acts which are suitable of themselves for the procreation of offspring are the acts which, by the very law of nature, are designed to lead to the *conception* of offspring, i.e. the use of the marriage right in a natural manner, without doing anything to prevent the natural consequence of conjugal union. If, therefore, the parties harbor a positive intention to effect the abortion of the offspring, or to kill the offspring or to abandon them completely, and a stipulation to such an effect is introduced into the marriage contract itself, they are guilty of a terrible crime against the law of God and against the law of nature, but there is no objective indication that the right in regard to the performance of acts suitable of themselves for the procreation of offspring necessarily is excluded.[59]

[59] Zeiger distinguished between the contribution which the contracting parties make towards the procreation of offspring and the contribution of nature herself as follows: "Tendentia sexualis ordinarie in unionem corporum tendit tamquam in finem suum proximum. Ope instinctus homines ad ineundum matrimonium et in eo ad commercium carnale impelluntur; hoc naturali modo ponentes (positivum elementum) nec effectus eius naturales impedientes (elementum negativum) satisfaciunt ei, quod in opere coniugii *opus humanum* [italics ours] dici potest. Ideo in copula rite posita satisfactio, quietatio tendentiae sexualis obtinetur, activitas humana sexualis interim sistit. At natura non sistit. Copula enim a natura non intenditur propter se ipsam, non ut finis ultimus, sed ut finis proximus, propter aliud, tamquam medium ad finem remotum, qui est procreatio prolis. Ad activitatem humanam (positivam et negativam) accedat oportet *opus naturae* [italics ours], scl. fecundatio et generatio. . . ."—"*Nova matrimonii definitio?*" *Periodica*, XX (1931), 55*.

If the contracting parties place a condition to not perform the act of conjugal union in the natural manner or to prevent the natural consequence of conjugal union, and the condition is made an essential part of the marriage contract itself, the marriage right is excluded and the marriage is invalid. If, however, they do not intend to interfere with the acts which are suitable of themselves for the procreation of offspring, but intend, by a positive act of the will, to tamper with the work of nature in the procreation of offspring by inducing the abortion of the offspring which may be conceived or by killing the offspring within the womb, it does not follow necessarily that the marriage is invalid. Zeiger expressed this view as follows: "Distinguenda est duplex finalitas: una, qua indoles sexualis in activitatem humanam (sec. elementum positivum et negativum) tendit, altera, qua ope activitatis humanae in opus

(*a*) *The Opinions of Authors*

The view advanced in the preceding paragraph is upheld by several outstanding, contemporary authors, i. e., the view that conditions which involve aborticide, infanticide or the abandoning of the offspring, if introduced into the marriage contract, are not in themselves incompatible with the giving of the marriage right. According to this view, such conditions are contrary to the boon of offspring, but they are not in themselves contrary to the essence of marriage. De Smet says, for example, that such conditions do not invalidate the marriage contract and should be regarded as if they never had been placed as such by the contracting parties.[60] Vromant holds the same opinion,[61] and adds that this opinion is in accordance with the text of the decretal in which Gregory IX mentions but one contrary condition (i. e. contrary to the boon of offspring) as contrary to the essence of marriage: "I contract marriage with you provided that you prevent the generation of offspring." [62] Other authors who

naturae (fecundationem etc.) est directa. Prior sola subest potestati nupturientium, altera eis manet subducta; prior ergo ipsum consensum matrimonialem, contractum coniugalem afficit, altera non."—*Ibid.*, 58*.

60 "Contrà non esset, salvo meliori iudicio, invalidum matrimonium contractum sub conditione occidendi prolem, eam abiiciendi, abortum provocandi, subeundi pro muliere, ovariotomiam, etc.: hae essent conditiones turpes (et, qua tales, pro non adiectis essent habendae), ac imo repugnantes matrimonio et obligationibus ex eo ortis, sed non essent repugnantes matrimonii *substantiae.*" —*De Sponsalibus et Matrimonio*, n. 155.

61 ". . . opinamur cum De Smet, matrimonium contractum sub condicione occidendi prolem, eam abiciendi, abortum provocandi, subeundi, etc. esse validum, atque has similesque condiciones quae adversantur *bono prolis etiam physico*, non esse repugnantes matrimonii substantiae, sed habendas esse uti turpes, et qua tales, tanquam contractui non adiectas; dummodo salvum maneat ius utriusque nupturientis *ad copulam per se generationi aptam. . .* ."—*De Matrimonio*, n. 175.

62 "Quae sententia convenit cum textu Gregorii IX (can. 7, X, IV, 5) ubi enumerans exempla condicionum contra substantiam matrimonii, praeter condiciones contra indissolubilitatem et unitatem, hanc solam praemittit: *'contraho tecum, si generationem prolis devites'* puta per copulam generationi ineptam."—*Ibid.*, note (2), (p. 145).

hold the same opinion are Ayrinhac,[63] Lydon,[64] Vermeesch and Creusen.[65] Claeys Bouuaert and Simenon agree with the doctrine of De Smet at least in principle.[66]

On the other hand, there is the fact that most authors have considered especially conditions which stipulate aborticide or infanticide as contrary to the essence of marriage.[67] Some authors state explicitly

[63] "De quibusdam defectibus in consensu matrimoniali," *Ius Pontificium* (Romae, 1921 ——), IX (1929), p. 33.

[64] *Marriage Legislation* (Ayrinhac-Lydon), n. 230, *in fine.*

[65] *Epitome Iuris Canonici* (3 vols., Vol. I, 6 ed., 1937; Vols. II et III, 5 ed., 1934-1936, Mechliniae-Romae: H. Dessain), II, n. 381, 2°.

[66] They admit that conditions which involve infanticide or the abandoning of the offspring do not invalidate the marriage contract: "Non tamen putamus extendi posse effectum irritandi matrimonium ad conditionem occidendi prolem natam, vel omnem prolis educationem negligendi, vel prolem exponendi aut in haeresi vel infidelitati educandi . . . non sunt directe contra essentiale matrimonii obiectum."—*Manuale Iuris Canonici,* II, n. 292, 3. In regard to conditions which involve the procuring of abortion, however, they depart from the doctrine of De Smet and maintain that such conditions invalidate the marriage contract: "quia prolis viventis emissio in lucem est quasi naturale complementum actus coniugalis."—*Loc. cit.*

[67] The following authors mention both conditions which stipulate aborticide as well as conditions which stipulate infanticide as contrary to the essence of marriage: c. 7, C. XXXII, q. 2; Chelodi, *Ius Matrimoniale,* n. 125; Payen, *De Matrimonio,* II, n. 1733, 1); Cappello, *De Sacramentis,* III, n. 631, 1; Knecht, *Handbuch des katholischen Eherechts* (Freiburg im Breisgau: Herder, 1928), 592; Sipos, *Enchiridion Iuris Canonici,* § 133, 4, b); Raus, *Institutiones Canonicae,* n. 306. Others mention only conditions which stipulate aborticide as contrary to the essence of marriage, e. g.: Noldin-Schmitt, *Summa Theologiae Moralis,* III, n. 631, 1, a); Blat, *Commentarium Textus Codicis Iuris Canonici* (5 vols. in 6, Vol. III, *De Rebus,* Pars I, Romae, 1924), III, Pars I, 601; Petrovitz, *The New Church Law on Matrimony* (second amplified and revised edition, Philadelphia: John Joseph McVey, 1926), n. 436. The following mention explicitly only conditions which stipulate infanticide: *glossa ordinaria* ad c. 6, C. XXXII, q. 2, s. v. *nolint;* Sanchez, *De Matrimonio,* lib. V, disp. IX, n. 12; Laymann, *Theologia Moralis,* lib. V, tr. 8, pars 2, c. 7, n. 8, cor. 1; Gonzalez-Tellez (+ after 1673), *Commentaria Perpetua in Singulos Textus Quinque Libros Decretalium Gregorii IX* (5 vols. in 4, Venetiis, 1699), lib. IV, tit. V, c. 7, n. 3 (cited hereafter as *Commentaria Perpetua*); Arregui, *Summarium Theologiae Moralis* (13 ed., Westminster, Maryland: The Newman Bookshop, 1944), n. 788, 2°; Genicot-Salsmans, *Institutiones Theologiae Moralis* (14 ed., 2 vols., Buenos Aires: Dedebec, 1942), II, n. 459.

that a condition which stipulates the abandonment of the offspring does not, in itself, indicate an exclusion of the essence of marriage.[68] Those who mention such a condition as having an invalidating effect upon the marriage contract apparently refer to the condition of abandoning the offspring completely i. e., so that they are left to die.[69] Other authors mention explicitly that the condition of abandoning the offspring does not invalidate the marriage if the parties intend to abandon the offspring in such a way as to allow for their care by others (e. g. leaving them at the doorstep of an orphanage).[70] If the contracting parties intend to feed the offspring, but not at the mother's breast (*alere proprio lacte*), the validity of the marriage contract is not affected.[71]

(*b*) *An Interpretation of the Majority Opinion*

It is not difficult to understand why the conditions of procuring the abortion of the offspring, or of killing them or abandoning them completely should be classed as conditions which are contrary to the essence of marriage. In actual cases such conditions usually would indicate a positive intention to preclude the conception of offspring entirely. Of the few cases as decided by the Sacred Roman Rota, which included a reference to the stipulated condition of procuring the abortion or the killing of the offspring, this evil intent or act apparently was considered as an added indication of a positive intention to preclude the conception of offspring.[72]

Considered from a purely objective viewpoint, however, such conditions do not indicate an intention to exclude the marriage right with reference to the acts which are suitable of themselves for the procreation of offspring, even though they are introduced into the

[68] ". . . si vero conditio sit, ut proles exponatur, licet pietatis officio repugnet, non tamen substantiae: . . ."—Gongalez-Tellez, *Commentaria Perpetua,* lib. IV, tit. V, c. 7, n. 3.

[69] Cf. Chelodi, *loc. cit.;* Payen, *loc. cit.;* Raus, *loc. cit.*

[70] Cf. Sanchez, *ibid.,* n. 13; Gasparri, *loc. cit.*

[71] Cf. Sanchez, *loc. cit.;* Gasparri, *loc. cit.;* Cappello, *loc. cit.*

[72] Cf. S.R.R., *Nullitatis Matrimonii,* 13 febr. 1925, coram R.P.D. Francisco Solieri, dec. X, nn. 5 and 8—*Decisiones,* XVII (1925), 77 and 79; 10 febr. 1926, coram R.P.D. Andrea Jullien, dec. V, n. 11—*Decisiones,* XVIII (1926), 29.

marriage contract itself. The mere fact that the parties are determined to prevent the birth of the offspring or to kill the offspring or to abandon it completely does not indicate necessarily that they intend to interfere with the acts which "are suitable in themselves for the procreation of offspring" (canon 1081, § 2). It is possible that such parties nevertheless may intend to perform the act of conjugal union in the natural manner without doing anything to prevent the natural consequence of conjugal union (conception), and without excluding the marriage right in regard to the acts which are suitable of themselves for the procreation of offspring, i. e., the acts which, by the law of nature, are designed to lead to the conception of offspring. In actual cases, however, it must be admitted that such conditions usually would indicate a positive intention to prevent the conception of offspring. Authors are justified, therefore, in classing such conditions as contrary to the essence of marriage. It is more accurate to say, however, that such conditions are invalidating not in themselves, inasmuch as they indicate necessarily a positive intention to prevent the birth or survival of the offspring, but only incidentally inasmuch as, in the given circumstances of a concrete case, such conditions usually indicate a positive intention to preclude or prevent the conception of offspring.

The present writer prefers the opinion of De Smet and others whereby the concept of conditions which are in themselves contrary to the essence of marriage (if introduced into the marriage contract) is limited to conditions which are expressive of positive opposition to the *conception* of offspring. The most common types of such conditions are those which involve a stipulation to not use the marriage right in the natural manner or to use contraceptive devices in married life. The opinion of De Smet is preferable primarily because it is more in conformity with what the Code of Canon Law requires as absolutely essential for a valid marriage contract, i. e. the giving and accepting of the "right over the body for the performance of acts suitable of themselves for the procreation of offspring" (canon 1081, § 2). Furthermore, the opinion of De Smet and the other authors cited above emphasizes the proper distinction between the ends of marriage and the essence of marriage, and between the sacred obligations which are incumbent upon married persons in regard to their offspring, and the essential marriage right and corresponding obligation in regard to the acts suitable of themselves for the procreation of offspring.

(c) *The Invalidating Effect of a Condition which Involves Surgical Sterility*

If the parties introduce into their marriage contract a condition whereby it is stipulated that the man undergo castration, which will render him impotent and incapable of performing the act of conjugal union in a manner suitable for the procreation of offspring, the marriage is invalid.[73] If, however, the condition contains the stipulation that the woman undergo an ovariotomy (removal of the ovaries), hysterectomy (removal of the womb) or fallectomy (removal of the Fallopian tubes), which will render her completely sterile, the marriage, according to some authors, would be invalid.[74] The present writer prefers the opinion of other authors, who maintain that such a condition, objectively considered, is not to be considered as contrary to the essence of marriage.[75] Such a condition, *objectively considered*, does not indicate necessarily that the party who places the condition as a part of the contract intends, by a positive act of the will, to preclude the conception of offspring. It is admitted readily, however, that *in the given circumstances* of an individual case, such a condition usually would indicate a positive intention to preclude the conception of offspring.

[73] Cf. De Smet, *De Sponsalibus et Matrimonio*, n. 155; Timlin, *Conditional Matrimonial Consent*, p. 288. For a discussion of the various opinions on this subject, cf. Vermeersch, "Aktuelle Fragen des Eherechts und der Ehemoral,"—*Theologisch-praktische Quartalschrift* (Linz, 1832 ——), LXXXIX (1936), 52 ff. (cited hereafter as *Quartalschrift*).

[74] Cf. Zeiger, "Nova matrimonii definitio?": "Quid vero, si coniuges, matrimonium ineuntes, condicionem pravam apponunt ut mulier (sine necessitate) operationem subeat qua generatio omnis futura excludatur? Resp. Si condicio haec apponitur in actu contrahendi matrimonii, est condicio contra bonum prolis, destruens activitatem humanam in opere coniugii (i. e. sec. elementum negativum) 'ne impediatur effectus actus coniugalis.' "—*Periodica*, XX (1931), 58*. Wernz-Vidal (*Ius Matrimoniale*, V, n. 518, note 31) apparently hold the same view as Zeiger on this question.

[75] Cf. De Smet, *loc. cit.;* Timlin, *loc. cit.*

If the condition is stated as follows, however: "I contract marriage with you provided that you *have* undergone an operation, so that you are completely sterile," most authors agree that the validity of the marriage is not affected.[76] The fact that the woman in such a case, in consequence of the operation, knows that she can not have children, furnishes an added indication that she very likely is not opposed to the giving of the marriage right with reference to the procreation of offspring at the time of the exchange of matrimonial consent:

> Nam fieri optime potest (et ob favorem iuris praesumendum est) ut haec mulier, cum matrimonium contrahit, velit tradere-acceptare ius in corpus in ordine ad actus *per se* aptos ad prolis generationem, perpetuum et exclusivum, eo vel magis quod iam persuasum habeat coitus esse infoecundos: quo posito consensus matrimonialis adesset . . . consensus matrimonialis est actus qui a nostra pendet voluntate.[77]

No one will deny, however, that when such a condition is added to the marriage contract, in an individual case, there is a foundation for the suspicion that the woman entered the marriage with the same intention as that which prevailed when she submitted to the operation.[78]

(2) The Moral Welfare of the Offspring

There is no need to insist that the primary end of marriage comprises both the procreation and the education of the offspring. In the words of Pius XI:

[76] Cf. Gasparri, *De Matrimonio*, II, n. 829; Cappello, *De Sacramentis*, III, n. 601, 4; Payen, *De Matrimonio*, II, n. 1732, 2); Davis, *Moral and Pastoral Theology* (4 ed., 4 vols., New York: Sheed and Ward, 1943), II, 190.

[77] Gasparri, *loc. cit.* Cf. also Cappello, *loc. cit.;* Oesterle, "Circa controversam validitatem matrimonii feminae recisae,"—*Ephemerides Theologicae Lovanienses* (Brugis, 1924 ——), III (1926), 353, note 39 (cited hereafter as *Ephem. Theol. Lovan.*). For a criticism of the contrary view as advanced by Arendt (1852-1937), cf. Arend, "De genuina ratione impedimenti impotentiae," *Ephem. Theol. Lovan.*, IX (1932), 51.

[78] "At certe in casu habetur grave indicium contra debitam intentionem mulieris; quod ex adiunctis augeri vel minui aut tolli potest."—Cappello, *loc. cit.* Gasparri made the same remark and added: ". . . igitur in casu practico recurratur ad S.C.S. Officii."—*Loc. cit.*

Procreationis autem beneficio bonum prolis haud sane absolvitur, sed alterum accedat oportet, quod debita prolis educatione continetur. Parum profecto generatae proli atque adeo toti generi humano providisset sapientissimus Deus, nisi, quibus potestatem et ius dederat generandi, iisdem ius quoque et officium tribuisset educandi.[79]

All that has been said in the preceding pages in regard to the procreation of offspring as an *end* of marriage applies with equal adaptation to the education of offspring as well. Together they constitute the primary *end* of marriage, giving rise to sacred obligations on the side of married persons in regard to the offspring of their union. If these obligations are spurned or rejected, however, it does not follow necessarily that the parties intend to exclude the marriage right with regard to the acts which of themselves are suitable for the procreation of offspring. The ends of marriage as such and the obligations associated with them do not constitute the essence of marriage.

(a) *The Opinion of Earlier Authors*

There are indications that some authors conceived of the education of offspring as pertaining to the physical welfare of the offspring. Píchler (1670-1736), for example, apparently used the word *educatio* as referring to the early care and development of the offspring.[80] The present discussion, however, concerns the education of offspring as understood in the usual sense, i. e., the moral and spiritual development of the offspring.

Böckhn (1690-1752) seems to have been the principal exponent of the view that if a condition contrary to the education of the offspring were introduced into the marriage contract, the marriage would be invalid.[81] The case he had in mind was an agreement be-

[79] Ex litt. encycl. *Casti Connubii*, 31 dec. 1930—*AAS*, XXII (1930), 545.

[80] "Substantiae matrimonii repugnare non solum illas conditiones turpes, quae tendunt ad impediendam positive generationem prolis . . . verum etiam quae educationi prolis, uti, *si prolem natam occides* . . ."—*Candidatus Iurisprudentiae Sacrae* (Ingolstadii, 1724-1728), lib. IV, tit. V, n. 12, *sub fine*.

[81] ". . . si id vere in pactum et animo se mutuo ad id obligandi deducatur: secus si (ut plerumque fit, quando fit) simpliciter contrahentes invicem intentionem declarent, . . ."—*Commentarium*, lib. IV, tit. V, n. 61. The same view had been advanced by Schmier (1680-1728) (*Iurisprudentia*, lib. IV, tr. III,

tween the contracting parties to rear the boys in the religion of the father and the girls in the religion of the mother, or to rear all of the offspring in heresy.[82] Others adopted the same view in principle, but distinguished by saying that a stipulated condition of educating the offspring in heresy, in schism or in the magic arts did not invalidate the marriage contract, but that a condition to educate them in infidelity (Judaism, paganism, etc.) did invalidate the contract.[83]

Pichler contested the doctrine of Schmier, and insisted that only the conditions which concern the natural or physical welfare of the offspring (*bonum prolis naturale*) affect the validity of the marriage contract.[84] Tropper reviewed the various opinions on the question in detail, and concluded that since no authors except Schmier, Böckhn and Schmalzgrueber adhered to the opinion expressed above, it was better to hold that only those conditions which affect the natural generation of offspring invalidated the marriage contract.[85]

c. 5, n. 56 ff.) and accepted by Schmalzgrueber (1663-1735) (*Ius Ecclesiasticum Universum*, lib. IV, tit. VI, n. 150). Cf. also De Camillis, *Institutiones Iuris Canonici* (3 vols., Parisiis: apud Ludovicum Vivès, 1889), II, p. 224.

[82] *Loc. cit.*

[83] Wernz-Vidal indicate not only who those authors were, but also point to the inconsistency of their opinion when they state: "Qua in controversia nequit teneri illa distinctio, quam *Haringer* [1817-1887], *Weber* [1830-1890], *Steyart* [fl. end of 17th cent.], *Dens* [+ 1775] defenderunt, quod conditio in pactum deducta educandi filios in *infidelitatè* v. g. in *Iudaismo* ipso iure naturali irritet matrimonium, at eadem conditio educandi prolem in *haeresi* (vel schismate vel aliis delictis) matrimonium *non* reddat invalidum. Nam utraque conditio est *turpis* atque maior *gradus* turpitudinis, si proles in infidelitate sit educanda non constituit differentiam essentialem; ergo etiam in altero casu educationis in haeresi matrimonium dicendum est aut cum *Schmier* aliisque paucis *invalidum* aut in utroque casu cum aliis *validum*.—*Ius Matrimoniale*, n. 518, note (32).

[84] *Candidatus Iurisprudentiae Sacrae*, lib. IV, tit. I, n. 131.

[85] "Ex quo manifestum est, omnes retro Auctores caput illud 7 [i.e. of Gregory IX] de conditione naturali dumtaxat generationi prolis apposita intellexisse, hocque ipso moraliter certum esse, non nisi de ea intelligi debere."—*Tractatus Duo in Quibus Impedimenta Matrimonii Contractum Impedientia et Dirimentia ex Theologiae, et Iuris fontibus utriusque fori . . . explanantur* (Monachii, 1753), Pars I, n. 130. Cf. also Feije (1820-1894), *De Impedimentis et Dispensationibus Matrimonialibus* (4 ed., Lovanii: Typis Caroli Peeters, 1893), n. 566, 461, note (3).

(b) *The Prevalent Opinion Among Later Authors*

Most of the authors deny that a condition or agreement to educate the offspring in heresy, in schism or in infidelity invalidates the marriage contract.[86] They insist that such conditions are to be regarded in the external forum as any other shameful conditions which are not contrary to the essence of marriage, i. e., to be regarded as if they never had been placed by the contracting parties (*pro non adiecta habeantur*).[87]

It seems logical to make the same remarks concerning the exclusion of the education of offspring as were applied to the question of stipulated conditions of abandoning, of killing or of procuring the abortion of the offspring. If the parties agree to neglect their sacred obligation in regard to the moral and spiritual formation of their children, it would be a very serious violation of the laws of God and of nature, just as a condition or agreement to procure the abortion of the offspring, for example, would be a crime against God and nature. In the latter instance there would be good reason to suspect that the parties harbor a positive intention to exclude both the conception of offspring, and the right itself with reference to the acts suitable of themselves for the procreation of offspring. In the former instance (conditions against the education of children), however, the presence of such an invalidating intention would be extremely improbable.

(c) *The Attitude of the Holy See*

In 1742, the Sacred Congregation of the Council decided a case in which the parties had made an agreement to rear the offspring

[86] "Communissime tenent D.D. eam [conditionem] non esse contra substantiam matrimonii, quia non est directe contra bonum physicum prolis."—De Becker (1857-1936), *De Matrimonio, Praelectiones Canonicae* (nova ed., Louvain: Ceuterick, 1931), p. 125 f. Cf. also Lehmkuhl. *Theologia Moralis*, II, n. 689, note 1; Craisson (+ 1881), *Manuale Totius Iuris Canonici* (5 ed., 4 vols., Pictavii: Ex Typis H. Oudin, 1877), II, n. 4090; Santi (1830-1885)—Leitner (1862-1929), *Praelectiones Iuris Canonici* (4 ed., 5 vols. in 2, Ratisbonae: Pustet, 1903-1905), lib. IV, tit. V, n. 19; Chelodi, *Ius Matrimoniale*, n. 125; Gasparri, *De Matrimonio*, II, n. 905; Wernz-Vidal, *Ius Matrimoniale*, n. 518, note 32; Cappello, *De Sacramentis*, III, n. 631, 4; Noldin-Schmitt, *De Sacramentis*, III, n. 631, 1, a); Sipos, *Enchiridion Iuris Canonici*, § 133, 4, b), note 4; Knecht, *Handbuch des katholischen Eherechts*, p. 592, note (1).

[87] Cf. De Becker, *loc. cit.;* Wernz-Vidal, *loc. cit.*

in the Lutheran religion of the mother.[88] The case stated briefly that authors did not agree as to whether such agreements like others which are contrary to the natural procreation of offspring, would invalidate the marriage.[89] The decision was that such agreements did not affect the validity of marriage.[90]

In another case which contained a reference to an agreement to rear the boys in the religion of the non-Catholic father, and the girls in the religion of the Catholic mother, the agreement merely was branded as evil and sacrilegious, inasmuch as it is contrary to the divine law, which obligates the parents to rear their children in the true religion.[91] Since the case was concerned primarily with the lawfulness of marriages between Catholics and non-Catholics, there was no decision as to the validity of marriages which were contracted with an agreement to rear some of the offspring in a non-Catholic religion.

B. The Indirect Exclusion of the Boon of Offspring

Thus far the discussion has concerned only those conditions which are expressive of positive opposition to the procreation of offspring in particular. The discussion has led to the conclusion that the only conditions of this type which are in themselves contrary to the essence of marriage, if introduced into the marriage contract, are those which are expressive of positive opposition to the conception of offspring. Such conditions, if introduced into the marriage contract as

[88] S.C.C., *Augustana, Matrimonii,* 24 nov. 1742—*Thesaurus,* XI (1742), 169.

[89] "At num eiusmodi pactum, quod veluti prorsus impium nulla potest ratione subsistere, neque servandum est, substantiae ipsius coniugii refragetur, ita ut irritum illud reddat, non secus ac aliae conditiones, et pacta quae vel bono fidei coniugalis, vel naturali liberorum procreationi adversantur, haud una est Doctorum opinio."—*Loc. cit.*

[90] "Siquidem Authores mox allegati, quamvis quaestionem hanc peculiariter non instituant, in eam facile coniiciuntur abire sententiam, quod pactum istud sit irritum, salvo tamen, et integro manente iure connubii; . . ."—*Ibid.,* n. 169 f.

[91] S.C.C., *Dubio super matrimoniis inter Catholicos et Haereticos Cliviensis Ducatus,* 15 iun. 1793, § 22: ". . . iniquum porro sacrilegumque hoc pactum cum *Iure* pugnat *Divino,* ex quo parentes educare tenentur filios in vera Religione, in qua una est salus. . . ."—*Thesaurus,* LXII (1793), 152.

an essential part of the contract, point ***directly*** to the exclusion of the marriage right with reference to the acts suitable of themselves for the procreation of offspring.[92] When such conditions are introduced into the marriage contract itself, it is clear that the preventing of the conception of offspring enters into the contract as a matter of obligation, so that the marriage right and the corresponding essential obligation with reference to the acts suitable of themselves for the procreation of offspring are excluded necessarily.

There are other conditions, however, which sometimes are mentioned by authors as expressive of positive opposition to the giving of the marriage right as such. If such conditions do indicate the exclusion of the marriage right as such, it follows that they ***indirectly*** indicate the exclusion of the marriage right with reference to the procreation of offspring as well. The conditions in question are the following: "I contract marriage with you, provided that you abstain from the use of the marriage right forever," or ". . . provided that you never request the use of the marriage right," or ". . . provided that I have no obligation to grant you the use of the marriage right." The first of these conditions has been discussed sufficiently in the preceding article of this study. The present author prefers the opinion that the condition, "I contract marriage with you, provided that you abstain from the use of the marriage right forever," even if introduced into the marriage contract itself, is not necessarily incompatible with the giving of the marriage right with reference to the procreation of offspring. In other words, such a condition is not, in itself, contrary to the essence of marriage.

The condition, "I contract marriage with you, provided that you never request the use of the marriage right (*debitum coniugale*)" apparently is another form of the condition just discussed above, and as such, is not incompatible with the giving of the marriage right with reference to the procreation of offspring. Some authors, how-

[92] Apparently Gregory IX referred only to such conditions when he mentioned but one condition (with reference to the boon of offspring) as contrary to the essence of marriage: "Contraho tecum, si generationem prolis evites, . . ." —C. 7, X, *de conditionibus appositis in desponsatione vel in aliis contractibus*, IV, 5—Potthast, n. 9664. Cf. Vromant, *De Matrimonio*, n. 175 (p. 145), note (2).

ever, insisted that such a condition is to be regarded as contrary to the essence of marriage.[93] It is to be noted, however, that these authors are among those who held that an agreement to abstain from the use of the marriage right forever indicates an exclusion of the marriage right itself.[94]

Obviously, if one of the contracting parties stipulates that the other contracting party must never request the use of the marriage right, or must abstain forever from the use of the right, and the circumstances in the individual case indicate the exclusion of the marriage right itself, there is no doubt about the invalidity of the marriage. The principal point of the present discussion, however, is to stress that such conditions, objectively considered, do not in themselves indicate an exclusion of the marriage right itself.

The condition "I contract marriage with you, provided that I have no obligation to grant you the use of the marriage right" amounts to a clear exclusion of an essential obligation in marriage, i. e., the obligation which corresponds to the right over the body for the performance of acts suitable of themselves for the procreation of offspring.[95] In fact, such a condition would invalidate the marriage contract even if it were modified to read "I marry you, provided that I have no obligation to grant you the use of the marriage right when you request it unlawfully," for the just right over the body of the consort in marriage extends even to cases in which one of the par-

[93] The reason for such an opinion was stated by Schmalzgrueber as follows: ". . . quia de ratione matrimonii est totalis corporum traditio, ex qua dimanat mutuum, et aequale ius in utroque ad corpus alterius; atqui in hoc casu haec totalis traditio non fieret; non enim traderetur ius petendi; neque exurgeret aequale ius ad corpus; quia alter haberet ius petendi, et reddendi, alter vero solum ius reddendi."—*Ius Ecclesiasticum Universum,* lib. IV, tit. V, n. 125. Cf. also Sanchez, *De Matrimonio,* lib. V, disp. X, n. 3 f.; Pirhing (1606-1679), *Ius Canonicum Nova Methodo Explicatum* (5 vols. in 4, Dilingae, 1674-1678), lib. IV, tit. V, n. 13, *in fine* (cited hereafter as *Ius Canonicum*); Laymann, *Theologia Moralis,* lib. V, tr. X, par. 2, cap. 7, n. 8, cor. 2.

[94] Sanchez, *ibid.,* nn. 1 ff; Schmalzgrueber, *ibid.,* 120; Pirhing, *op. cit.,* lib. IV, tit. I, n. 69, and tit. V, n. 13; Laymann, *op. cit.,* lib. V, tr. 10, par. 2, cap. 7, n. 9.

[95] "Convenit inter DD. si simpliciter ineatur matrimonium sub conditione non reddendi debitum, ea conditione vitiari matrimonium; quia est contra bonum prolis, et contra bonum fidei."—Schmalzgrueber, *ibid.,* n. 126.

ties may exceed the bounds of temperance or religion (i. e., as contrary to a vow) in requesting the act of conjugal union.[96] If the condition were modified, however, to read, "I marry you, provided that I have no obligation to grant you the use of the marriage right when you are without a right in justice to request it," then there would be no question of an invalid marriage in consequence of the placing of the condition.[97]

Some authors maintained that a condition to exclude cohabitation forever had an invalidating effect upon the marriage contract.[98] Modern authors maintain, however, that such a condition does not invalidate the marriage contract, for cohabitation pertains not to the essence of marriage, but to the integrity of marriage.[99]

It is important to note that no condition has an invalidating effect upon the validity of the marriage contract, unless it proceeds from a positive act of the will. This important point will be emphasized and illustrated in the following chapter.

[96] Cf. Schmalzgrueber, *ibid.*, n. 127; Sanchez, *op. cit.*, lib. V, disp. XI, n. 2.

[97] "Si tamen apponatur conditio, ut possit coniux debitum negare, quoties id sibi licet, quia alter non habet ius iustitiae ad petendum, ut si alter adulteretur, vel petat in loco sacro, valet conditio, nec vitiat; quia iure inest."—Sanchez, *ibid.*, n. 3; Schmalzgrueber, *loc. cit.*

[98] "Consensus ab uno ex coniugibus praestito sub conditione nunquam cum altero cohabitandi, est causa dispensandi. Imo haec conditio nullum reddit matrimonium."—Coscius (fl. 1766-1773), *De Separatione Tori Coniugalis* (Florentiae, 1856), cap. 16, n. 271 f. Cf. also Schmalzgrueber, *Ius Ecclesiasticum Universum*, lib. IV, tit. V, n. 124.

[99] Cf. Wernz-Vidal, *Ius Matrimoniale*, n. 600; Cappello, *De Sacramentis*, III, nn. 6, 3 and 574, 3°; Gasparri, *De Matrimonio*, II, n. 905, as well as a recent decision of the Sacred Roman Rota: *Romana, Nullitatis Matrimonii et Dispensationis super Rato*, 22 ian. 1944, coram R.P.D. Arcturo Wynen, n. 24—*AAS*, XXXVI (1944), 189.

CHAPTER II

TYPES OF OPPOSITION TO THE BOON OF OFFSPRING

In the preceding chapter, the question of opposition to the boons of marriage has been discussed by referring to both intentions and conditions which militate against the boons of marriage. Each of these two types of opposition to the boons of marriage will be discussed separately in the present chapter (Articles 2 and 3 respectively). In order to present a clear concept of each of these types of opposition to the boons of marriage, it may be well to devote a preliminary article to a comparison between the two.

Article I. Intentions and Conditions Compared

In order to determine the validity of consent to the marriage contract, it is important to investigate not only whether the parties actually intended to contract marriage, but also whether anything which is incompatible with the essence of marriage was added to the object of their consent, as a part of the contract. When the contracting parties express consent to the marriage contract externally, it is presumed that their internal intention in regard to the marriage contract is in conformity with their external consent,[1] i. e., that they intend internally to enter a true marriage contract with all of its essential obligations. If there is convincing evidence in the external forum that the parties actually did not intend to contract marriage, a declaration of nullity is possible. In such a case, the immediate reason for the invalidity of the marriage lies with the contracting parties themselves.

If, on the other hand, there is every indication that the parties themselves intended to contract marriage, but there is convincing evidence in the external forum that they added something to the object of their consent (as a part of the contract) which is incompatible with the essence of marriage, a declaration of nullity likewise

[1] Canon 1086, § 1.

is possible; but the *immediate* reason for the invalidity of the marriage lies not with the parties themselves, but with the object of their consent.[2] The marriage is invalid not precisely inasmuch as the parties themselves lack an intention to contract marriage, but inasmuch as the presence of something which is incompatible with the essence of marriage, as a part of their contract, indicates a positive intention to exclude one of the essential obligations of marriage, and hence vitiates their consent necessarily.

If one or both of the parties harbor a positive intention to exclude one of the essential obligations of marriage, their consent necessarily is vitiated and cannot give rise to a valid marriage contract. A true intention to contract marriage cannot exist side by side with a positive intention to exclude something which pertains to the very essence of marriage.[3] In such cases, therefore, there is no absolute need to investigate whether the person actually intended either to

[2] As indicated in the foreword of this study, the lack of an intention to contract marriage amounts to a case of total simulation, whereas the presence of a positive intention to exclude an essential obligation of marriage amounts to a case of partial simulation. In referring to this distinction between total and partial simulation, Roberti ("Quaestiones quaedam de identificatione actionum ob vitia consensus in causis matrimonialibus") stated as follows: "Simulatio quae totalis appellatur non est nisi simulatio simpliciter considerata; eademque *subiectum* respicit cuius externa manifestatio non respondet internae voluntati. Contra ea quae simulatio partialis dicitur respicit *obiectum* consensus eo quod non totum illud praestatur quod praestari debet, e. g. ius in corpus sed non exclusivum vel non perpetuum."—*Apollinaris* (Romae, 1928 ——), VI (1933), 107.

[3] "Quicumque contractum vult, necesse est, ut eiusdem substantiam velit; ideoque, si contrahentes in matrimonii foedere ineundo, conditionem apponunt illius substantiae contrariam, certissimum hoc est argumentum, nequaquam eos in veri matrimonii contractum consentire: sine contrahentium autem consensu, matrimonium esse non potest."—Benedictus XIV, *De Synodo Dioecesana,* lib. XIII, cap. 22, n. 7. Cf. also Payen, *De Matrimonio,* II, n. 1675; Cappello, *De Sacramentis,* III, n. 598, 2, and the comments of contemporary authors in regard to the distinction between the intention of contracting marriage (*intentio contrahendi*), the intention of not obligating oneself to essential obligations of marriage (*intentio sese non obligandi*), and the intention of not fulfilling the obligations (*intentio obligationes non implendi*), e. g. (besides those authors mentioned on page 12) Vlaming, *Praelectiones Iuris Matrimonii,* II, n. 534; Gasparri, *De Matrimonio,* II, n. 814 ff.

contract marriage at the time of his exchange of consent, or to withhold his consent until some future time, for as long as something which is contrary to the essence of marriage remains as an integral part of the object of his consent, the intention to contract marriage can not be anything else but vitiated and invalid. The direct cause of the invalidity of the marriage is to be traced not to the person who gave consent to the marriage (*ex parte subiecti*), but to the deficient object of that person's consent (*ex parte obiecti*). In such cases, the marriage is invalid not precisely because of a lack of consent to the marriage contract as such, but because of the presence of a vitiated matrimonial consent.

The intention to exclude something which pertains to the essence of marriage may be expressed either by a direct and absolute act of the will: "I intend to contract marriage but I intend to preclude the conception of offspring," or by an indirect and hypothetical act of the will: "I intend to contract marriage, provided that you prevent the conception of offspring." In the former case the consent is absolute, in the latter case it is conditional. Since every positive act of the will which is expressive of opposition to something which pertains to the essence of marriage presupposes a vitiated consent, and since every condition necessarily includes an intention,[4] the fact whether the intention was expressed in an absolute manner or in a conditional manner is of secondary importance in so far as the internal validity or invalidity of the marriage is concerned.

A. *The Character of Conditions Which Are Contrary to the Essence of Marriage*

It must be remembered that conditions which are expressive of positive opposition to the essence of marriage are in a class by themselves. The conditions which are considered as capable of invalidating a marriage precisely *as conditions* are those which presuppose an intention to contract a true marriage.[5] Provided that the con-

[4] "Conditio distinguitur ab intentione, sed eam necessario includit in ipso conceptu, . . ."—Cappello, *De Matrimonio,* III, n. 625 f.). Cf. also Ford, *The Validity of Virginal Marriage,* p. 95.

[5] "Conditio semel apposita et non revocata: . . . 3°. Si de futuro licita,

ditions do not involve something which is contrary to the essence of marriage, there is no question of an underlying intention to exclude one or the other of the essential obligations of marriage. Nor is there any question of a total simulation, for an intention to contract marriage as such is implied in the condition itself: "I intend to contract marriage, provided that you become a Catholic within a year." Such conditions indicate merely that the intention to enter the marriage contract irrevocably, with the recognition of all its essential obligations, depends upon whether or not the stipulated condition is verified.[6] If the condition is not verified, the intention to contract marriage does not take effect, and the marriage is demonstrated to be invalid.

In the case of conditions which are contrary to the essence of marriage, however, the verification of the condition is incapable of determining the validity or invalidity of the marriage for the simple reason that the marriage was invalid from the very moment of the exchange of external consent. Since such stipulations invalidate the marriage contract not precisely as conditions, but as indicative of a positive intention to exclude all recognition of one of the essential obligations of marriage, it is only proper to classify them as examples of a simulated or vitiated consent.[7]

The following conclusions may serve to emphasize the special character of conditions which are contrary to the essence of marriage:

(1) If intentions are compared with conditions, but in abstraction from whether or not either the former or the latter involve something

valorem matrimonii suspendit; 4°. Si de praeterito vel de praesenti matrimonium erit validum vel non, prout id quod conditioni subest, exsistit vel non."—Canon 1092.

[6] ". . . consensus conditionatus est consensus *verus*, sed nondum *irrevocabilis* et *efficax* ad producendum effectum *principalem*, i. e., *vinculum* matrimonii, *ante* verificatum eventum; . . ."—Wernz-Vidal, *Ius Matrimoniale*, n. 512, note 13, *in fine*.

[7] As one Rota decision stated in reference to the condition of precluding the procreation of offspring in particular: ". . . haec conditio, . . . non est vera et propria conditio, sed potius voluntas contraria substantiae matrimonii, . . ."—S.R.R., *Nullitatis Matrimonii*, 31 oct. 1919, coram R.P.D. Aloisio Sincero, dec. XVII, n. 2—*Decisiones*, XI (1919), 146.

which is contrary to the essence of marriage, the principal difference between them is that in the case of an intention (an absolute act of the will) the question of the validity or invalidity of the marriage is settled at the time of consent. In the case of a condition the question of the validity or invalidity of the marriage is not settled until the stipulated condition is verified.[8]

(2) If *intentions* which involve an exclusion of something which pertains to the essence of marriage are compared with *conditions* which are *not* contrary to the essence of marriage, a considerable difference is noted between them. The former presuppose vitiated consent, whereas the latter presuppose an intention to contract a true marriage. This amounts to a comparison between a simulated consent on the one hand and a lawful but conditional consent on the other. In the former instance the marriage is invalid from the moment of the exchange of the apparent consent, and never can be valid as long as such a contrary intention prevails. In the latter instance (conditional consent) the marriage will be valid if and when the stipulated condition is verified.[9]

(3) If *intentions* which are contrary to the essence of marriage are compared with *conditions* which are contrary to the essence of marriage, the principal point of difference concerns the manner in which the positive opposition to the essence of marriage is manifested in the external forum.[10] Naturally it is less difficult to prove that a contracting party intended to exclude one of the essential obligations of marriage if the intention has been expressed as a condition. Since this difference is purely incidental, it is logical to conclude that whatever is said in regard to intentions which are con-

[8] ". . . intentio est actus voluntatis simpliciter elicitus, conditio est idem actus voluntatis non simpliciter positus, sed alicui circumstantiae necne alligatus."—Cappello, *De Sacramentis,* III, n. 625, *in fine.* Cf. also *ibid.,* n. 593, 1.

[9] Cf. S.R.R., *Monacen. et Frisingen., Nullitatis Matrimonii,* 25 febr. 1929, coram R.P.D. Ubaldo Mannucci, dec. XV, n. 4—*Decisiones,* XXI (1929), 134 f.

[10] S.R.R., *Nullitatis Matrimonii,* 12 aug. 1929, coram R.P.D. Francisco Parrillo, dec. LII, n. 2: ". . . differentia inter utrumque, ad effectus quod attinet, vix nominis est, si excipias diversam voluntatis manifestationem, quae proprius attingit probationem in foro externo."—*Decisiones,* XXI (1929), 435.

trary to the essence of marriage generally may be applied to conditions which are contrary to the essence of marriage.[11]

(4) If conditions which are contrary to the essence of marriage are compared with lawful conditions (canon 1092, 3° and 4°), the same observations apply as those which were stated in conclusion n. (2). Since conditions which are contrary to the essence of marriage indicate vitiated consent, their invalidating force is not to be attributed primarily to their character as conditions, but to the fact that they indicate an underlying positive intention to exclude one of the essential obligations of marriage.

B. *The Value of Conditions As Indicative of Vitiated Consent*

Since the term *condition* applies in a strict sense only to a stipulation which, when added to the expression of consent, suspends the effectiveness of that consent until some future, uncertain time,[12] it is apparent that a stipulation which indicates a vitiated consent, and hence precludes the possibility of a valid marriage at some future time, can not be considered as a condition in the strict sense. The latter stipulation nevertheless is to be classed as a condition inasmuch as the validity of the consent, and consequently of the marriage contract as well, is made dependent upon some circumstance, e. g., the future preventing of conception in married life. For the essential element in all true conditions is that the validity of an act is made dependent upon some circumstance.[13]

In order to be a true condition, however, capable of affecting the validity of matrimonial consent, it is essential that the condition be intended as a part of the marriage contract itself. Otherwise, the

[11] Cf. Cappello, *De Sacramentis,* III, n. 593, 1.

[12] "Conditio . . . sensu stricto est circumstantia actui legitimo adiecta, quae illius valorem in tempus futurum et incertum *suspendit.*"—Wernz-Vidal, *Ius Matrimoniale,* n. 510. Cf. also Chelodi, *Ius Matrimoniale,* n. 123; Gougnard, *Tractatus de Matrimonio* (7 ed., Mechliniae: H. Dessain, 1931), n. 30, p. 142; Vermeersch-Creusen, *Epitome Iuris Canonici,* II, n. 379; Cappello, *De Sacramentis,* III, n. 625, 2).

[13] "Conditio late sumpta est circumstantia ("si") actui legitimo (v. g., contractui, testamento) adiecta, ex qua consensus pendet . . ."—Wernz-Vidal, *loc. cit.;* Gougnard, *loc. cit.;* Payen, *De Matrimonio,* II, n. 1725, 3).

most it indicates is that one of the parties intends to obligate the other party to something in married life itself—a *post*-contractual obligation.[14] Just as a stipulation to suspend consent until some future time does not have the force of a true condition unless the intention is to contract *only*, e. g., "provided that you become a Catholic within a year," so a stipulation which is expressive of opposition to the essence of marriage has not the force of a true condition unless there is present a positive intention to enter *only* such a union in which, e. g., the conception of offspring is precluded.[15] In the latter case the condition, as part of the very contract of marriage, indicates that the positive intention to exclude the essential obligation with regard to the boon of offspring actually prevails over the externally expressed intention to contract a true marriage.

It is rare that a positive intention contrary to the boon of offspring is expressed clearly enough to indicate, in the external forum, that the party who expressed the intention intended to exclude the marriage right or reject the essential obligation with regard to the boon of offspring. If such an intention is expressed as a *true condition,* however, and the condition involves something which, objectively considered, is incompatible with the essence of marriage, it is apparent not only that the party who placed the condition did not intend to contract a true marriage, but also that he or she could not have intended to contract a true marriage. When the consent of the parties is vitiated, inasmuch as the object of their consent includes something which is incompatible with the essence of marriage, their consent can not give rise to the true marriage union, as established by Christ. Hence when there is evidence that one of the contracting parties has placed a *true condition* contrary to the

[14] This type of stipulation, which is known as a *mode,* will be discussed in the final article of this study.

[15] ". . . tunc habetur contra matrimonii substantiam *vera conditio,* ac reapse de futuro, si pars, positivo voluntatis actu, *suum consensum alligat* exclusioni alicuius obligationis essentialis, ita ut eatenus velit contrahere *quatenus haec obligatio a se excluditur.* Si id sit, condicio adiecta ingreditur ipsum contractum matrimonialem: . . ."—Payen, *De Matrimonio,* II, n. 1732, 1). Cf. also S.R.R., *Nullitatis Matrimonii,* 10 dec. 1914, coram R.P.D. Ioanne Prior, dec. XXXIII, n. 4—*Decisiones,* VI (1914), 341; 8 febr. 1915, coram R.P.D. Ioanne Prior, dec. III, n. 4—*Decisiones,* VII (1915), 22.

boon of offspring, it is less difficult to establish the invalidity of the marriage in the external forum.[16]

To say that a condition invalidates a marriage only if it is placed as a *true* condition is equivalent to saying that it must be placed as a condition apart from which consent would not have been given (*conditio sine qua non*). The mere fact that the contracting parties intend, by a positive act of the will, to exclude something which pertains to the very essence of marriage is sufficient to invalidate the marriage. Such an intention is incompatible with an intention to contract a true marriage. In actual cases, however, it is necessary to establish that the intention entered into the marriage contract itself. The best means of establishing this fact is to investigate whether the parties expressed such an intention as a condition, and whether they would have consented to the marriage apart from such a condition. In other words, the best means of verifying that the parties actually harbored a positive intention of excluding one of the essential obligations of marriage is to seek evidence that the parties were determined to withhold consent to the marriage altogether, rather than accept, for example, the essential obligation with reference to the procreation of offspring. It seems, therefore, that the only conditions which can be accepted in the external forum as true conditions are those which are known as *sine qua non* conditions. For it is only such a type of condition which furnishes convincing evidence in the external forum that the intention to exclude one of the essential obligations of marriage prevailed over the externally expressed intention to contract marriage.

[16] Of the fifty-nine cases decided by the Sacred Roman Rota on the score of the exclusion of the boon of offspring from 1909 and 1931 inclusively, forty-three were distinct cases. Each of the remaining sixteen cases was a review of a case which previously had been decided by the Rota. Of the forty-three cases, twenty resulted in a declaration of nullity: thirteen cases furnished sufficient evidence of a *sine qua non* condition contrary to the boon of offspring, and seven cases furnished evidence of a positive intention to exclude the marriage right itself with reference to the boon of offspring. Cf. *infra*, Chapter V.

Article 2. Invalidating Intentions

Despite the strong presumption that the internal consent of the contracting parties is in conformity with their consent as expressed externally,[17] the Code of Canon Law establishes clearly that if one or both of the contracting parties, by a positive act of the will, exclude either the marriage itself or all right to the conjugal act, or one of the essential properties of marriage, the contract is invalid.[18] The purpose of the present article is to analyze each phrase of this important canon (1086, § 2). It will be helpful to preface such an analysis with a brief review of both the canonical principles and the practice of the Holy See relative to the question of simulated consent.

A. *Principles and Practice in Regard to Simulated Consent*

1. Discussions Among the Authors

Authors agree that even an implicit intention contrary to the boon of sacramental stability is sufficient to invalidate matrimonial consent.[19] There was considerable discussion among the authors, however, on the question of just what kind of intention contrary to the boons of offspring and conjugal fidelity indicated an exclusion of the marriage right itself with reference to either of these two boons of marriage. Some maintained that even an unexpressed implicit intention (*in mente retenta*) contrary to any one of the three boons of marriage invalidated the marriage contract.[20] Others took the view that an intention contrary to any of the three boons of marriage did not invalidate the marriage, unless it was expressed ex-

[17] "Internus animi consensus semper praesumitur conformis verbis vel signis in celebrando matrimonio adhibitis."—Canon 1086, § 1.

[18] "At si alterutra vel utraque pars positivo voluntatis actu excludat matrimonium ipsum, aut omne ius ad coniugalem actum, vel essentialem aliquam matrimonii proprietatem, invalide contrahit."—Canon 1086, § 2.

[19] Cf. Sanchez, *De Matrimonio*, lib. II, disp. XXIX, n. 11. This follows from the fact that the boon of sacramental stability always pertains to the essence of marriage. Cf. *supra*, p. 6 f.

[20] Sanchez mentions this view (*ibid.*, n. 9) without, however, approving of it.

plicitly and agreed upon by both parties.[21] The favored opinion, however, involved a distinction between the boon of sacramental stability and the other two boons of marriage. According to this opinion, even an implicit intention contrary to the boon of sacramental stability invalidated the contract. Intentions contrary to the boons of offspring and conjugal fidelity did not invalidate the contract unless they were expressed explicitly and agreed upon by both parties (*deducta in pactum*).[22] This view is based on the fact that in regard to the boons of offspring and conjugal fidelity, there is always the possibility that the parties do not intend to exclude the marriage right or corresponding essential obligation with reference to the boons of offspring and conjugal fidelity, but merely intend to abuse the right or neglect the fulfillment of the corresponding obligation.[23]

The distinction employed by contemporary authors between the intention of not contracting marriage and the intention of not acknowledging the essential obligations of marriage has been mentioned previously in this study.[24] There is no need to explain further why both intentions indicate an invalid marriage. The same authors make a further distinction between an intention not to acknowledge the essential obligations of marriage, and an intention of acknowledging those obligations, but of neglecting the fulfillment of them in married life.[25] This distinction applies only to the boons of offspring and conjugal fidelity.[26] This distinction emphasizes the

[21] Cf., for example, Lancelotti (1522 ——), *Institutiones Iuris Canonici* (Lugdini, 1579), lib. II, col. 139.

[22] Cf. Sanchez, *Ibid.*, n. 11; Gonzalez-Tellez, *Commentaria Perpetua*, lib. IV, tit. V, c. 7, n. 9; Laymann, *Theologia Moralis*, lib. V, tr. X, par. 2, c. 7, n. 8. In confirmation of this view, Sanchez makes the following statement: "Et confirmatur, quia stat velle obligari ad aliquid faciendum, et adesse animum non implendi; ut qui vere iurat animo violandi iuramentum: nec ea intentio tollit obligationis valorem."—*Loc. cit.*

[23] Cf. *supra*, p. 6 ff.

[24] Cf. *supra*, p. 8.

[25] Cf. *supra*, p. 37.

[26] For the boon of sacramental stability is enjoyed at the moment that the parties consent to the marriage contract, and always pertains to the essence of marriage. Cf. *supra*, p. 6.

view expressed in the preceding paragraph, i. e., if the contracting parties intend not to acknowledge one or the other of the essential obligations of marriage, the marriage is invalid; if, however, they intend to obligate themselves to all that pertains to the essence of marriage, but intend to neglect the fulfillment of one or the other of those obligations, the validity of the marriage is not necessarily affected by such an intention.[27] These same distinctions are employed in the decisions of the Sacred Roman Rota.[28]

In actual cases, however, most conditions which are expressive of opposition to the boon of offspring indicate merely an intention to neglect the fulfillment of the obligation with reference to the procreation of offspring, by abusing the marriage right. Although the contracting parties frequently intend to prevent the conception of offspring, the condition whereby they give expression to their opposition to the boon of offspring usually does not indicate a positive intention to exclude the essential obligation in regard to the procreation of offspring. In other words, the condition usually is not placed as a part of the marriage contract itself.

Unless the intention or condition to preclude the conception of offspring is introduced into the marriage contract itself as an essential part of the contract, the validity of the marriage is not affected. No condition logically can be regarded as contrary to the essence of marriage in a given case unless it enters into the contract itself. When Sanchez and other authors said that a condition contrary to the boon of offspring did not invalidate the marriage contract unless

[27] "Cum *valido* contractu matrimoniali cohaeret voluntas seu intentio positiva non implendi obligationes, quas secum affert; harum enim adimpletio supervenit matrimonio in suo esse constituto nec defectus adimpletionis actus essentiam mutare potest: voluntas obligationem assumendi et eam violandi non necessario se invicem excludunt."—Wernz-Vidal, *Ius Matrimoniale*, n. 462. Cf. also Gasparri, *De Matrimonio*, II, n. 814; Payen, *De Matrimonio*, II, n. 1677; Chelodi, *Ius Matrimoniale*, n. 117; Cappello, *De Sacramentis*, III, n. 601.

[28] Cf., for example, S.R.R., *Nullitatis Matrimonii*, 11 febr. 1929, coram R.P.D. Francisco Guglielmi, dec. XI, n. 3—*Decisiones*, XXI (1929), 93; 15 ian. 1931, coram R.P.D. Henrico Quattrocolo, dec. II, n. 5 ff.—*Decisiones*, XXIII (1931), 2 ff.; 16 iul. 1931, coram R.P.D. Francisco Guglielmi, dec. XXXV, n. 2 f.—*Decisiones*, XXIII (1931), 293; 20 nov. 1931, coram R.P.D. Ubaldo Mannucci, dec. LIII, n. 2—*Decisiones*, XXIII (1931), 457.

it was reduced to a pact (*deducta in pactum*),[29] they apparently referred primarily not to the marriage pact itself (*pactum matrimoniale*) but to a separate agreement between the contracting parties concerning the contrary condition, e. g., the preventing of the conception of offspring. This does not mean that these authors held that the marriage was invalid in the internal forum only if there was evidence of such an agreement, but rather that they were insisting upon the need of an indication in the external forum that the condition was introduced into the marriage pact itself. Although the fact that the contracting parties express their intention to prevent the procreation of offspring as a condition and agree upon such a condition does not indicate necessarily that the condition becomes a part of the marriage contract itself, such an external pact or agreement does justify a presumption to that effect. The question will be discussed at length in Chapter III of this study. The few remarks presented here may serve to furnish a clearer concept of invalidating intentions.

2. The Historical Background of Canon 1086

Until the time of Pope Innocent III (1198-1216), authors offered slight hope for a declaration of nullity on the score of simulated consent once the parties had pronounced the words of consent. Gratian stated in his *Decretum* (ca. 1140) that the marriage was invalid if one of the contracting parties was insane at the time of the exchange of consent,[30] and the great theologian Peter the Lombard (ca. 1100-ca. 1164) implied that the marriage was invalid if one of the parties consented through force or deception,[31] but no exception was made for those who claimed to have given only a fictitious or simulated consent.[32] Joyce (1864-1943) interpreted the view of

[29] Cf. *supra*, p. 44 f.

[30] C. 26, XXXII, q. 7.

[31] "Si autem verbis explicant quod tamen corde non volunt: si non sit ibi coactio vel dolus, obligatio illa verborum, quibus consentiunt dicentes: Accipio te in virum, et ego te uxorem: matrimonium facit."—*Petri Lombardi Libri IV Sententiarum* (2. ed., 2 vols., Quaracchi: Ex Typographia Collegii S. Bonaventurae, 1916), lib. IV, dist. XXVII, cap. 3.

[32] *Loc. cit.* For a more detailed study of this subject, cf. Esmein (+ 1913) —Génèstal (1872-1931)—Dauvillier, *Le Mariage en Droit Canonique* (2. ed., 2 vols., Paris, 1929-1935), I, 334 ff.

Peter the Lombard as indicating that the Church could only judge by externals, and therefore could not take account of a man's declaration that he had not intended to give true consent.[83]

In the year 1212, however, Pope Innocent indicated that if there was proof in the external forum that one of the parties did not give internal consent, the marriage could not be upheld as valid.[84] The declaration of the pontiff was a response in answer to a question concerning the validity of a marriage in which the young man, not wishing marriage but mere concubinage, used a fictitious name when giving consent.[85] It is to be noted that the young man in the case considered the marriage invalid in view of his use of a fictitious name.[86]

The response of Innocent III indicated that he was inclined to uphold the validity of the marriage, for it was clear that the young man spoke for himself, and the presumption in favor of the validity of the union was confirmed by the subsequent act of conjugal union between the two.[87] The rest of the response, however, was a source of embarrassment to many of the early commentators:

> . . . videtur forte pro coniugio praesumendum, nisi tu nobis expresse scripsisses, quod ille nec proposuit, nec consentit illam ducere in uxorem, quod qualiter tibi constiterit non videmus. Nos autem, quid iuris sit rescribentes, [*hoc*] dicimus, quod, si res ita se habuerit, videlicet, quod ille eam non proposuit ducere in uxorem, nec unquam consentit in praedictam personam, non debet

[83] *Christian Marriage: An Historical and Doctrinal Study* (London and New York: Sheed and Ward, 1933), p. 75.

[84] C. 26, X, *de sponsalibus et matrimoniis,* IV, 1—Potthast, n. 4379. The same text had been incorporated into the *Compilatio Quarta,* c. 1, IV, 1.

[85] ". . . quum quandam mulierem quidam aliter inducere nequivisset, ut sibi commisceretur carnaliter, nisi desponsasset eandem, nulla solennitate adhibita vel alicuius praesentia, dixit illi: 'te Ioannes desponsat,' quum ipse Ioannes non vocaretur, sed finxit se vocari Ioannem, non credens esse coniugium eo, quod ipse non vocaretur hoc nomine, nec haberet propositum contrahendi, sed copulam tantum exsequendi carnalem, . . ."—*Loc. cit.*

[86] *Loc. cit.*

[87] "Super quod tibi respondemus, quod, quum praefatus vir praedictam desponsaverit mulierem in propria persona et sub nomine alieno, quo tunc vocari se finxit, et inter eos sit carnalis copula subsecuta, videtur forte pro coniugio praesumendum, . . ."—*Loc. cit.*

> ex illo facto coniugium iudicari, quum in eo nec substantia coniugalis contractus, nec [*etiam*] forma contrahendi coniugium valeat inveniri, quoniam ex altera parte dolus sollummode adfuit, et defuit omnino consensus, sine quo cetera nequeunt foedus perficere coniugale.[38]

Some commentators, while admitting that simulated consent can not give rise to a valid marriage, nevertheless thought that the response of Innocent III should apply only in the internal forum.[39]

Although such an interpretation involved a distortion of the text of Innocent III's response,[40] it was based on several sound, juridical considerations, e. g., that the law must presume good faith on the part of persons who enter any legal engagement,[41] and that no one should be allowed to profit by his own evil action.[42]

The gloss on the response of Innocent III stated that even if the person previously had told others of his intention to simulate consent so that witnesses were available to prove a lack of consent, the validity of the marriage had to be upheld, for the man could well have changed his evil intention before giving consent to the marriage.[43] Later, Hostiensis stated that the protestation of one of the

[38] *Loc. cit.*

[39] Cf. *Glossa ordinaria* ad c. cit., s. v. *qualiter tibi constiterit;* Hostiensis (+ 1271), *Commentaria in Quinque Decretalium Libros* (5 vols. in 3, Venetiis, 1581), lib. IV, tit. I, c. 26, nn. 1-6 (cited hereafter as *Commentaria*); Ioannes Andreae, *Commentaria,* lib. IV, tit. I, c. 26, n. 9; Abbas Panormitanus (1386-1453), *Commentaria in Quinque Libros Decretalium* (5 vols. in 7, Venetiis, 1588), lib. IV, tit. I, c. 26, n. 8 (cited hereafter as *Commentaria*).

[40] "Néanmoins, cette solution [i. e., the response of Innocent III] était tellement extrême, tellement antijuridique, que beaucoup de docteurs, faisant violence au text, l'entendaient autrement."—Esmein—Généstal—Dauvillier, *Le Mariage en Droit Canonique,* I, 339.

[41] ". . . nemo existimandus est dixisse quod non mente agitaverit."—D. (33.10) (7, 2).

[42] C. 1, X, *de eo, qui duxit in matrimonium, quam polluit per adulterium,* IV, 7

[43] "Sed pone quod aliquis protestetur coram pluribus, quod omnia quae dicet vel faciet, non faciet animo contrahendi matrimonium, et postea publice dicat, consentio in te: nunquid est hic matrimonium, vel non? In casu isto dico quod ecclesia iudicare debet pro matrimonio: quia recurrendum est ad communem verborum intelligentiam . . . Talia enim verba non possunt servire suae intentioni, praeterea si probet, quod illa verba protestatus fuit primo,

contracting parties that true consent actually was not intended should be accepted in the external forum if the external consent had been given because of fear or for some other reasonable cause.[44] This view was accepted by later commentators.[45] In other words, an exception to the rule as stated in the gloss mentioned above was admitted in cases in which the party who protested that his or her consent was stimulated or fictitious had a just reason for doing so.

3. The Practice in the Tribunals of the Holy See

The response of Innocent III discussed above referred to a case of total simulation. That it was accepted as a guiding norm in cases of total simulation is evidenced by a considerable number of decisions as issued by both the Sacred Congregation of the Council[46] and the Sacred Roman Rota.[47] The proof demanded by the tri-

potuit postea recedere ab illa voluntate, et consentire in illam, et hoc videtur per illud quod postea publice facit: et si dicat quod adhuc tempore contractus erat in eadem voluntate, non creditur ei: quia contra eum debet fieri interpretatio, qui dolum adhibet, . . ."—*Glossa ordinaria* ad c. 26, X, *de sponsalibus et matrimoniis*, IV, 1, s. v. *mulierem*.

[44] *Commentaria*, lib. IV, tit. I, c. 26, n. 6.

[45] "Aut enim fuit iusta causa protestandi, puta metus, et iuvat protestatio, nec ab ea videtur recessum per contrarium factum . . . nisi postmodum sequatur copula . . . . Aut non suberat iusta causa protestandi, et procedit determinatio glossae. . . ."—Abbas Panormitanus, *Commentaria*, lib. IV, tit. I, c. 26, n. 9. Cf. also Ioannes Andreae, *Commentaria*, lib. IV, tit. V, c. 26, n. 14; Bohic (ca. 1310-ca. 1350), *In Quinque Decretalium Libros Commentaria* (Venetiis, 1576), lib. IV, tit. I, c. 26, n. 4 f.

[46] Cf. S.C.C., *Mutinen, Matrimonii*, 19 aug. 1724 et 9 iun. 1725—*Thesaurus*, III (1724-1726), 66 ff. and 161 ff., Fontes, nn. 3282 and 3299; *Compostellana, Matrimonii*, 19 aug. 1730 et 10 mart. 1731—*Thesaurus*, V (1730-1732), 29 ff. and 83, *Fontes*, nn. 3363 and 3371; *Capauna seu Calven., Matrimonii*, 9 iul. 1757 et 13 dec. 1757 et 28 ian. 1758—*Thesaurus*, XXVI (1757), 57 and 87 and XXVII (1758), 8, *Fontes*, nn. 3674 and 3678; *Parisien, Matrimonii*, 7 iul. 1883 et 7 mart. 1885—*Thesaurus*, CXLII (1883), 429-451 and 639, CXLIV (1885), 61-69, *Fontes*, nn. 4259 and 4266.

[47] As representative of numerous decisions in cases of total simulation, the following cases may be consulted: S.R.R. *Massilien, Nullitatis Matrimonii*, 10 aug. 1912, coram R.P.D. Ioanne Prior, dec. XXXV—*Decisiones*, IV (1912),

bunals of the Holy See over and above the confession of the party who gave the simulated consent to the marriage contract consisted of the proof of a proportionate cause or reason which was sufficient to account for a simulated consent in the individual case as well as proof from the circumstances which preceded, accompanied and followed the marriage that the party concerned actually withheld true consent to the marriage contract.[48] Although the early commentators insisted upon a rather rigorous interpretation of the text of Innocent III's response, the tribunals of the Holy See seem to have been guided by a more literal interpretation of the response itself.[49]

Since the exclusion of one of the essential elements in marriage likewise amounts to simulated consent (at least in effect), the response of Innocent III is the basic norm to be applied in cases of partial simulation as well. As stated before, if one of the contracting parties harbors a positive intention to not obligate himself or herself in regard to one or the other of the essential elements of marriage, it is impossible for that person to have an intention to contract a true marriage. The difficulties which for a time stood in the way of applying the response of Innocent III to cases of partial simulation will be discussed in the following pages.

401 ff.; *Vicariatus Apostolici Novae Pomeraniae, Nullitatis Matrimonii,* 30 apr. 1913, coram R.P.D. Seraphino Many, dec. XXV—*Decisiones,* V (1913), 283 ff.; *Oregonopolitana, Nullitatis Matrimonii,* 6 iul. 1914, coram R.P.D. Ioanne Prior dec. XXII—*Decisiones,* VI (1914), 244 ff.

[48] Cf. in addition to the cases cited in the two preceding footnotes: S.R.R. *Nullitatis Matrimonii,* 13 dec. 1912, coram R.P.D. Ioanne Prior, dec. XL, n. 5 f.—*Decisiones,* IV (1912), 461; 6 mart. 1929, coram R.P.D. Francisco Guglielmi, dec. XVII, n. 5—*Decisiones,* XXI (1929), 146; 16 iul. 1931, coram R.P.D. Francisco Guglielmi, dec. XXXV, n. 4—*Decisiones,* XXIII (1931), 293 f.

[49] S.C.C., *Mutinen., Nullitatis Matrimonii,* 19 aug. 1724: "Fundamentum Annae constituitur in hoc, quod matrimonium ab ipsa contractum cum Annibale fuit simulatum, in quo themate non est obligatorium iuxta *Textum in cap. tua nos de sponsalibus,* et quia ad effectum probandi in foro fori simulationem, doceri debet de causa simulandi, et de coniecturis, et circumstantiis simulationem suadentibus."—*Thesaurus,* III (1724-1726), 66 f. Cf. also. S.R.R., *Nullitatis Matrimonii,* 6 iul. 1914, coram R.P.D. Ioanne Prior, dec. XXII, n. 4—*Decisiones,* VI (1914), 245 f. and Gasparri, *De Matrimonio,* II, n. 821.

B. *An Analysis of Canon 1086, § 2*

The following analysis will touch only that portion of canon 1086 which refers to partial simulation. The principal aspects of that portion of the canon may be singled out as follows: there is question of partial simulation if (1) one or both of the contracting parties, (2) by a positive act of the will, (3) exclude (4) all right to the conjugal act or one of the essential properties of marriage. This is stated in canon 1086, § 2 as follows:

> . . . si alterutra vel utraque pars positivo voluntatis actu excludat . . . omne ius ad coniugalem actum, vel essentialem aliquam matrimonii proprietatem, invalide contrahit.

Each of the four principal aspects of this canon as indicated above will be discussed separately.

(1) Mutual Consent Is Not Required

(*Si alterutra vel utraque pars excludat* . . .)

Although it is difficult to prove that one of the contracting parties did not intend to consent to the marriage contract as such, it is even more difficult to prove that those who intended to contract marriage, nevertheless intended not to acknowledge all of the essential obligations of marriage. In regard to the boon of offspring and the boon of conjugal fidelity, there is the possibility that the intention may have been merely to exclude the proper *use* of the marriage right, and not the marriage right itself, or to exclude the fulfillment of the corresponding essential obligation and not the obligation itself. In regard to the boon of sacramental stability in particular, there is the possibility that the contrary intention may have been based merely on an error on the part of the intellect, and not on a positive act of the will. At any rate, the commentators insisted that intentions or conditions contrary to any of the three boons of marriage did not invalidate the marriage contract unless such intentions or conditions were agreed upon by both of the contracting parties.[50] This view apparently was based on a literal in-

[50] "Nam nisi ambo consentiant, non impedit matrimonium."—Ioannes Andrea, *Commentaria*, lib. IV, tit. V, n. 2. Cf. also c. 7, C. XXXII, q. 2, *casus*.

terpretation of the decretal of Gregory IX.[51] The argument was that if only one of the parties expressed opposition to something which pertained to the essence of marriage, but consent to the marriage contract subsequently was given and the marriage consummated, the presumption applied that the party who had placed the contrary condition, retracted it before consenting to the marriage contract.[52]

The commentators adopted certain presumptions which reduced considerably the possibility of a declaration of nullity in cases of partially simulated consent. Thus, if one of the parties objected to the proposed condition of the other, the presumption was that the latter party retracted the condition and gave absolute consent to the marriage contract.[53] The same presumption was applied if the other party merely kept silent when the condition was proposed. Such silence was considered as tantamount to an objection to the proposed condition.[54]

Modern authors do not reject the above mentioned presumptions

[51] C. 7, X, *de conditionibus appositis in desponsatione vel in alliis contractibus,* IV, 5—Potthast, n. 9664. Fagnanus (1598-1678), for example, made the following comment on Gregory's IX's decretal in regard to the invalidating effect of conditions which are contrary to the essence of marriage: "At haec consideratio cessat, quando unus tantum intendit detrahere, et alius non exprimit, . . ."—*Ius Canonicum seu Commentaria Absolutissima in Quinque Libros Decretalium* (Romae, 1661), lib. IV, tit. V, n. 4 (cited hereafter as *Ius Canonicum*).

[52] ". . . quia tunc descendendo postea ad actum, qui mutuo censensu perficit, et matrimonium consummando, ex quo utraque pars non consentit turpitudini contra substantiam actus, censetur recessum a conditione seu protestatione . . ."—Fagnanus, *loc. cit.*

[53] "Ratio est, quia si apponens eiusmodi conditionem, alterius contradictione non obstante, ad contractum matrimonialem processit, favore matrimonii a conditione apposita recessisse praesumitur; . . ."—Schmalzgrueber, *Ius Ecclesiasticum,* lib. IV, tit. V, n. 116. Cf. also Ioannes Andreae, *Commentaria,* lib. IV, tit. V, c. 7, n. 2; Fagnanus, *ibid.,* n. 3; Pirhing, *Ius Canonicum,* lib. IV, tit. V, n. 14; Sanchez, *De Matrimonio,* lib. II, disp. XLV, n. 19 f.

[54] Cf. Ioannes Andreae, *loc. cit;* Fagnanus, *loc. cit.;* Sanchez, *loc. cit.* In fact, some authors suggested that the young women be instructed to keep silent when contrary conditions were placed: ". . . nam sequuta copula, erit matrimonium."—Fagnanus, *ibid.,* n. 5. Cf. also Hostiensis, *Commentaria,* lib. IV, tit. V, c. 7, n. 1.

entirely, but hold that they are mere presumptions which lose their force whenever evidence is at hand that the condition or intention actually was not retracted.[55] Some authors, however, explicitly reject the presumption that the silence of one of the parties points to a retraction of the condition by the other party.[56] Since this question will be discussed fully in the second section of this study, it may here suffice to mention that the Sacred Roman Rota does not require evidence of even an implicit agreement between the contracting parties (in regard to conditions which are expressive of opposition to the essence of marriage) as a requisite for a declaration of nullity in the external forum.[57]

It may be well to add that if evidence is insufficient in the external forum to warrant a declaration of nullity, but true consent was not given internally, then there is an unfortunate conflict between the internal and the external forum. Since the lack of internal consent precludes the possibility of a valid marriage, the parties may not live together as man and wife. Yet, due to lack of evidence, the validity of the marriage must be upheld in the external forum. In fact, the ecclesiastical judge can force the parties to remain together.[58] The situation becomes even more complicated if the party who is guilty of simulated consent gives a true consent for marriage with another person. In the internal forum

[55] Cf. Gasparri, *De Matrimonio,* II, n. 895; Cappello, *De Sacramentis,* III, n. 634, 3.

[56] "Si conditio contra substantiam ab *uno* contrahentium apponitur, alter contradicit et tamen ad celebrationem matrimonii devenitur, aliqua praesumptio est illum a conditione recessisse: non vero si alter tantum tacet."—Chelodi, Ius *Matrimoniale,* n. 125. Cf. also Payen, *De Matrimonio,* II, n. 1732, 3; Wanenmacher, *Canonical Evidence in Marriage Cases* (Philadelphia, Pa.: Dolphin Press, 1935), n. 474.

[57] S.R.R., *Nullitatis Matrimonii,* 5 iul, 1923, coram R.P.D. Francisco Parrillo, dec. XVI, n. 3: ". . . satis est ad matrimonii nullitatem evincendam, ut vel unam partem positivam intentionem habuisse et explicitam sese non obligandi, utcumque tandem, dummodo concludenter, probetur."—*Decisiones,* XV (1923), 143. Cf. also 17 aug. 1926, coram R.P.D. Francisco Guglielmi, dec. XLIV, n. 8—*Decisiones,* XVIII (1926), 357: 5 dec. 1927, coram R.P.D. Francisco Parrillo, dec. LV, n. 3—*Decisiones,* XIX (1927), 499.

[58] Cf. Gasparri, *De Matrimonio,* 11, n. 817; Cappello, *De Sacramentis,* III, n. 595.

the first marriage is invalid, and the second valid. In the external forum, however, the first marriage has to be considered as valid as long as the presence of simulated consent has not been proved, and the second marriage has to be considered as invalid.[59] To obviate scandal, the person would have to obey the command of the ecclesiastical judge by returning to the consort of the first marriage even though it was contracted with simulated consent. Yet, under no circumstance would such a person be allowed to act against his conscience either by requesting or by granting the act of conjugal union.[60] The full blame for such an unfortunate state of affairs rests solely upon the shoulders of the person who simulated the consent to the marriage contract.[61]

(2) Only *Positive* Intentions Invalidate the Marriage Contract

(Si alterutra vel utraque pars positivo voluntatis actu excludat . . .)

Only positive intentions can have an invalidating effect upon the marriage contract. A negative intention really is not an act of the will, but rather, as Cappello points out, it consists in a lack of inclination on the part of the will in regard to a specified object.[62] A positive intention is a resolute act of the will whereby a person takes a definite stand regarding the object in question, e. g.: "I intend to prevent the conception of offspring." The mere fact that one or both of the parties have no inclination to remain faithful one to the other or to have children is an indication of no more than a so-called negative intention with reference to the boon of conjugal fidelity or the boon of offspring—a disposition of the will which is compatible entirely with the all-important giving and accepting of the rights and obligations which are essential to a valid marriage contract. It is only when one of the parties harbors a *positive* intention

[59] Gasparri, *loc. cit.;* Cappello, *loc. cit.;* Wernz-Vidal, *Ius Matrimoniale,* n. 460; Chelodi, *Ius Matrimoniale,* n. 155.

[60] Gasparri, *loc. cit.;* Cappello, *loc. cit.*

[61] Gasparri, *loc. cit.;* Cappello, *loc. cit.*

[62] "Dicitur *actu positivo* voluntatis, ut excludatur actus mere *negativus* qui reipsa non exsistit, cum consistat in defectu tendentiae seu inclinationis ex parte voluntatis in determinatum obiectum."—*De Sacramentis,* III, n. 598, 1.

contrary to one of the essential elements of marriage that the validity of the marriage is questioned.

(a) The Mere Pursuit of a Contrary Objective Does Not Indicate Invalidity

As an example of a mere negative intention contrary to the boon of offspring, there is the recurrent case in which one or both of the contracting parties are determined to preclude the conception of offspring merely in the sense that they are opposed to the idea of having children. In one case in 1931, for example, evidence was at hand that the man had done everything possible to prevent the conception of offspring in his conjugal life. Because of the lack of evidence of a *positive* and *specific* intention to that effect at the time when he consented to the marriage contract, however, the validity of the marriage was upheld.[63] The same case affords a good example of another type of negative intention, known as an interpretative intention. The man testified that *if* he had been given the alternative, at the time of marriage, either of marrying the woman and of having children, or of not marrying at all, he *would* have chosen the latter alternative.[64] Since such an intention actually did not exist in the mind of the contracting party when giving consent, it did not affect the validity of the contract. Hence authors insist—and this point will be discussed presently—that the validity of a marriage contract may be affected on this score only by an *actual* intention (positive and specific) formed at the time of the giving of consent, or previously formed but still persisting in force at the time of the exchange of consent as expressive of the will of the party with reference to the procreation of offspring in marriage life (*virtual* intention).

[63] S.R.R., *Nullitatis Matrimonii,* 15 ian. 1931, coram R.P.D. Henrico Quattrocolo, dec. I—*Decisiones,* XXIII (1931), 1 ff. As other examples, cf. 10 aug. 1929, coram R.P.D. Ubaldo Mannucci, dec. LI, n. 11—*Decisiones,* XXI (1929), 431; 14 ian. 1930, coram Rmo P.D. Maximo Massimi, Decano, dec. IV, n. 14 ff. —*Decisiones,* XXII (1930), 52 ff.; 20 nov. 1931, coram R.P.D. Ubaldo Mannucci, dec. LIII, n. 7—*Decisiones,* XXIII (1931), 460. Among the authors, cf. Chelodi, *Ius Matrimoniale,* n. 117; Wernz-Vidal, *Ius Matrimoniale,* n. 462.

[64] *Ibid.,* n. 12 (p. 6).

(b) Other Examples of Negative Intentions

Another noted example of a so-called negative intention is found in the cases of those who contract marriage with simple erroneous views concerning the indissolubility or unity of marriage.[65] If it is a simple error, i. e., purely on the part of the intellect, there is no indication of any intention or of any act of the will contrary to the blessing of sacramental stability or contrary to the blessing of conjugal fidelity.[66] If such an error, however, has led to the formation of a positive act of the will whereby the essential property of unity or of indissolubility is excluded in the giving of consent, then the marriage is invalid.[67] It may happen that one of the contracting parties is in error or ignorance in regard to the precise manner of physical union which leads to the conception of offspring. As long as such a person has sufficient knowledge in regard to the essential object of marriage, i. e., as long as the person knows that, in giving consent to the marriage contract, a right over the body is given and accepted for the performance of acts suitable of themselves for the procreation of offspring, an erroneous view with reference to the precise manner of physical union which leads to the conception of offspring would not affect the validity of the marriage contract. This is true even though the person concerned would not have consented to the marriage contract if a fuller knowledge regarding the act of conjugal union had been present at the time of the exchange of matrimonial consent. Since such an attitude of mind points to nothing more than an interpretative intention, which is of a purely negative import, it could not affect the validity of the marriage.[68]

[65] Canon 1084.

[66] "Agitur de *simplici errore*, qui est actus *intellectus*, qui *manet* in intellectu in eoque *terminatur*. Ideo dicitur *'simplex error,'* ut excludatur positiva intentio vel conditio seu influxus positivus in voluntatem."—Cappello, *De Sacramentis*, III, n. 588, 2. Cf. also Payen, *De Matrimonio*, II, n. 1675.

[67] Cf. Cappello, *loc. cit.*

[68] "Nec refert quod ignorantia dederit causam contractui, ita ut, cognita veritate, pars nuptias non celebrasset, v.g. mulier quae ignorabat ea quae propius spectant ad modum et rationem copulae seu generationis. Agitur sane de ignorantia quae non excludit obiectum essentiale contractus matrimonialis, et consequenter de voluntate mere *interpretativa* quae in rerum natura non

(3) Only Actual or Virtual Intentions Invalidate the Marriage Contract

(*Si alterutra vel utroque pars positivo voluntatis actu* excludat . . .)

Since the boons of offspring and conjugal fidelity admit of the distinction between the accepting of the respective essential obligations and the fulfillment of such obligations and between the giving of the marriage right and the use of that right,[69] it is logical to conclude that the word *exclude* as used in canon 1086, § 2 takes on a special meaning in relation to the boon of offspring and the boon of conjugal fidelity. Indissolubility and unity, as essential properties of marriage, are excluded by the mere fact that one of the parties forms a specific, positive intention contrary to a perpetual or exclusive union. Conjugal fidelity and the procreation of offspring, however, as blessings which are dependent upon the use of the marriage right for their enjoyment, are not excluded unless one of the parties, by a specific and positive act of the will, denies the marriage right itself or refuses to accept the corresponding essential obligation in regard to conjugal fidelity or the procreation of offspring. In all cases, however, there is no question of the exclusion of any essential element in the contracting of marriage unless the opposition proceeds from an *actual* intention formed at the time of the giving of the matrimonial consent, or from an actual intention which, though previously formed, persists in its force at the time when the matrimonial consent is given. In the latter case, the intention indicates an exclusion of an essential element in marriage *in virtue of* a previous *actual* intention which never was retracted. Hence it is called a *virtual* intention. These points pertain to the treatise of the sacraments in general, and scarcely require a thorough discussion in the present study. It may be advisable, however, to consider briefly the discussion with reference to the sufficiency of habitual intentions as distinquished from virtual intentions.

exsistit, et quae proinde nihil operatur."—Cappello, *De Sacramentis,* III, n. 583. Cf. also S.R.R., *Nullitatis Matrimonii,* 5 dec. 1927, coram R.P.D. Francisco Parrillo, dec. LV, n. 10—*Decisiones,* XIX (1927), 502 f.

[69] Cf. *supra*, p. 6 f.

(a) The Difference Between Habitual and Virtual Intentions

Although some authors consider a habitual intention as a synonym for a virtual intention,[70] most authors hold that a habitual intention is somewhat akin to an interpretative intention, and as such it is incapable of affecting the validity of the marriage.[71] The following statement indicates that the Sacred Roman Rota shares this view:

> . . . mera *dispositio* in qua quis sit, denegandi consensum si sciret compartem carere aliqua qualitate, non est nisi *habitualis* vel *interpretativa* intentio, quae nihil operatur cum non sit in mundo, ut aiunt pragmatici. . . .[72]

Habitual and virtual intentions have this in common, that both are based upon an abiding disposition or inclination of the will which has not been changed or revoked. But a virtual intention differs from a habitual intention inasmuch as the latter intention is not preceded by an actual, positive act of the will.[73] In this sense a habitual intention, like an interpretative intention, represents merely an inclination or disposition of the parties with reference, for example, to the procreation of offspring, and not a positive act of the will which is indicative of an exclusion of the boon of offspring.

(b) The Need of Caution in Reviewing Actual Cases

In many cases, persons who are opposed to the procreation of offspring in their married life have not formed an actual intention to prevent the conception of offspring. As stated in a decision rendered in 1931, the mere fact that some are accustomed to make adverse remarks regarding the procreation of children does not mean

[70] Gasparri, for example, states: ". . . nomine consensus virtualis seu habitualis intelligitur idem consensus primitivus non revocatus; . . ."—*De Matrimonio*, II, n. 781.

[71] Cf. D'Annibale (1815-1892), *Summula Theologiae Moralis* (5. ed., 4 vols., Romae, 1908), I, 135; Payen, *De Matrimonio*, II, n. 1675.

[72] S.R.R., *Nullitatis Matrimonii*, 13 iul. 1926, coram R.P.D. Ubaldo Mannucci, dec. XXIX, n. 2—*Decisiones*, XVIII (1926), 230.

[73] Cf. Ferraris, *Prompta Bibliotheca Canonica Iuridica Moralis Theologica nec non Ascetica Polemica Rubricistica Historica* (9 vols., Romae, 1885-1899), V, v. *intentio* (cited hereafter as *Bibliotheca Canonica*).

that they intend to deny the essential obligation or withhold the giving of the marriage right in regard to the boon of offspring.[74] Since it is easy to confuse habitual intentions with virtual intentions [75] the Sacred Roman Rota has adopted the policy of insisting strictly upon the distinction between the two.[76]

The entire subject of the invalidating effect of opposition to the procreation of offspring may be summarized as follows: although the *lack of an intention* to accept the obligations of marriage does not affect the validity of the contract, the marriage is invalid if the parties positively *exclude* any of the essential obligations of marriage when giving consent to the marriage contract. This thought was expressed in one decision of the Sacred Roman Rota as follows:

> At si consensus deficere nequit ob omissam onerum acceptationem, nec expresse nec tacite necessariam, inficiari tamen potest, si aliquid ei adiiciatur, quod coniugii substantiae, seu eius bonis adversetur: quo in casu consensus labefactaretur non ob defectum alicuius elementi essentialis positive *non intenti,* sed positive a consensu *exclusi.*[77]

(4) The Two Principal Types of Partial Simulation

According to canon 1086, § 2, a marriage is invalid not only if one or both of the parties, when exchanging matrimonial consent externally, actually do not intend internally to contract marriage as such (total simulation), but also if one or both of the parties, by a positive act of the will, exclude (a) all right to the conjugal act

[74] S.R.R. *Nullitatis Matrimonii,* 20 nov. 1931, coram, R.P.D. Ubaldo Mannucci, dec. LIII, n. 7: ". . . Solent quidam contra prolem iactare verba, quin tamen insana ista verba concludere faciant contra suscipiendas obligationes, et ius coëundi in comparte."—*Decisiones,* XXIII (1931), 460.

[75] As evidenced in a case which was reviewed in 1893. Cf. *AAS,* XXVI (1893-1894), 335.

[76] Cf. S.R.R., *Cameracen, Nullitatis Matrimonii,* 23 iun. 1911, coram R.P.D. Iosepho Mori, dec. XXVII, n. 24 f.—*Decisiones,* III (1911), 306; *Nullitatis Matrimonii,* 6 aug. 1915, coram R.P.D. Ioanne Prior, dec. XXXIV, n. 3 f.—*Decisiones,* VII (1915), 371; 18 aug. 1916, coram R.P.D. Seraphino Many, dec. XXVIII, n. 3—*Decisiones,* VIII (1916), 315.

[77] S.R.R., *Nullitatis Matrimonii,* 7 ian. 1929, coram R.P.D. Francisco Parrillo, dec. II, n. 4—*Decisiones,* XXVI (1929), 14.

or (b) one of the essential properties of marriage (partial simulation). These two types of partial simulation will be discussed separately.

(a) The Positive Exclusion of the Marriage Right Itself

(. . . *si alterutra vel utraque pars . . . excludat . . .* omne ius *ad coniugalem actum . . .*)

The portion of canon 1086, § 2, which states that the marriage is invalid if one or both of the contracting parties exclude *all right* to the conjugal act must not be understood in the sense that the marriage is invalid only if the marriage right is excluded forever.[78] It is accepted canonical doctrine that if the marriage right is excluded only for a limited period of time, the marriage is invalid. Authors admit, however, that this doctrine is not expressed explicitly in canon 1086, § 2. Mahoney, for example, made the following remarks:

> The doctrine is expressed clearly enough in Canon 1081, § 2: "Ius in corpus perpetuum." The equivalent rule of Canon 1086: "Si . . . excludat matrimonium ipsum, aut omne ius ad coniugalem actum" is not so clear. This phrase appears to be capable of the sense that the contract is invalid only if the right is *perpetually* excluded. That this is not the meaning of *omne ius* is evident from all published judgments which interpret the phrase.[79]

[78] Some authors apparently understood the canon in that sense. Cerato, for example, stated: "Si *Caius vel Caia* matrimonium inierint non cum voluntate excludendi *omne* ius ad actum coniugalem, sed ius huiusmodi solum *una vel altera vice* admittendi, *valide* contrahunt. Item *valide* etiamsi voluntatis propositum habeant *matrimonio abutendi*."—*Matrimonium a Codice Iuris Canonici Integre Desumptum* (Editio altera locupletior, Patavii: Typis Seminarii, 1919), n. 82, § 2 f.

[79] "Matrimonial Consent and 'the Safe Period'," *The Clergy Review* (London, 1931), XIII (1937), 128. Salsmans referred to the same difficulty when he stated: "Dolendum est Canonem 1086, § 2 non esse ita concinnatum ut ad motam quaestionem clara appareat responsio [i.e. the question of the invalidating effect of the temporary exclusion of the marriage right]."—"Sterilitas facultativa licita?"—*Ephem. Theol. Lovan.*, XI (1934), 568.

(1) *Principles Concerning the Perpetuity of the Marriage Right*

The marriage right essentially is a perpetual right.[80] The fact that it is a perpetual right implies necessarily that it is also a continuous right: "The perpetuity or indissolubility of marriage means that it creates between husband and wife a permanent bond so that at no moment do they cease to be husband and wife with the rights and obligations of such." [81] If the contracting parties, by a positive act of the will, intend to exclude the marriage right only for a certain period of their married life, their intention is contrary to the very essence of marriage.[82] The fact that marriage is indissoluble signifies not only that the bond which results from the mutual exchange of matrimonial consent is perpetual, but also that the rights and obligations which constitute the object of matrimonial consent are perpetual.[83]

If the contracting parties place the condition that the conception of offspring be prevented after the birth of one or two children and intend thereby to exclude the marriage right itself after the birth of one or two children (i. e., *ius in corpus . . . in ordine ad actus per se aptos ad prolis generationem*), the condition is contrary to the perpetuity of marriage and affects the validity of the marriage.[84]

[80] "Consensus matrimonialis est actus voluntatis quo utraque pars tradit et acceptat ius in corpus, perpetuum et exclusivum, in ordine ad actus per se aptos ad prolis generationem."—Canon 1081, § 2. Cf. also Gasparri, *De Matrimonio*, II, n. 825.

[81] Browne, *The Irish Ecclesiastical Record* (Dublin, 1864—[5th. series, 1913—]), XLIX (1937), 86. The statement above was contained in an answer to a question concerning a "safe period" agreement [i.e. the "rhythm" practice] between the contracting parties. The same author continued: "It seems to us clear that a right which is partial in regard to duration is opposed to perpetuity: perpetual signifies, in ordinary usage, unbroken, uninterrupted."—*Loc. cit.* Cf. also Wanenmacher, "Some questions on vitiated marital consent," *The Ecclesiastical Review* (Philadelphia, 1889—), C (1939), pp. 491 and 496.

[82] "Dicitur: *omne ius ad coniugalem actum*. Statim ac formaliter excluditur *quodcumque ius, etiam ad tempus tantum*, invalidum est matrimonium. Exempla: exclusio iuris, *usquedum melior fortuna arrideat*; vel *post natam unam prolem*."—Claeys Bouuaert-Simenon, *Manuale Iuris Canonici*, II, n. 292, 3.

[83] Cf. canons 1081, § 2, 1110.

[84] "Conditio quae in corruptis populorum moribus saepe apponitur:

The same applies if the parties marry with the condition of preventing the conception of offspring until their financial status is better, and intend thereby to exclude the marriage right itself during that period.[85] The view that even the temporary exclusion of the marriage right affects the validity of the marriage contract is expressed clearly in the decisions of the Sacred Roman Rota.[86]

The mere fact that the contracting parties express an intention or even enter an agreement to prevent the conception of offspring, however, does not indicate necessarily that they intend to exclude the marriage right itself. If the condition or agreement concerns merely the temporary preventing of the conception of offspring, the presumption is that the parties intend merely to abuse the marriage right. Hence the marriage is to be regarded as valid. If, however, the condition or agreement concerns the absolute and perpetual preventing of the conception of offspring, there is a very strong presumption that the parties intend to exclude the marriage right itself.[87]

dummodo post primum vel alterum filium prolem evitemus, est contra perpetuitatem, si coniux intendit ipsum matrimoniale ius tradere—acceptare temporaneum, idest usque ad primum vel alterum filium; . . ."—Gasparri, *De Matrimonio,* II, n. 906. Cf. also *ibid,* n. 898; Lehmkuhl, *Theologia Moralis,* II, n. 689; Cappello, *De Sacramentis,* III, n. 631, 5.

[85] Such a condition may be intended also as a true suspensive condition. Even though the parties do not intend to exclude the marriage right itself, they may intend to withhold consent to the marriage contract as such until their financial status improves. Cf. Gasparri, *ibid.,* n. 898; Lehmkuhl, *loc. cit.;* Cappello, *loc. cit.*

[86] S.R.R., *Nullitatis Matrimonii,* 14 mart. 1924, coram R.P.D. Raphaele Chimenti, dec. XIV, n. 3: "Quamvis enim ordinario per eam conditionem [i.e. de vitanda ad tempus prole] non indicetur nisi abusus, salvo iure coeundi, tamen verba apta sunt ad ipsum ius enecandum. Revera, ut dictum est, simulatione partiali invalide contrahit non tantum qui excludit, sed etiam qui limitat matrimoniale ius. Et Lehmkuhl . . „ ita pergit: 'At si demum de ipso matrimonii abusu (nempe de vitanda ad tempus prole) tanquam de vera conditione *sine qua non, seu* de conditione mutua iura restringente (constet) matrimonium nullum est' . . ."—*Decisiones,* XVI (1924), 108 f. Cf. also 23 mart. 1925, coram R.P.D. Andrea Jullien, dec. XVIII, n. 2—*Decisiones,* XVII (1925), 132; 6 aug. 1929, coram R.P.D. Francisco Morano, dec. XLV, n. 4—*Decisiones,* XXI (1929), 382; 10 febr. 1931, coram R.P.D. Arcturo Wynen, dec. VII, n. 11 —*Decisiones,* XXIII (1931), 49 f.; 23 iun. 1931, coram R.P.D. Francisco Morano, dec. XXX, n. 6—*Decisiones,* XXIII (1931), 260 f.

[87] Cf. Gasparri, *De Matrimonio,* II, n. 898; Lehmkuhl, *Theologia Moralis,*

This does not preclude the possibility, however, that the temporary exclusion of the boon of offspring may, in the given circumstances of an individual case, indicate the exclusion of the marriage right itself or the possibility that the perpetual and absolute exclusion of the boon of offspring may, in an individual case, indicate merely an intention to abuse the marriage right. The former possibility has been discussed sufficiently in the preceding paragraphs. The possibility that the perpetual and absolute exclusion of the blessing of offspring may indicate merely an intention to abuse the marriage (in an individual case) will be discussed in the article on presumptions in Chapter IV of this study.

(2) *The Interpretation of the Expression* Omne Ius

The portion of canon 1086, § 2, which states that the marriage is invalid if one or both of the contracting parties exclude *all right* to the conjugal act apparently means that the marriage is invalid on the score of the exclusion of the boon of offspring or of the boon of conjugal fidelity only if the *marriage right itself* is excluded in a positive manner, i. e., the fundamental right (*ius radicale*) to the conjugal act as distinguished from the use or abuse of that right. The canon thereby implies that even the perpetual exclusion of the *use* of the marriage right is, of itself, insufficient to invalidate the marriage contract:

> . . . in can. 1086, § 2, perspicue cavetur, invalide contrahi matrimonium ab eo, qui positivo voluntatis actu excludit *omne*

II, n. 689. Cappello, *De Sacramentis*, n. 600, 2, 3° f. As evidence that the Sacred Roman Rota follows the view stated above, cf. S.R.R. *Nullitatis Matrimonii*, 5 dec. 1927, coram R.P.D. Francisco Parrillo, dec. LV, n. 8: "Conditio autem vel propositum, etsi in pactum deductum, tunc solum praesumptionem favore matrimonii excludit, iuxta dicta, cum absolute et absque temporis limitatione fuerit elicitum; secus contraria militat praesumptio de simplici matrimonii abusu . . ."—*Decisiones*, XIX (1927), 502. Cf. also 23 mart. 1925, coram R.P.D. Andrea Jullien, dec. XVIII, n. 2—*Decisiones*, XVII (1925), 131 f.; 30 iun. 1925, coram R.P.D. Francisco Parrillo, dec. XXXIV, n. 3—*Decisiones*, XVII (1925), 270; 7 ian. 1929, coram R.P.D. Francisco Parrillo, dec. II, n. 6—*Decisiones*, XXI (1929), 15; 15 jan. 1931, coram R.P.D. Henrico Quattrocolo, dec. I, n. 6—*Decisiones*, XXIII (1931), 3.

> *ius* ad coniugalem actum, nempe obligationem ipsam, seu *ius radicale,* ut aiunt, utendi matrimonio, vel, iuxta doctrinam D. Thomae, prolem *in suo principio,* ut pro prole accipiatur *intentio prolis.* . . . Praesumendum autem non est voluisse legislatorem otiosa vel superflua verba usurpari, praecise in quaestione diu et acriter inter Doctores disceptata, unde citata canonis verba, *excludat omne ius ad coniugalem actum,* ita sunt accipienda, ut non sufficiat *usum* etiam per pactum et *perpetuo* adimere, sed necesse prorsus quod ipsa obligatio vel facultas utendi positive excludatur. . . .[88]

Since the marriage right essentially is a perpetual right, the mere temporary limitation of that right is, in effect, equivalent to its exclusion.[89]

(3) *The "Rhythm" Practice and the Validity of the Marriage Contract*

When Gregory IX stated that the condition, "provided that you prevent the procreation of offspring" was contrary to the essence of marriage, he gave no indication that he referred only to the pre-

[88] S.R.R., *Nullitatis Matrimonii,* 5 dec. 1927, coram R.P.D. Francisco Parrillo, dec. LX, n. 7—*Decisiones,* XIX (1927), 501. Cf. also 29 apr. 1922, coram R.P.D. Francisco Parrillo, dec. XIV, n. 12—*Decisiones,* XIV (1922), 123; 4 aug. 1922, coram R.P.D. Raphaele Chimenti, dec. XXVII, n. 3—*Decisiones,* XIV (1922), 254; 19 apr. 1926, coram R.P.D. Iulio Grazioli, dec. XVIII, n. 10—*Decisiones,* XVIII (1926), 144.

[89] Cf. S.R.R., *Nullitatis Matrimonii,* 14 mart. 1924, coram R.P.D. Raphaele Chimenti, dec. XIV, n. 2, where the view of Gasparri [*De Matrimonio,* 3. ed., 1909, n. 919] is compared to the wording of canon 1086, § 2, as follows: "Ita et in Codice (can. 1086, § 2) simulatio huiusmodi partialis aequiparatur totali, ad effectum nullitatis matrimonii: . . . Ut patet, verba Gasparri probe conveniunt cum citato canone. Apud Gasparri: 'Si contrahens excludit vel limitat (iuris coeundi) ordinationem ad prolem, vel perpetuitatem, vel unitatem';—et in Codice: 'Si pars excludit *omne* ius ad coniugalem actum, vel essentialem aliquam matrimonii proprietatem.' Itaque quod est in Codice 'excludit *omne* ius ad coniugalem actum,' aequivalet formulae, 'excludit *vel limitat* (iuris coeundi) ordinationem ad copulam.' Habetur itaque nullitas matrimonii, si quis non concedit *omne* ius ad coniugalem actum, sed hoc ius limitat."—*Decisiones,* XVI (1924), 107 f. For another interpretation of the expression *omne ius,* which, however, is not at variance with the interpretation discussed above, cf. Cappello, *De Sacramentis* (4 ed., 1939), III, n. 598, 2.

venting of the conception of offspring by shameful means.[90] If the contracting parties intend to prevent the conception of offspring by having recourse to the so-called "rhythm" practice[91] and intend, by a positive act of the will, to exclude the marriage right itself during the fertile periods of the woman, it is logical to conclude that the marriage is invalid. Such is the opinion of an increasing number of contemporary theologians and canonists. Noldin-Schmitt say, for example:

> Qui contrahunt sub condicione *nonnisi diebus infecunditatis* congrediendi, invalide contrahunt, si excludere volunt ipsum ius continuum in corpus coniugis, similiter ac si solum pro aliquot annis tradere vellent ius in corpus. Si autem volunt continuum ius tradere et mere non uti quibusdam temporibus, valide contrahunt.[92]

In actual practice, however, it is difficult to establish whether the parties who entered the marriage contract with an agreement to prevent the conception by adopting the "rhythm" practice intended to exclude the marriage right itself during the fertile days, or merely the use of the right. It is difficult to conceive that they would consider themselves as having the marriage right only during the sterile periods of the woman. As Mahoney says: ". . . it would be ex-

[90] Cf. c. 7, X, *de conditionibus appositis in desponsatione vel in aliis contractibus,* IV, 5—Potthast, n. 9664.

[91] This practice is referred to variously as "periodic continence," "facultative sterility," "the 'safe-period' practice," and "the Ogino-Knaus method."

[92] *Summa Theologiae Moralis,* III, n. 631, 1, a. Cf. also Mancini, *Palaestro del Clero* (Ravigo, 1922—), XIV (1935, 71; Lavaud, *Le Monde Moderne et le Mariage,* pp. 421 ff.; Salsmans, "Sterilitas facultativa licita?"—*Ephem. Theol. Lovan.,* XI (1934), 568; Vermeersch, "De prudenti ratione iudicandi sterilitatem physiologicam,"—*Periodica,* XXIII (1934), 241*; and "De moralitate sic dictae abstinentiae periodicae in matrimonio,"—*Periodica,* XXIV (1935), 169*, 4); Flieszer, "Ehewille und *bonum prolis,*"—*Quartalschrift,* XC (1937), 440; Mahoney, "Matrimonial Consent and 'The Safe Period',"—*The Clergy Review,* XIII (1937), 129; Wanenmacher, "Some questions on vitiated marital consent,"—*The Ecclesiastical Review,* C (1939), 491;' Browne, *The Irish Ecclesiastical Record,* XLIX (1937), 86; anonymous author, *L'Ami du Clergé* (Paris, 1878—), LI (1934), 751.

tremely odd for any normal person to regard himself as properly married only for eleven days or so in each month!"[93] It seems that the presumption in favor of the validity of the marriage would be stronger in the case of a "rhythm" agreement than in the case of an agreement to prevent the conception of offspring by abusing the marriage right. To cite Wanenmacher:

> Catholic couples who thus agree beforehand to engage in coition only during the sterile period, whether they agree because of reasons that are grave and allowable, or from reasons that are frivolous and hence culpable, do so, generally, because they want their marriage to be nevertheless sacred and free from the unnatural irregularities of modern contraceptive practices. Hence, when they have reduced their intent to bilateral pact, it is much easier to overcome the presumption against validity than it is when there has been a pact against the natural use of marriage, or against the exclusive use of one spouse, or against indissolubility by divorce.[94]

As a means of determining whether the parties of such an agreement actually intended to exclude the marriage right itself during the fertile periods, it may be well to ask them if they meant that neither of them had a right to break the agreement and request the payment of the marriage debt during the fertile periods, or if they meant that neither of them had the strict right to conjugal union during the fertile days. If they meant that the very right to conjugal union was excluded during the fertile periods of the woman, the marriage is invalid.[95] Likewise, it would be prudent to ask them if they thought that after the marriage they could change their mind in this matter and therefore engage lawfully in conjugal relations during the sterile periods, or whether they thought that the children born of their relations during the fertile periods were born of lawful wedlock.[96]

[93] *The Clergy Review,* XIII (1937), 131.

[94] *The Ecclesiastical Review,* CI (1939), 138.

[95] Mahoney, *The Clergy Review,* XIII (1937), 131.

[96] Wanenmacher, *The Ecclesiastical Review,* C (1939), 491.

(b) The Positive Exclusion of the Essential Properties of Marriage

(*Si alterutra vel utraque pars . . . excludat . . .* essentialem aliquam proprietatem)

Since unity and indissolubility are essential properties of the marriage bond, the mere fact that one or both of the contracting parties, by a positive act of the will, intend to contract a non-exclusive or a dissoluble union is sufficient to indicate the invalidity of the marriage. In regard to the indissolubility of marriage, the statement above follows logically from the fact that the distinction between the acknowledgement of the obligation and the fulfillment of the obligation does not apply to the boon of sacramental stability. Since marriage is an indissoluble union from the very moment of the exchange of matrimonial consent, an intention not to fulfill the obligation which indissolubility implies would be tantamount to an intention to exclude that obligation itself. The same applies to positive intentions which are directly contrary to the unity of marriage.[97] In actual cases, however, it is rare that a contracting party harbors a positive intention which is directly contrary to the unity of marriage, e.g., by intending to reserve the right to take another woman as a true wife later on (polgamy). Usually the contracting parties are opposed to the essential property of unity only in an indirect manner, i.e., intentions which are contrary to conjugal fidelity.[98]

As stated frequently throughout this study, an intention or condition does not affect the validity of the marriage contract unless it enters into the marriage contract itself as an essential part of it. An intention which is contrary to the indissolubility of marriage

[97] "Unitati autem directe contrarius est animus viri qui, volens tradere et acceptare ius *exclusivum,* sibi reservat *potestatem* aliam mulierem sibi, *ut veram uxorem,* postea coniungendi."—Payen, *De Matrimonio,* II, n. 1677, 2). Cf. also Vlaming, *Praelectiones Iuris Matrimonii,* II, n. 535.

[98] Thus Gasparri distinguishes between a condition which is contrary to unity, and a condition which is contrary to conjugal fidelity: "Contra *unitatem* est conditio: *Dummodo mihi liceat aliam assumere;* contra *fidelitatem* coniugalem: *Si pro quaestu adulterandam te tradas, . . .*"—*De Matrimonio,* II, n. 906.

(or directly contrary to the unity of marriage) enters into the contract itself as an essential part by the mere fact that the intention proceeds from a positive act of the will.[99] The problem of proving in the external forum that the opposition to the indissolubility of marriage, for example, proceeds from a positive act of the will and not merely from an error on the part of the intellect is, however, a very difficult matter. The question will be discussed from a more practical aspect in the following chapter of this study. On the other hand, the mere fact that one of the contracting parties harbors a positive intention contrary to the boon of offspring or the boon of conjugal fidelity is not sufficient to indicate that the intention enters into the marriage contract itself as a matter of obligation. Since it is possible that the party may intend merely to abuse the marriage right or violate conjugal fidelity, there is no question of an invalid marriage unless there is evidence that the party intended to exclude the marriage right itself either by an express declaration or by expressing the intention as a true condition (*conditio sine qua non*). An analysis of the invalidating force of such conditions will be presented in the following article of this study.

ARTICLE 3. INVALIDATING CONDITIONS

Canon 1092, 2°, states simply that conditions which concern the future, if they are contrary to the essence of marriage, invalidate the marriage.[100] The important aspects of this canon will be discussed in the following order: (1) the condition must concern the future; (2) it must concern something which, objectively considered, is incompatible with the essence of marriage; and (3) it must be stipulated as a *true condition*. The last two aspects were discussed several times thus far in the present study.[101] The purpose of the present

[99] Cf. S.R.R., *Neo-Eboracen., Nullitatis Matrimonii,* 8 febr. 1915, coram R.P.D. Ioanne Prior, dec. III, n. 5—*Decisiones,* VII (1915), 22. This question will be discussed further in the following chapter of this study.

[100] "Conditio semel apposita et non revocata: . . . Si de futuro contra matrimonii substantiam, illud reddit invalidum; . . ."

[101] The fact that the condition must retain its force at the time of the exchange of matrimonial consent (". . . semel apposita et non revocata: . . .") likewise has been discussed sufficiently in the preceding article (p. 58 ff.).

article is to repeat briefly some of the things discussed heretofore, and to add what is lacking, in order to present a coherent analysis of the wording of canon 1092, 2°. As a preliminary, however, the counterpart to the text of canon 1092, 2°, in the Gregorian Decretals will be analysed as briefly as possible.

A—The Counterpart to Canon 1092, 2°, *in the Gregorian Decretals*

Gregory IX (1227-1241) stated the doctrine on conditions which are contrary to the essence of marriage with such clarity and precision, that scarcely any commentary is required. He stated that if one party said to the other: "I contract with you if you prevent the procreation of offspring;" or "until I find another person richer and more honorable than you;" or "if for gain you give yourself to adultery," the marriage contract was invalid.[102] The first of these conditions is contrary to the blessing of offspring, the second is contrary to the blessing of conjugal fidelity and the third is contrary to the blessing of sacramental stability.[103] He added that if the conditions concerned something which was shameful or impossible, but not contrary to the essence of marriage, they were to be considered as if they never had been placed, and the validity of the marriage was not affected.[104]

All three of the conditions mentioned by Gregory IX concerned the future. Authors concluded that only such conditions which concerned a future event could be considered as being contrary to the essence of marriage.[105] Sanchez pointed out that Gregory IX merely

[102] "Si conditiones contra substantiam coniugii inserantur, puta, si alter dicat alteri: 'contraho tecum si generationem prolis evites,' vel: 'donec inveniam aliam honore vel facultatibus digniorem,' aut: 'si pro quaestu adulterandam te tradas,' matrimonialis contractus, quantumcunque sit favorabilis, caret effectu; . . ."—C. 7, X, *de conditionibus appositis in desponsatione vel in aliis contractibus,* IV, 5; Potthast, n. 9664.

[103] Cf. *supra,* p. 5.

[104] ". . . licet aliae conditiones appositae in matrimonio, si turpes aut impossibiles fuerint, debeant propter eius favorem pro non adiectis haberi." *Loc. cit.*

[105] Cf. Sanchez, *De Matrimonio,* lib. V, disp. IX, n. 6; Schmalzgrueber, *Ius Ecclesiasticum Universum,* lib. IV, tit. V. n. 115; Reiffensteul (1642-1703),

emphasized the natural law when he presented the three examples given as conditions which are contrary to the substance of marriage.[106] No one will deny that a condition which concerns the future dissolution of the marriage bond necessarily invalidates the marriage. Regarding the condition which Gregory IX mentioned as contrary to the boon of conjugal fidelity, i.e. that the woman engage in the practice of adultery, it may suffice to mention that such a stipulation, if intended as an essential part of the marriage contract, is incompatible with true matrimonial consent. The character of the condition, "if you prevent the procreation of offspring," as contrary to the essence of marriage if introduced into the marriage contract itself, has been discussed sufficiently in the third article of Chapter I of this study.[107]

Gregory IX apparently meant not only that the conditions had to concern the future and, objectively considered, involve something which was incompatible with the essence of marriage, but also that they had to be placed as *true* conditions, i.e., in effect, *sine qua non* conditions.[108] The entire context of the decretal justifies the conclusion that he considered such conditions as invalidating only if they were placed as an essential part of the marriage contract itself.[109]

It may be noted that Gregory IX did not indicate that his list of conditions was exhaustive in the sense that other conditions than the ones exemplified by him could not be added to the list.[110] In the opinion of the present writer, however, the only conditions contrary to the blessing of offspring which then as now could be considered as incompatible with the essence of marriage, if introduced

Ius Canonicum Universum (5 vols. in 7, Paris, 1864-1870), lib. IV, tit. V, n. 40; Pirhing, *Ius Canonicum*, lib. IV, tit. V, n. 14.

106 *Ibid.*, n. 4.

107 Cf. *supra*, p. 19 ff.

108 Cf. Payen, *De Matrimonio*, II, n. 1732, 1).

109 This is indicated especially by the phrase: "Si conditiones contra substantiam coniugii inserantur . . ." C. 7, X, *de conditionibus appositis in desponsatione vel in aliis contractibus*, IV, 5—Potthast, n. 9664.

110 Cf. Pirhing, *Ius Canonicum*, lib. IV, tit. V, n. 13; Gasparri, *De Matrimonio*, II, n. 892.

into the marriage contract itself, are those which indicate an intention to preclude the *conception* of offspring.[111]

B—An Analysis of Canon 1092, 2°

(1) The Conditions Must Concern the Future

(*Conditio* . . . de futuro *contra matrimonii substantiam* . . .)

Conditions which are expressive of opposition to the boon of offspring but which regard the past or present do not in themselves indicate an intention to do anything in married life which is incompatible with the essence of marriage, e. g. the condition: "I intend to contract marriage provided that you *have* used contraceptives." [112] Such a condition is no indication that the parties intend to obligate themselves to the preventing of conception. Hence there is no objective indication that they intend to exclude an essential right or obligation of marriage at the time when matrimonial consent is expressed by them. Since marriage as an established status (i.e. in facto esse) is *future* with regard to conditions placed at the time of the exchange of consent, such conditions necessarily must regard the *future* if they are to affect the validity of the marriage bond.[113] On the other hand, a condition which concerns the past or the present is something which is completed and antecedent in relation to the marriage obligations which arise with the giving of matrimonial consent.[114]

It is possible, however, that conditions which in their wording point to the present or the past actually indicate that the intention

[111] Cf. Vromant, *De Matrimonio,* n. 175, note (2), (p. 145).

[112] ". . . quando est conditionio de praesenti, aut praeterito, tantum continet executionem contrariam, non vero obligationem."—Sanchez, *De Matrimonio,* lib. V, disp. IX, n. 6. Cf. also Wernz-Vidal, *Ius Matrimoniale,* n. 518, note 31.

[113] Cf. Ford, *The Validity of Virginal Marriage,* p. 90.

[114] Cf. Cappello, *De Sacramentis,* III, n. 642, 4° If a condition which concerns the past or present is not incompatible with the essence of marriage, objectively considered, it may affect the validity of the marriage. It may indicate a withholding of consent which proceeds from a lack of knowledge or from the presence of a doubt whether the condition actually has been verified. Cf. Wernz-Vidal, *Ius Matrimoniale,* n. 511, note 3, and n. 513.

of the person who placed the condition is focused on the future. The condition, "I intend to contract marriage provided that you *have* used contraceptives," may mean in the individual case, ". . . provided that you have means of contraception to use in our conjugal life," or ". . . provided that you know how to use contraceptives so as to be able to prevent conception in our conjugal life." [115] This only serves to confirm the conclusion that the concept of conditions which are contrary to the essence of marriage must be limited to those which, in actual intent, regard the future.[116]

(2) The Conditions Must be Incompatible with the Essence of Marriage

(*Conditio . . . de futuro* contra substantiam *illud reddit invalididum*)

To say that the conditions which are expressive of opposition to the boon of offspring invalidate the marriage contract only if they are incompatible with the essence of marriage means that they must involve something which, *if* introduced into the marriage contract as an essential part, is repugnant to the very essence of marriage.[117] Since such conditions indicate the presence of a vitiated consent at the time when the marriage is contracted, it is clear that they can not be understood either as suspensive conditions or as voiding or resolutory conditions, i. e., conditions which, when verified, terminate the contract. This is further emphasized by the fact that such conditions usually concern not one future event or act, but a series of acts, e. g. the future and perpetual preventing of the conception of offspring. If such stipulations were intended as true suspensive conditions, it would mean that the validity of the marriage would be suspended indefinitely. If they were intended as voiding conditions, it would mean that the marriage would be

115 "Ut, 'Contraho tecum, si invenisti, vel habes venena sterilitatis ad utendum in matrimonio,' vitabit enim conditio haec matrimonium."—Sanchez *De Matrimonio*, lib. V, disp. IX, n. 7.

116 "Huiusmodi conditio, saltem reductive, est semper et necessario *de futuro*, . . ."—Cappello, *De Sacramentis*, III, n. 630, 2.

117 Cf. *supra*, p. 41 f.

dissolved just as soon as the other party failed to use contraceptives.[118]

As to external form, however, conditions which are contrary to the essence of marriage usually are worded as suspensive conditions. Of the three conditions mentioned by Gregory IX, two were worded as suspensive (". . . si generationem prolis evites," and ". . . si pro quaestu adulterandam te tradas,") while the third was worded as a voiding condition (". . . donec inveniam aliam honore vel facultatibus digniorem,").[119] Obviously, every condition which is worded as a voiding condition is contrary to the essence of marriage, that is, all but those voiding conditions which are mentioned in the law itself.[120]

The fundamental reason why conditions which are contrary to one of the three boons of marriage are not considered as having a suspensive effect on matrimonial consent, if they enter into the marriage contract itself, has been stressed in the first article of this chapter, i. e. such conditions indicate *vitiated* consent.[121] If, however, the object of conditions which are expressive of opposition to one of the three boons of marriage is something which is *not* incompatible with the essence of marriage, the conditions are to be rejected as incapable of affecting the validity of the marriage.[122] But if such a condition is placed as an essential part of the marriage

[118] Cf. S.R.R., *Nullitatis Matrimonii et Dispensationis super Rato,* 25 iul. 1930, coram R.P.D. Iulio Grazioli, dec. XL, n. 6—*Decisiones,* XXII (1930), 453 ff.; also Wernz-Vidal, *Ius Matrimoniale,* n. 518, note 33.

[119] C. 7, X, *de conditionibus appositis in desponsatione vel in aliis contractibus,* IV, 5—Potthast, n. 9664.

[120] Cf. Wernz-Vidal, *Ius Matrimoniale,* n. 513; Cappello, *De Sacramentis,* III, n. 633. The two exceptions mentioned in the law itself as these: a *non-consummated* marriage may be dissolved either by solemn religious profession or in consequence of a papal dispensation. Cf. also De Smet, *De Sponsalibus et Matrimonio,* n. 152, 1.

[121] Cf. *supra,* p. 36 ff.

[122] "Conditio . . . Si sit de futuro necessaria vel impossibilis vel turpis, sed non contra matrimonii substantiam, pro non adiecta habeatur; . . ."—Canon 1092, 1°. The expression *pro non adiecta habeatur* sometimes is paraphrased thus: *conditio vitiatur et non vitiat.* In other words, if the condition is immoral but not contrary to the essence of marriage, the condition loses its force and is vitiated, and hence is incapable of affecting the validity of the marriage. Cf. Chelodi, *Ius Matrimoniale,* p. 124; Wernz-Vidal, *Ius Matrimoniale,* n. 517.

contract, i. e. as a condition apart from which consent would not be given (*sine qua non* condition), it undoubtedly affects the validity of the marriage contract.[123] The marriage contract is invalid in such cases not precisely because of a vitiated consent, but because the party who places the condition lacks an intention to contract marriage as such. Even if the parties agreed to such an immoral condition, neither of them would be obligated to abide by the agreement and await the fulfillment of the condition.[124]

Needless to say, a condition is considered as contrary to the essence of marriage only if it affects the individual marriage in question, not marriage in general or someone else's marriage. Thus the condition, "I intend to contract marriage provided that you will induce Peter's wife to commit adultery," would not be contrary to the essence of marriage.[125] Since Gregory IX did not make a distinction between immoral and respectable conditions when he spoke of conditions which are contrary to the essence of marriage, it follows that, at least in principle, conditions which do not involve anything immoral likewise may be considered as contrary to the essence of marriage.[126] An illustration of this principle was presented in the previous article of this chapter when the question of the preventing of conception by means of the "rhythm" practice was discussed briefly.

(3) Only *True Conditions* Invalidate the Marriage Contract

Only those stipulations are considered as contrary to the essence of marriage which concern the future married life of the contracting

[123] ". . . si revera serio adserta fuerit [i.e. an impossible condition, or an immoral condition which is not contrary to the essence of marriage], non vitiatur sed *vitiat* matrimonium, perinde ac ceteros contractus, quia ea deficiente corruit consensus . . ."—Chelodi, *loc. cit.;* Wernz-Vidal, *loc. cit.;* Cappello, *De Sacramentis,* III, n. 629, 3.

[124] Cf. Reiffenstuel, *Ius Canonicum Universum,* lib. IV, tit. V, n. 44; Chelodi, *loc. cit.;* Wernz-Vidal, *loc. cit.;* Cappello, *ibid.*, n. 629, 4.

[125] Cf. Sanchez, *De Matrimonio,* lib. V, disp. IX, n. 5.

[126] This interpretation of Gregory IX's decretal was insisted upon especially by those who held that a condition to abstain perpetually from the use of the marriage right invalidated the marriage contract. Cf. Schmalzgrueber, *Ius Ecclesiasticum Universum,* lib. IV, tit. V, n. 120.

parties, and which involve something, which, objectively considered, is incompatible with the essence of marriage *if* introduced into the marriage contract itself. If, however, such conditions are to affect the validity of the particular marriage in question, they actually must be introduced into the marriage contract, i.e. placed in such a way that the validity of the consent is made dependent upon that stipulation. This is equivalent to saying, in effect, that the stipulation must be intended as an essential part of the marriage contract.[127] If such is not the case, the stipulation is considered as a *mode* or as some other addition in the giving of consent which does not affect the validity of the marriage contract itself. The principal additions of this type will be discussed briefly.

(*a*) *Conditions and Modes*

A mode is similar to a condition in that it gives rise to an obligation between the contracting parties, but differs from a condition inasmuch as the obligation in the case of a mode is intended to arise only after the marriage has been contracted, that is, in the nature of a post-contractual obligation.[128] Whereas conditions usually are introduced by means of conditional conjunctions (if, provided that, as long as, etc.), modes usually are introduced by means of final conjunctive phrases (with a view to, with the purpose of, etc.), e.g.: "I intend to marry you with a view to your preventing of conception."[129] They are called *modes,* for, objectively considered, they indicate not an intention to exclude any of the essential obligations of marriage, but rather an intention to neglect the fulfillment or the proper fulfillment of the obligations which were assumed in the

[127] ". . . tunc habetur contra matrimonii substantiam *vera condicio,* ac reapse de futuro, si pars, positivo voluntatis actu, *suum consensum alligat* exclusioni alicuius obligationis essentialis, ita ut eatenus velit contrahere *quatenus haec obligatio a se excluditur."*—Payen, *De Matrimonio,* II, n. 1732, 1).

[128] "Modus est *adiectio oneris ad quod post contractum volumus obligare contrahentem."*—Santi-Leitner, *Praelectiones Iuris Canonici,* lib. IV, tit. V, n 36. Cf. also Wernz-Vidal, *Ius Matrimoniale,* n. 98 and n. 510, note 2; Gasparri, *De Matrimonio,* II, n. 879; Cappello, *De Sacramentis,* III, nn. 100 and 644, 2.

[129] Cf. Wernz-Vidal, *ibid.,* n. 510, note 2.

contracting of the marriage. They pertain, therefore, to the manner of fulfilling the obligations involved (*modus implendi obligationes*).

As long as there is no convincing evidence that a stipulation which is expressive of opposition to the boon of offspring was intended as an essential part of the marriage contract itself, the stipulation is considered as indicative of no more than an intention to abuse the marriage right.[130] Even though such stipulations frequently may be worded as conditions, they are at most to be considered as modes until evidence is at hand that they actually were intended as true conditions.

Stipulations which have the external form of modes may, at times, be intended as true conditions. The stipulation, "I intend to contract marriage with you, with a view to your preventing of conception," may mean in reality, ". . . provided that you preclude the conception of children." Some authors held that all such stipulations, even though expressed as modes, were contrary to the essence of marriage.[131] Although it may not be imprudent to follow this view in practice,[132] still it is important to note the distinction between modes and conditions. For if a stipulation is intended *as a mode,* i.e., as pointing to a post-contractual obligation, it does not invalidate the marriage even though it concerns something which, objectively considered, is incompatible with the essence of marriage.[133]

130 S.R.R., *Nullitatis Matrimonii,* 31 iul. 1928, coram R.P.D. Iosepho Florczak, dec. XXXVI, n. 2: "Quodsi non excludatur *ipsa ordinatio ad prolem* et contrahens vult sibi fieri ab altera parte unam promissionem de iuris matrimonialis abusu, contractus valet: non esset enim positiva intentio aut propria conditio matrimonii substantiae contraria, sed *modus* implendae obligationis, qui validum contractum praesupponit . . ."—*Decisiones,* XX (1928), 334. Cf. also 9 mai. 1928, coram Rmo P.D. Maximo Massimi, Decano, dec. XVIII, n. 3 f.—*Decisiones,* XX (1928), 178 f.

131 Cf. Sanchez, *De Matrimonio,* lib. V, disp. XIX, n. 5; Santi-Leitner, *Praelectiones Iuris Canonici,* lib. IV, tit. V, n. 37.

132 "Cui sententiae facile *in praxi* standum est, quoniam onus in forma modi contractui matrimoniali adiectum, re et intentione contrahentium saepe potest esse nihil aliud quam *simulata conditio* in pactum deducta."—Wernz-Vidal, *Ius Matrimoniale,* n. 519.

133 "At *theoretice verus modus* pro natura sua oneris *adiecti* ad contractum *iam perfectum* non irritat contractum matrimonialem, etiamsi sit contra substantiam matrimonii."—Wernz-Vidal, *loc. cit.* Cf. also Reiffenstuel, *Ius*

This emphasizes the need of investigating above all the actual *intention* of the contracting parties in all cases of stipulations which are expressive of opposition to the essence of marriage in particular.

(*b*) *Conditions, Demonstrative Declarations and Recited Causes*

Another type of addition to the declared matrimonial consent is known as a demonstration (*demonstratio*). Such a declaration implies neither an obligation in the contract itself nor a post-contractual obligation, but merely is expressive of some desired quality in the other contracting party, e.g.: "I intend to contract marriage with you whom I know to be given to the use of contraceptives." [134] A somewhat similar type of addition to the declared matrimonial consent is known as a cause (*causa*), wherein the motive or the reason for consenting to the marriage contract is expressed, e.g.: "I intend to contract marriage with you for the reason that (*quia*) you use contraceptives." Authors agree that, objectively considered, both of these types of additions to the matrimonial consent merely indicate opinions or motives in the mind of one of the contracting parties in regard to the other. They do not have an invalidating force with reference to the expressed matrimonial consent.[135] Such additions to the matrimonial consent may in unusual circumstances invalidate the marriage contract, for instance, if they amount to an error concerning the physical identity of the other contracting party, or regarding the freedom of status (i. e. freedom from slavery) of that party.[136] Furthermore, it is possible that such demonstrative declarations and recited causes may be intended as *true conditions*.[137]

Canonicum Universum, lib. IV, tit. V, n. 64. Cappello, *De Sacramentis*, III, n. 644, 2.

[134] Cf. Sanchez, *De Matrimonio*, lib. V, disp. XIX, n. 2; Schmalzgrueber, *ibid.*, n. 136; Wernz-Vidal, *ibid.*, n. 510, note 2; Cappello, *ibid.*, nn. 100, 2 f. and 644, 3.

[135] Wernz-Vidal (*ibid.* n. 519) state: "*Causa* vel *demonstratio* qualiscunque sive vera sive falsa honesta vel turpis et substantiae matrimonii contraria vel non contraria non vitiat vel suspendit matrimonium, nisi reducatur ad *errorem* personae et conditionis servilis aut transeat in veram *conditionem*." Cf. also Schmalzgrueber, *loc. cit.*; Cappello, *ibid.*, n. 644, 3.

[136] Cf. Wernz-Vidal, *loc. cit.*; Cappello, *loc. cit.*, and canon 1083.

[137] "Si apponatur per modum conditionis, iudicandum est de illis, sicut de conditionibus."—Sanchez, *De Matrimonio*, lib. V, disp. XIX, n. 2 f. Cf. also Wernz-Vidal, *loc. cit.*; Cappello, *loc. cit.*

CONCLUSIONS TO SECTION ONE

I. Only those intentions or conditions which, if introduced into the marriage contract, are inconsistent with the essential object or the essential properties of marriage are to be considered as contrary to the essence of marriage. Opposition to the ends of marriage, *as ends*, does not constitute the exclusion of any of the essential rights or obligations of marriage.

II. An intention or condition is contrary to the essence of marriage in the strict sense of the word only if it involves something which, when introduced into the *marriage contract itself* as a matter of obligation, is incompatible with the giving of the marriage right or the accepting of one or the other of the essential obligations of marriage. In the case of an intention or of a condition which is contrary to the boon of sacramental stability, the mere fact that the intention or condition proceeds from a positive and specific act of the will indicates that it enters into the marriage contract itself as a matter of contrary obligation, thereby contravening the element of indissolubility which always is inherent in and essential to a valid matrimonial contract. In the case of an intention or of a condition which is contrary to the boon of offspring or the boon of conjugal fidelity, however, the intention or condition enters into the marriage contract itself as a matter of obligation only if the opposition to either of these two boons of marriage is expressed *directly* as an exclusion of the marriage right itself, or *indirectly* as a *true condition*, that is, in effect, a condition apart from which consent would not be given to the marriage contract (*conditio sine qua non*).

III. The only intentions or conditions contrary to the boon of offspring which are in themselves incompatible with the essence of marriage, if introduced into the marriage contract, are those which are expressive of positive opposition to the *conception* of offspring. Intentions or conditions which relate to the procuring of abortion or to the killing or the abandoning of the offspring are incompatible with the essence of marriage, if introduced into the marriage contract, only in so far as such intentions or conditions, in the given circumstances of each individual case, indicate a positive intention to prevent the conception of offspring. Intentions or conditions which are expressive of opposition to the *education* of the begotten offspring do not affect the validity of marriage.

IV. Since conditions which are contrary to the essence of marriage indicate a vitiated consent, and hence preclude the possibility of a valid marriage from the very moment of the exchange of consent, they cannot be understood as conditions in the strict sense of the word, i. e. as suspending the validity of the consent until a future time. Voiding conditions, inasmuch as they are contrary to the indissolubility of marriage, always are contrary to the essence of marriage and accordingly are invalidating in their effect.

Section II

Proofs of the Exclusion of the Boon of Offspring

The discussions in the preceding chapters should suffice to establish that invalidating opposition to the three boons of marriage amounts to a question of vitiated consent. The difficulty of proving the invalidity of a marriage in the external forum in such cases likewise is implied in the preceding chapters. The purpose of the following chapters is to establish that it is possible, however, to arrive at sufficient proof of vitiated consent in the external forum. As a preliminary to the discussion of the main elements of such proof (Chapter IV), the first chapter of this section will be devoted to a review of several important, practical considerations of a more general nature (Chapter III).

CHAPTER III

PRACTICAL CONSIDERATIONS OF PRIMARY IMPORTANCE

In handling marriage cases which involve the exclusion of one of the boons of marriage in particular, the ecclesiastical tribunal must keep in mind the attitude and practice of the Holy See in regard to such cases (Article 1). Furthermore, it must be remembered that no matter how clearly the intention or condition, objectively considered, is incompatible with the essence of marriage, it does not invalidate the marriage unless it has been introduced into the marriage pact itself (Article 2). As a final consideration, it may be well to emphasize that the Holy See has limited considerably the right to impugn the validity of the marriage in the cases here under discussion (Article 3).

Article 1. The Attitude and Practice of the Holy See

A. The Attitude of the Holy See

Since the Church is the guardian of christian marriage, she would rather tolerate the continued union of those who may be married invalidly in the internal forum, than risk the violation of God's laws by declaring a marriage invalid in the absence of convincing evidence of nullity in the external forum.[1] She is mindful of the fact that the presumptions in favor of the validity of marriage "must be safeguarded particularly in cases involving defects of consent, exclusion of the *bona matrimonii* and the like. For it is here that laxity may arise and the faithful, and perhaps even non-Catholics, be shocked and scandalized."[2] Although the ecclesiastical tribunals should manifest every kindness in examining marriage cases presented by the laity, "it would be a mistake to consider the ecclesiastical tribunal as a kind of clinic for unhappy marriages where the judges are bound to adjust unfortunate situations at all costs, or at least with exaggerated leniency. Such an erroneous attitude would wound the sacred bond of marriage, indissoluble by divine origin, and harm the very solidity of the family and society."[3]

The same source presents the following observation in regard to the exclusion of the boon of offspring in particular:

> In cases of exclusion of the *bona matrimonii,* conditions, simulations and the like, judges should bear in mind that ordinarily consorts who claim to have excluded the *bonum prolis,* have in reality agreed to exclude the proper exercise of marriage prerogatives and duties, but not its basic rights. Hence, in such

[1] "Tolerabilius est enim, aliquos contra statuta hominum dimittere copulatos, quam coniunctos legitime contra statuta Domini separare."—C. 47, X, *de testibus et attestationibus,* II, 20.

[2] *Letter of Apostolic Delegate on handling of marriage cases in the United States* (Apostolic Delegation, U. S., 23 Sept., 1938) *Private*—Bouscaren, *The Canon Law Digest* (2 vols., Milwaukee: Bruce, 1934-1943), II, 532. This letter will be cited hereafter as *Apos. Delegate's letter,* 1938. As stated in Bouscaren (*ibid.,* 531), the Apostolic Delegate in the United States sent this letter to the bishops of the United States at the direction of the Sacred Congregation of the Sacraments.

[3] *Ibid.,* 532.

cases, the marriage is valid, except, of course, in the very rare instances where the evidence proves that the consorts have effectively excluded the very *ius radicale* and have had the positive will *se non obligandi* and not merely *obligationem assumptam violandi*.[4]

B. The Practice of the Holy See

Since its re-organization in 1908,[5] the Sacred Roman Rota has issued comparatively few declarations of nullity in cases which involved the exclusion of the boon of offspring. Although the decisions of the Rota after the year 1931 are not available at the present time, information as to the number of such cases decided up to the year 1944 inclusively can be gleaned from the available volumes of the *Acta Apostolicae Sedis*. The writer was enabled to form the following table by consulting the indexes of the Decisions of the Sacred Roman Rota, volumes one to twenty-three inclusively, and supplying the figures for the subsequent years (after 1931) through a consulting of the annual lists of cases reviewed by the same tribunal—lists which are published each year in the *Acta Apostolicae Sedis*.

Year	Number of Marriage Cases (*Nullitatis Mat.*) Reviewed	Exclusion of the Boon of Offspring Involved	Nullity Declared	Validity Upheld
1909	9	1	....	1[6]
1910	19	0	....	....
1911	26	0	....	....
1912	23	1	....	1
1913	23	0	....	....
1914	16	2	1	1
1915	21	1	....	1
1916	18	1	1	....
1917	19	1	....	1
1918	17	0	....	....
1919	12	1	1	....
1920	24	0	....	....
1921	26	0	....	....
1922	34	4	3	1
1923	31	2	2	....
1924	42	1	1	....

[4] *Ibid.*, 533.

[5] Const. *Sapienti Consilio*, 29 iun. 1908—*AAS*, I (1909), 7 ff.

Year	Number of Marriage Cases (*Nullitatis Mat.*) Reviewed	Exclusion of the Boon of Offspring Involved	Nullity Declared	Validity Upheld
1925	48	4	1	3[6]
1926	45	7	3	4
1927	53	6	3	3
1928	49	7	4	3
1929	58	6	1	5
1930	54	7	1	6
1931	56	7	2	5
1932	51	4	1	3
1933	72	12	4	8
1934	93	13	4	9
1935	80	8	2	6
1936	76	12	7	5
1937	76	10	2	8
1938	72	13	2	11
1939	56	6	2	4
1940	76	7	1	6
1941		Figures not available.		
1942		Figures not available.		
1943	90	10	6	4
1944	66	9	6	3
	1,531	163	59	104

The table above indicates that about 10 per cent of the cases (i. e. *nullitatis mat.*) reviewed by the Sacred Roman Rota from 1909 to 1944 inclusively involved the exclusion of the boon of offspring. Of this 10 per cent, the validity of the marriage was upheld in almost two-thirds of the cases. Furthermore, a considerable number of the cases which did result in a declaration of nullity involved the exclusion of other boons of marriage besides the boon of offspring—usually the boon of sacramental stability. This was true especially in 1943 when three of the four declarations of nullity on the score of the exclusion of the boon of offspring involved the exclusion of the boon of sacramental stability as well.[7]

[6] One of these decisions was reversed by the Sacred Tribunal of the Apostolic Signatura (July 26, 1926).

[7] Cf. *AAS*, XXXVI (1944), decisions 4, 60 and 81, pp. 105, 117 and 121 respectively.

ARTICLE 2. AN ANALYSIS OF THE EXPRESSION *Deducta in Pactum*

Once it has been established that the intention or condition in the individual case, objectively considered, concerns something which is incompatible with the essence of marriage, it remains to be established by proof that the intention or condition actually was introduced into the marriage contract itself as part of the contract. If such is the case, then the corresponding essential obligation of marriage is excluded necessarily, e. g. the essential obligation in regard to the procreation of offspring. If the intention or condition is not placed as part of the marriage contract, whatever obligation is implied therein refers only to the future married life of the contracting parties, and not to the contract itself.[8] In this sense, it is logical to say that an intention or condition does not invalidate the marriage unless it is introduced into the marriage pact itself (*deducta in pactum matrimoniale*).

More frequently, however, the expression *deducta in pactum* is understood to refer not to the marriage pact itself, but to an added pact or agreement between the contracting parties, e. g., when one of the parties either directly or indirectly (as in a condition) expresses an intention to prevent the conception of offspring in married life, and the other party agrees to the same. In this sense, the expression *deducta in pactum* refers rather to a *means for proving* that the adverse intention or condition was introduced into the marriage pact itself. Although there is no question of the invalidity of a marriage unless the adverse intention or condition has been introduced into the marriage pact itself, a declaration of nullity in the external forum is possible, even though the intention or condition has not been reduced to a pact or agreement between the parties. In order to clarify this important question, it may be wise

[8] "At in matrimonio conditio contraria quando apponitur in ipso contractu, repugnat eius substantiae, quia apponitur tamquam pars contractus, quo solo modo repugnat substantiae matrimonii, sed quando apponitur matrimonio iam contracto, cum iam dissolvi nequeat, non est pars eius contractus, et sic non adversatur ei, neque ipsum vitiat."—Sanchez, *De Matrimonio*, lib. V, disp. IX, n. 14; cf. also Payen, *De Matrimonio*, II, n. 1732, 1).

to discuss separately the two distinct aspects of the expression *deducta in pactum* as outlined above.

A. *The Adverse Intention or Condition Must Enter Into the Marriage Pact*

If the expression *deducta in pactum* is understood to refer to the marriage pact itself, it signifies an essential factor for the invalidity of a marriage. To introduce a condition into the marriage pact means simply that the condition is made a constitutive part of the marriage contract.[9] This is equivalent to saying that the intention or condition is, in effect, a *sine qua non* condition for the consent, i. e., that the party is so intent upon precluding the procreation of offspring, for example, that consent to the marriage contract is bound up with such an intention as by a condition, apart from which the consent would not have been given. This is sufficient to invalidate a marriage, even though such an intention or condition is introduced into the marriage pact by only one of the contracting parties, and without the knowledge of the other.[10]

Understood in this sense, an intention or condition contrary to the blessing of sacramental stability enters into the marriage pact itself by the mere fact that one of the contracting parties harbors a positive intention contrary to the indissolubility of the marriage

[9] S.R.R., *Oregonopolitana, Nullitatis Matrimonii,* 6 iul. 1914, coram R.P.D. Ioanne Prior, dec. XXII, n. 10: "Deducere aliquam conditionem in pactum matrimoniale nihil aliud significat quam facere talem conditionem partem constitutivam contractus matrimonialis . . .;"—*Decisiones,* VI (1914), 248 f. and *AAS,* VI (1914), 520 ff. Cf. also Payen, *De Matrimonio,* n. 1677, 2), 3°; O'Donnell, "Matrimonial Consent in the New Code," *The Irish Ecclesiastical Record,* XII (1918), 278.

[10] S.R.R., *Nullitatis Matrimonii,* 10 dec. 1914, coram R.P.D. Ioanne Prior, dec. XXXIII, n. 4: "Si vero ita intendit positive iure coëundi abuti, ut consensus matrimonio praestitus hac intentione ligetur, tamquam a conditione sine qua non fuisset datus consensus, seu ut aiunt, si intentio abutendi copula maritali deducta fuerit in pactum matrimoniale, etiam ab uno solo coniugum, altero inscio, matrimonium est nullum."—*Decisiones,* VI (1914), 341; cf. also *Neo-Eboracen., Nullitatis Matrimonii,* 8 febr. 1915, coram R.P.D. Ioanne Prior, dec. III, n. 4—*Decisiones,* VII (1915), 22.

bond.[11] In the case of an intention or condition which is contrary to the boon of offspring or the boon of coniugal fidelity, however, there must be evidence that the stipulation was placed in such a manner as to prevail over the intention, presumed in all marriages, that the parties wished to enter marriage as established by Christ, with all its inherent obligations.[12] Such evidence is present if the positive intention, in regard to something which is incompatible with the essence of marriage, was expressed as a condition apart from which the consent to the marriage would not have been given (*conditio sine qua non*) or if one of the contracting parties expressed a positive intention to exclude the marriage right itself or the corresponding essential obligation in regard to the boon of offspring or the boon of conjugal fidelity. Otherwise it is presumed that the parties gave the marriage right and accepted the essential obligations, but intended merely to abuse the marriage right and neglect the fulfillment of the essential obligation in regard to offspring or conjugal fidelity.

In 1680, the Sacred Congregation of the Holy Office apparently used the expression *deducta in pactum* as referring to the marriage pact itself.[13] In answer to the question whether an intention to abuse or to dissolve the marriage would invalidate a marriage between a Catholic and a schismatic, that sacred congregation answered that if such an intention is introduced into the [marriage] pact, or if

[11] S.R.R., *Neo-Eboracen.*, *Nullitatis Matrimonii,* 8 febr. 1915, coram R.P.D. Ioanne Prior, dec. III, n. 5: ". . . intentio, igitur, contrahentis huic indissolubilitati contraria, eo ipso contraria est matrimonii substantiae; etenim nativo suo pondere pactum matrimoniale ingreditur, quin ad hoc requiratur specialis ex parte contrahentis vel contrahentium voluntas, et unum ex constitutivis elementis contractus matrimonialis reiicit, perpetuitatem nempe, sine qua matrimonium concipi nequit."—*Decisiones,* VII (1915), 22. Cf. also 6 iul. 1914, coram R.P.D. Ioanne Prior, dec. XXII, n. 10—*Decisiones,* VI (1914), 248 f.

[12] S.R.R., *Oregonopolitana, Nullitatis Matrimonii,* 6 iul. 1914, coram R.P.D. Ioanne Prior, dec. XXII, n. 10 ". . . ut talis conditio [i.e. contra fidem vel prolem] in contractum ipsum ingrediatur, et consequenter illum irritum reddat, requiritur specialis actus voluntatis, quo non solum positive intenditur conditio contra bonum fidei et prolis, sed etiam ut ita intendatur ut praevaleat intentioni generali contrahendi matrimonium prout ordinarie contrahitur, . . ." —*Decisiones,* VI (1914), 249.

[13] S.C.S. Off. (*Bosniae*), 2 dec. 1680—*Fontes,* n. 755.

marriage is contracted with such a condition, the marriage is invalid.[14] It seems, therefore, that a condition is made part of the marriage pact (*deducta in pactum*) by the fact that it is placed as a true condition, fully determinative of the validity of consent, and that an intention enters into the marriage pact inasmuch as it determines directly the validity of consent. But if neither the contrary intention nor the contrary condition enters into the contract itself to effect the essential element of consent, the marriage is valid. This concept of the expression *deducta in pactum* is advanced by outstanding authors.[15]

B. *Evidence of an Added External Pact Is Not Required for Invalidity*

As stated in the previous chapter (p. 52 f.), the early commentators interpreted Gregory IX's decretal on conditions which are contrary to the essence of marriage [16] as referring only to an express, mutual agreement in regard to the prevention of the conception of children, the violation of conjugal fidelity and the future dissolution of the marriage bond. This interpretation implies that the expression *deducta in pactum* is to be understood as a means for proving in the external forum the presence of a vitiated consent, and not as an implication that the marriage is invalid in the *internal* forum only if there is evidence of such an agreement between the parties. In this, the usual interpretation of the expression *deducta in pactum,* a pact may be defined as a stipulation added to marriage by the con-

[14] The question was stated as follows: "An sit validum matrimonium contractum inter catholicum et schismaticum haereticum cum intentione foedandi vel solvendi matrimonium?" The Holy Office replied: "Si ista sint deducta in pactum, seu cum ista conditione sint contracta, matrimonia sunt nulla; sin aliter, sunt valida." *Loc. cit.* Cf. also S.C.S. Off. instr. (*ad Ep. S. Alberti*), 9 dec. 1874—*Fontes,* n. 1036.

[15] Cf. Payen, *De Matrimonio,* II, n. 1677 2), 3°; Gougnard, *Tractatus de Matrimonio,* n. 30 (p. 143); De Smet, *De Sponsalibus et Matrimonio,* n. 151, note 1; Ayrinhac, "De quibusdam defectibus in consensu matrimoniali, *Ius Pontificium* (Romae, 1921—), IX (1929), 29.

[16] C. 7, X, *de conditionibus appositis in desponsatione vel in aliis contractibus,* IV, 5; Potthast, n. 9664.

tracting parties, whereby they come to a decision in regard to something which is contrary to the essence of marriage.[17]

If the expression *deducta in pactum* is interpreted to refer not to the marriage pact, but to an added pact or agreement between the contracting parties, two important points must be emphasized: (1) the expression signifies a means of proving in the external forum the presence of a vitiated consent; (2) evidence of such a pact is not required absolutely for a declaration of nullity in the external forum.

(1) Character of a Mutual Pact As An External Means of Proof

As an external proof of an internally vitiated consent, a mutual pact between the contracting parties has nothing to do with the inherent validity of the marriage.[18] The *means of proof* must not be confused with the object of proof. As an external means of proof, the presence of such a pact serves to prove that a condition or intention was expressed by one of the contracting parties, and *demonstrates* that, inasmuch as the other party consented to the condition or concurred in the intention, the condition or intention entered into the marriage pact itself.[19]

The presence of such a mutual agreement, therefore, does not serve to prove, but serves merely to indicate or to demonstrate that the condition was placed as a true condition (i. e., *sine qua non*), or that at least one of the contracting parties intended to exclude the marriage right itself or the corresponding essential obligation in re-

[17] Cf. S.R.R., *Nullitatis Matrimonii,* 29 apr. 1922, coram R.P.D. Francisco Parrillo, dec. XIV, n. 14, where a pact is defined as follows: "Stipulatio a contrahentibus matrimonio adiecta, qua statuitur aliquid contrarium essentiae matrimonii."—*Decisiones,* XIV (1922), 123.

[18] "Pactum nequaquam influit in validitatem aut nullitatem matrimonii, sed solum potest et debet considerari tamquam medium aptissimum, non tamen unicum, ad probandum intentionis factum."—Cappello, *De Sacramentis,* III, n. 599, 2.

[19] "Pactum vim habet dumtaxat *demonstrativam* et *probativam.* Demonstrat nempe agi de vera conditione, quae, alia parte consentiente, tamquam pars constitutiva contractus apposita est; probat factum, i.e. exsistentiam conditionis."—Cappello, *ibid.*, n. 634, 4.

gard to one of the boons of marriage. The mere fact that the contracting parties are of one mind in regard to something which, objectively considered, is incompatible with the essence of marriage does not in itself constitute sufficient proof in the external forum of a vitiated consent. In every case decided by the Sacred Roman Rota in which there was evidence of such a mutual pact contrary to the blessing of offspring, the tribunal sought evidence that the condition was placed as a *sine qua non* condition for the consent, or evidence of a positive intention to exclude the marriage right itself or corresponding essential obligation, before issuing a declaration of nullity.[20]

(2) Vitiated Consent Can Be Proved Without Evidence of a Mutual Pact

Even though there is no evidence of a pact or agreement between the contracting parties, the mere fact that one of the parties expressed a positive intention to exclude the marriage right itself or reject one of the essential obligations of marriage is sufficient to invalidate a marriage.[21] If the contrary intention or condition has

[20] Cf. *infra,* Chapter V, cases nn. 1-10 inclusively.

[21] S.R.R., *Nullitatis Matrimonii,* 23 nov. 1923, coram R.P.D. Raphaele Chimenti, dec. XXXII, n. 2: "In iuridica aestimatione conditionis, hodie vera censenda est doctrina, per can. 1086, § 2, clariore luce nitescens, quae tenet non requiri ut pars comparti suum propositum non aliter contrahendi manifestet, prout vetus effatum 'conditionem non attendi nisi sit in pactum deducta,' nonnullis scriptoribus suggesserat; sufficit enim ex laudato canone, 'ut *alterutra* pars positivo voluntatis actu' propositum suum perficiat. Ad rem N.S.O. in una Romana.—*Nullitatis Matrimonii*—coram Sebastianelli, 7 februarii 1914: 'Parum refert, an haec intentio fuerit in pactum deducta, i.e. intentio uti conditio fuerit inserta in ipso contractu, vel non fuerit in pactum deducta; contractus enim essentialiter in ipso consensu consistit . . . Quidquid enim olim scripserint Auctores non minimi subsellii, hodie apud omnes certa rest est, ad valide contrahendum requiri consensum, saltem implicitum, in substantiam matrimonii, seu in tria ipsius matrimonii bona . . . Si quis contrahentium ita statuat *apud se* consensum matrimonialem, ut excludat ipsasmet obligationes, vel unam tantum, bonum v.g. prolis, vel absque ullo pacto cum altera parte, vel etiam *sine scientia* alterius partis, matrimonium est nullum'."—*Decisiones,* XV (1923), 275. Cf. also 7 febr. 1914, coram R.P.D. Guilelmo Sebastianelli, dec. V, n. 3—*Decisiones,* VI (1914), 58; 10 maii. 1916, coram Rmo P.D. Guilelmo Sebastianelli, Decano, dec. XIII, n. 2—*Decisiones,* VIII (1916), 140.

been reduced to a pact or agreement between the contracting parties, however, the task of proving in the external forum the presence of a vitiated matrimonial consent will be less difficult.[22] The essential thing is to prove that the intention or condition entered into the marriage pact itself. In as far as the *possibility* of such proof is concerned, the question whether or not the parties have entered a pact or agreement in regard to the contrary condition or whether or not the one party knew of the contrary intention or condition of the other is of secondary importance.[23]

A review of the actual decisions of the Sacred Roman Rota (from 1909 to 1931 inclusively) will demonstrate that, in exactly half of the cases which resulted in a declaration of nullity, there was no evidence or only insufficient evidence of a mutual pact between the parties with regard to the exclusion of the boon of offspring. In those cases, however, there was sufficient evidence either of a *sine qua non* condition or of a positive intention to exclude the marriage right with reference to the boon of offspring, or to reject the corresponding essential obligation.

[22] S.R.R., *Nullitatis Matrimonii,* 17 iul. 1929, coram Rmo P.D. Maximo Massimi, Decano, dec. XXXIV, n. 3: ". . . de obligatione non suscepta, id est de iure excluso, longe facilius constabit, si intentio bonis prolis et fidei contraria deducta fuerit in pactum. Neque tamen id necessario requiritur, cum satis sit ad nullitatem matrimonii evincendam, ut vel unam partem positivam intentionem habuisse et explicitam sese non obligandi, utcumque tandem, dummodo concludenter probetur."—*Decisiones,* XXI (1929), 290. Cf. also 1 dec. 1928, coram R.P.D. Andrea Jullien, dec. LV, n. 2—*Decisiones,* XX (1928), 484; 12 aug. 1931, coram Exc. mo. P.D. Maximo Massimi, Decano, dec. L, n. 3—*Decisiones,* XXIII (1931), 424.

[23] "Nihil autem refert quoad effectum iuridicum, utrum conditio apposita fuerit in actu celebrationis an antea nec revocata; utrum in pactum deducta vel non; utrum ab una tantum parte, an ab utraque; utrum apposita fuerit publice, an occulte ita ut in foro externo probari non possit; utrum quae ab una dumtaxat parte fuerit apposita alteri parti fuerit cognita, vel non. At conditionis occulte appositae et in foro externo non probatae in hoc foro nulla habenda est ratio."—Wernz-Vidal, *Ius Matrimoniale,* n. 514. Cf. also Gasparri, *De Matrimonio,* II, n. 817 ff.; De Smet, *De Sponsalibus et Matrimonio,* n. 151; Cappello, *De Sacramentis,* III, nn. 599, 603 and 634; Claeys Bouuaert-Simenon, *Manuale Iuris Canonici,* II, nn. 292, 6 and 297, III, 3.

C. The Practice of the Sacred Congregation of the Council

As stated in Chapter II of this study (p. 44 f.), the more common opinion among the authors was that an intention or condition contrary to the boon of offspring or the boon of conjugal fidelity invalidated a marriage contract only if the intention or condition was reduced to a pact between the contracting parties, whereas even an undisclosed intention contrary to the boon of sacramental stability (indissolubility) was considered as having an invalidating effect upon the marriage contract.[24] Without denying this doctrine, the Holy See nevertheless required evidence of an external pact for several centuries in all cases which involved the exclusion of any one of the three boons of marriage. This is clear from a series of declarations of the Sacred Congregation of the Holy Office.[25] Some of these declarations indicated that such pacts could be implicit, i. e., if reference to the dissolution of the marriage in the event of adultery was implied in the formulae used in the contracting of the marriage.[26]

It seems that in the practice of the Sacred Congregation of the Council, an express condition was considered as equivalent to a pact as evidence in particular of the exclusion of the blessing of sacramental stability.[27] Apparently the doctrine of Sanchez was adhered

[24] ". . . si haberet animum etiam corde retentum, adversum bono sacramenti quia scilicet intenderet non contrahere matrimonium, nisi ad tempus, non esset verum matrimonium; si tamen haberet intentionem adversam aliis duobus matrimonii bonis, corde solo retentam, nec in pactum deductam, valeret utique: . . ."—Sanchez, *De Matrimonio,* lib. II, disp. XXIX, n. 11.

[25] Cf. S.C.S. Off. (Mission. Capuccin.), 23 iul. 1698, ad I—*Fontes,* n. 761; (*Promont. Bonae Spei*), 22 iul. 1840, ad II—*Fontes,* n. 883; (Vic. Ap. Sandwic), 11 dec. 1850, ad 25 et 26—*Fontes,* n. 913; (*Iaponiae*), II mart. 1868, ad II—*Fontes,* n. 1005; instr. (*ad Ep. Nesquallien.*), 24 ian. 1877, n. 3—*Fontes,* n. 1050; instr. (*Mongoliae*), 29 nov. 1882—*Fontes,* n. 1075; instr. (*ad Vic Ap. Iapon. Merid*), 4 febr. 1891—*Fontes,* n. 1130; (*Siouxormen*), 18 mai. 1892, ad I—*Fontes,* n. 1155.

[26] Cf. S.C.S. Off. instr. (*ad Vic. Ap. Oceaniae*). 6 apr. 1843—*Fontes,* n. 894; instr. (*ad Vic. Ap. Gallas*), 28 mart. 1860, ad VI—*Fontes,* n. 957.

[27] S.C.C., *Parisien., Matrimonii,* 31 ian. 1891: "Non abs re erit notare quod in stylo S.C. *expressa* conditio valeat 'pactum' . . ."—*Thesaurus,* CL (1891), 19; cf. also Benedictus XIV, *De Synodo Dioecesana,* lib. XIII, cap. 22,

to by the same sacred congregation in regard to the exclusion of the boon of offspring and the boon of conjugal fidelity, i.e., the invalidity of the marriage was not admitted in the external forum unless there was evidence of a pact or agreement between the contracting parties relative to the preventing of the procreation of offspring or the violating of conjugal fidelity.[28]

In regard to the boon of sacramental stability, that is, the indissolubility of marriage, it seems clear that the Sacred Congregation of the Holy Office required evidence of a mutual pact or of an express condition not as an indication that the marriage was considered invalid in the *internal* forum only if such a condition or pact had been placed or agreed upon by the contracting parties,[29] but as an indication that there must be evidence in the external forum that the intention to contract a dissoluble marriage was based on a positive act of the will and not merely on an erroneous view in regard to the indissolubility of marriage.[30] Unless the intention to contract a dis-

n. 7. Likewise, a declaration of the Sacred Congregation of the Holy Office stated clearly: "Si vero expressa illa conditio de matrimonio pro aliquo casu dissolvendo, apposita minime fuerit . . . standum pro valore contractus; exceptio enim intentionis in foro externo non admittitur nisi probetur, et probari nequit nisi per externam declarationem."—S.C.S. Off. (*Tahiti*), 19 aug. 1857, ad I—*Fontes,* n. 945; cf. also (*Iaponiae*), 11 mart. 1868—*Fontes,* n. 1005.

[28] This seems to be indicated in a case decided as late as 1904 on the score of the exclusion of the boon of offspring. Cf. S.C.C. *Parisien., Matrimonii—Thesaurus,* CLXIII (1904), 801 ff.

[29] Cf. S.R.R. *Neo-Eboracen., Nullitatis Matrimonii,* 8 febr. 1915, coram R.P.D. Ioanne Prior, dec. III, n. 7, wherein it is stated that the declarations of the Holy Office, relative to the requirement of a mutual pact, do not refer to the validity of the marriage in the internal forum: ". . . cum S. Cong. de quaestione speculativa . . . directe non agat; . . ."—*Decisiones,* VII (1915), 24. Cf. also Wernz-Vidal, *Ius Matrimoniale,* n. 461; Cappello, *De Sacramentis,* III, n. 599, 2, note (17).

[30] S.R.R., *Oregonopolitana, Nullitatis Matrimonii,* 6 iul. 1914, coram R.P.D.Ioanne Prior, dec. XXII, n. 14: "In huiusmodi vero documentis [i.e. the declarations of the Holy Office] clarum est ex contextu non agi de distinctione inter contrahentem simpliciter cum positiva intentione matrimonium solubile ex una parte, et ex altera contrahentem cum tali positiva intentione in pactum deducta, sed potius inter illum qui contrahit cum errore concomitanti de indissolubilitate coniugii, menti quidem inhaerenti, quin tamen actu positivo

soluble marriage was placed as an express condition or as an agreement between the contracting parties, the marriage was regarded as valid in the external forum.[31]

Although it became the policy of the Holy See to require evidence of an express condition or mutual pact even in cases which involved the exclusion of the boon of sacramental stability, it was decided clearly in 1724 that such a pact or condition did not have to be placed at the time of the exchange of matrimonial consent in order to serve as an indication of the invalidity of the marriage.[32] The noted canonist, Prosper de Lambertini (later, Benedict XIV) was secretary of the Sacred Congregation at the time when the 1724 decision was given. The import of the decision, as indicated by his discussion of the case, was that the marriage could be declared invalid provided that the circumstances which preceded, accompanied and followed the marriage indicated that the parties had not revoked the condition or pact.[33]

Later authors attached less importance to evidence of a mutual pact between the contracting parties, and conceded at most that without evidence of such a *means of proof* the marriage would be presumed valid in the external forum.[34] Other authors insisted that the declarations of the Holy Office which seem to require evidence of a mutual pact as an absolute requirement for a declaration of

voluntatis coniugium dissolubile intendat, et ex alia parte contrahentem cum positiva intentione matrimonium dissolubile."—*Decisiones*, VI (1914), 250 f. Cf. also Doheny, *Canonical Procedure in Matrimonial Cases* (2 vols., Vol. I, Milwaukee: Bruce, 1938) I, 616 ff.

[31] Cf. Benedictus XIV, *De Synodo Dioecesana*, lib. XIII, cap. 22, n. 7.

[32] Cf. S.C.C. *Ulixbonen, Occidentalis, Matrimonii*, 8 iul. 1724—*Thesaurus*, III (1724-1726), 39 ff. and *Fontes*, n. 3278.

[33] ". . . attamen, omnibus praecedentibus, et subsequentibus simul iunctis, simulque perpensis, nullus erat locus suspicandi, coniuges ab iis promissis, et conditionibus, de quibus invicem convenerant, recessisse: . . ."—*De Synodo Dioecesana*, lib. XIII, cap. 22, n. 10. It may be noted, however, that the revocation of a pact or condition is not presumed, but must be proved. Cf. *infra*, Chapter IV, p. 122 ff.

[34] Cf. De Angelis (1824-1881), *Praelectiones Iuris Canonici* (5 vols., Vol. III, Romae, 1880), lib. IV, tit. V, 5°; Santi-Leitner, *Praelectiones Iuris Canonici*, lib. IV, tit. V, n. 16 f.; Gury (1801-1866)-Ballerini (1805-1881), *Compendium Theologiae Moralis* (7. ed., 2 vols. Romae, 1887), 724.

nullity were to be interpreted to refer to the presumption of law in favor of validity when there is no evidence of an express condition or mutual pact, or that the word *pact* was to be interpreted to mean a unilateral intention which is expressed in the marriage contract itself.[35] At any rate, the mere fact that the Holy See followed a policy of requiring evidence of an express condition or mutual pact does not justify the conclusion that a declaration of nullity was considered an impossibility without evidence of an express condition or mutual pact.

D. The Practice of the Sacred Roman Rota

In a few of the early decisions of the Sacred Roman Rota in cases which involved the exclusion of the boon of sacramental stability the tribunal insisted upon evidence of an express condition or mutual pact.[36] According to some authors these decisions indicate that the Sacred Roman Rota at first followed the jurisprudence of the Sacred Congregation of the Council (up until about 1912) in its interpretation of the expression *deducta in pactum*.[37] Doheny, however, maintains that these decisions do not indicate a change in the jurisprudence of the Sacred Roman Rota, but that these few decisions simply were not in accord with the Rota's usual interpretation of the expression *deducta in pactum*.[38]

As to the policy of the Sacred Roman Rota in regard to cases which involve the exclusion of the boon of offspring in particular, a review of the actual decisions of the Rota in Chapter V of this study will demonstrate sufficiently that a declaration of nullity is pos-

[35] Cf. Cappello, *De Sacramentis,* III, n. 599, 2; Chelodi, *Ius Matrimoniale,* n. 116.

[36] S.R.R., *Nullitatis Matrimonii,* 24 iul. 1909, coram R.P.D. Iosepho Mori, dec. XII, n. 6: ". . . non quaecumque intentio etiam exterius manifestata ad foedandum vel solvendum matrimonium dici debet sufficiens ad illud irritandum, sed tantum ea quae in pactum vel conditionem in celebratione matrimonii fuit deducta."—*Decisiones,* I (1909), 106 ff. Cf. also 17 mart. 1910, coram R.P.D. Iosepho Mori, dec. XII, n. 9—*Decisiones,* II (1910), 121.

[37] Cappelo, *De Sacramentis,* III, n. 599, note (18); Chelodi, *Ius Matrimoniale,* n. 116, 2.

[38] *Canonical Procedure in Matrimonial Cases,* I, 617, note 96.

sible even though there is no evidence of an express condition or mutual pact in each individual case. As indicated in one decision in 1912, the requirements in regard to an express condition or mutual pact merely emphasize the presumption in favor of the validity of the marriage when such means of proof are lacking.[39] More will be said about the probative value of pacts and express conditions in the following chapter when the question of presumptions enters into the discussion.

ARTICLE 3. THE RESTRICTION OF THE RIGHT TO IMPUGN THE VALIDITY OF A MARRIAGE

A thorough discussion of the right to impugn the validity of marriage would constitute a thesis in itself. By way of general comment on the subject, it may suffice to cite a paragraph from the private letter of the Apostolic Delegate to the United States, which was referred to in the first article of this chapter:

> As is well known, the Holy See has been constrained to recall to mind, not without good results, first through the Commission for the Interpretation of the Code, and again in the Instruction of August 15, 1936, the inability of consorts to impugn a marriage whose nullity was caused by their own culpability or vitiated consent. To permit such persons to prove their guilt, and so be liberated from a burdensome bond, would be to reward the guilty party. Such procedure, by encouraging violations of the law, would be tantamount to its abrogation.[40]

It remains to discuss the documents here referred to, and others of later date, in so far as they concern the question of intentions and conditions which run counter to the very essence of marriage.

[39] S.R.R., *Nullitatis Matrimonii,* 17 ian, 1912, coram Rmo P.D. Michaele Lega, Decano, dec. V, n. 26: "Quae tamen praxis [i.e. of requiring evidence of an express condition or pact], cum nitatur sola praesumptione, non obstat quominus haberi possit matrimonium nullum ex intentione substantiae matrimonii contraria, etiam in pactum non deducta, quando concludentissime demonstretur."—*Decisiones,* IV (1912), 50. Cf. also 7 febr. 1914, coram R.P.D. Guilelmo Sebastianelli, dec. V, n. 3—*Decisiones,* VI (1914), 58.

[40] *Apost. Delegate's Letter,* 1938—*Canon Law Digest,* II, 532.

A. The Right to Impugn the Validity of a Marriage

(1) Prior to the Year 1929 (March 12)

According to the Code of Canon Law, there is no indication that those who are the cause of the nullity of their marriage because of an intention or condition contrary to the essence of marriage are to be prohibited from impugning the validity of the marriage. Canon 1971, § 1, 1 states merely that those who have been the cause of the *impediment* involved in an invalid marriage lose their right to impugn the validity of the marriage.[41] Since the word "impediment" is applied properly only to whatever hindrance is mentioned in canons 1067 to 1080 (inclusively) of the Code of Canon Law, the logical conclusion was that those who caused the nullity of their marriage on the score of defective consent or of the lack of the proper cononical form [42] still retained the right to impugn the validity of the marriage. Hence it was not uncommon to find cases in the decisions of the Sacred Roman Rota, in which the contracting parties had agreed to an express condition contrary to the substance of marriage, and yet were not prevented from impugning the validity of the marriage.[43]

(2) The Response of March 12, 1929

On March 12, 1929, the Commission for the Interpretation of the Code declared, in effect, that canon 971, § 1, 1 is to be interpreted in the sense that the right to impugn the validity of a marriage is lost likewise by those who are the cause of the nullity due

[41] "Habiles ad accusandum sunt: 1° Coniuges, in omnibus causis separationis et nullitatis, nisi ipsi fuerint impedimenti causa; . . ."

[42] Canons 1081 to 1103 inclusively.

[43] Cf., for example, S.R.R., *Nullitatis Matrimonii,* 31 mart. 1922, coram Rmo P.D. Ioanne Prior, Decano, dec. X—*Decisiones,* XIV (1922), 83 ff. 10 iun. 1922, coram Rmo P.D. Ioanne Prior, Decano, dec. XVIII—*Decisiones,* XIV (1922), 179 ff.; 5 iul. 1923; coram R.P.D. Francisco Parrillo, dec. XVI—*Decisiones,* XV (1923), 142 ff.; and the final decision of the same case, 26 iun. 1925, coram R.P.D. Andrea Jullien, dec. XXXIII—*Decisiones,* XVII (1925), 262 ff.; 23 nov. 1923, coram R.P.D. Raphaele Chimenti, dec. XXXII—*Decisiones,* XV (1923), 273 ff.; 30 mart. 1926, coram R.P.D. Andrea Jullien, dec. XIII—*Decisiones,* XVIII (1926), 103 ff.; 11 febr. 1929, coram R.P.D. Francisco Guglielmi, dec. XI—*Decisiones,* XXI (1929), 91 ff.

to defective consent or lack of the proper canonical form.[44] This response was clarified in 1933 (July 17) by another, which specified that the parties lose the right to impugn the validity of their marriage if they are the *culpable* cause either of the impediment or of the nullity of the marriage.[45]

Since the response of March 12, 1929, clearly amounts to a restriction of the right to impugn the validity of the marriage, which otherwise is the prerogative of all married persons in regard to their own marriage, it follows that this new interpretation of canon 1971, § 1, 1 must be interpreted strictly.[46] This means that the interpretation "would be favorable to the party accused."[47] Another reason why the strict interpretation must be applied is furnished by the fact that this restriction of the right to impugn the validity of marriage has the nature of a penalty.[48] Finally, ignorance of the comprehensive import of canon 1971, § 1, 1°, as extended by the response of March 12, 1929, or of the penalty imposed in the case of a violation of the canon, does not afford protection against the loss of the right to impugn the validity of the marriage.[49]

[44] In answer to the question: "Utrum vox *impedimenti canonis* 1971, § 1, n. 1 intelligenda sit tantum de impedimentis proprie dictis (cann. 1067-1080), an etiam de impedimentis improprie dictis matrimonium dirimentibus (cann. 1081-1103)," the Code Commission answered: '*Negative ad primam partem, affirmative ad secundam*."—*AAS*, XXI (1929), 171.

[45] "II. An, ad normam eiusdem canonis 1971, § 1, n. 1, habilis sit ad accusandum matrimonium etiam coniux, qui fuerit causa culpabilis sive impedimenti sive nullitatis matrimonii." "Resp. ad II, *negative*."—*AAS*, XXV (1933), 345, ad. II.

[46] "Leges quáe poenam statuunt, aut liberum iurium exercitium coartant, aut exceptionem a lege continent, strictae subsunt interpretationi."—Canon 19.

[47] Francis F. Reh, "Guilt of the Plaintiff in a Marriage Case," *The Jurist* (Washington, D. C., 1941-), III (1943), 405.

[48] Cf. Gasparri, *De Matrimonio*, II, n. 1260; Cappello, *De Sacramentis*, III, n. 878, 5; Doheny, *Canonical Evidence in Matrimonial Cases*, I, 88; Reh, *loc. cit.;* S.R.R., *Nullitatis Matrimonii*, 11 aug. 1928, coram R.P.D. Arcturo Wynen, dec. XLVI, n. 5—*Decisiones*, XX (1928), 405. Inasmuch as a penalty is imposed, the law is to be interpreted according to canon 19: "Leges quae poenam statuunt . . ."

[49] Inasmuch as there is question of an inhabilitating law, canon 16 applies; if the restriction is acknowledged as a penalty, surely it is a vindictive penalty, so that canon 2229, § 3 applies as well.

(3) Later Directives from the Holy See

The application of the foregoing norms to the case of vitiated consent (intentions and conditions which are contrary to the essence of marriage) may be explained best in the light of a recent response of the Commission for the Interpretation of the Code. Although the Instruction of the Sacred Congregation of the Sacraments of August 15, 1936, repeated the same norm as that stated above,[50] it was still rather difficult to establish just what was intended by the expression *causa culpabilis*. In a response dated July 27, 1942, the Code Commission clarified the situation to some extent by stating that the married parties were to be considered as deprived of the right to impugn the validity of their marriage only if they were *both* the *direct and the malicious* cause of the nullity: *"qui . . . causa fuit et directa et dolosa."* [51]

The meaning of the word *malicious* (*dolosa*) is gleaned from canon 2200, § 1: *"Dolus . . . est deliberata voluntas violandi legem,* . . ." A person who expressed a positive intention or condition contrary to the very essence of marriage, and thus caused the nullity of the marriage, does not lose his or her right to impugn the validity of that marriage unless that person knew that it was gravely wrong to place such an intention or condition, and yet did so with a free act of the will.[52] As to the meaning of the expression "malicious *and direct* cause," it seems logical to apply the Thomistic distinction between a direct voluntary and an indirect voluntary act

[50] S.C. de Sacr., *Instructio servanda a tribunalibus dioecesanis in pertractandis causis de nullitate matrimoniorum*, 15 aug. 1936, article 37, § 1: "Coniux inhabilis est ad accusandum matrimonium, si fuit ipse causa culpabilis sive impedimenti sive nullitatis matrimonii."—*AAS*, XXVIII (1936), 321 (cited hereafter as *Instr.*, S.C. de Sacr., 1936).

[51] "D. Utrum, secundum canonem 1971, § 1, 1° et responsum diei iulii 1933 ad II, inhabilis ad accusandum matrimonium habendus sit tantum coniux, qui sive impedimenti sive nullitatis matrimonii causa fuit et directa et dolosa, an etiam coniux qui impedmenti vel nullitatis matrimonii exstitit vel indirecta vel doli expers." "R. *Affirmative ad primam partem; negative ad secundam.*" —*AAS*, XXXIV (1942), 241.

[52] Cf. Doheny, *op. cit.*, I, 88; Reh, *ibid.*, p. 410.

of the will.[53] A person would be the direct and malicious cause of the nullity of the marriage, therefore, if he or she knew the grave and evil effect of an intention or condition which is contrary to the very essence of marriage, and yet harbored that intention or condition with a positive act of the will. On the other hand, the person would be the malicious but indirect cause of the nullity of the marriage, if he or she knew the grave and evil effect of consenting to a marriage contract when the *other contracting party* harbored an intention or condition contrary to the essence of marriage, and, although not wishing to co-operate in an invalid marriage, nevertheless entered the marriage contract.[54] If both parties agree to such an intention or condition, i. e., reduce the intention or condition to a mutual pact, it appears that, by way of a general rule, each of the parties is a direct and malicious cause of the nullity, and both in consequence would lose the right to impugn the validity of the marriage.

Although the Code of Canon Law states in canon 2200, § 2 that, in the external forum, the violation of a law is presumed to have been malicious until the contrary is proved, there is at least a slight possibility that the party involved may have been ignorant of the grave evil of harboring a positive intention or condition which is contrary to the essence of marriage.[55] At any rate, it will be up to the parties who wish to impugn the validity of their marriage to convince the members of the tribunal that they are not the malicious cause of the nullity, or at least not the direct cause. It is not to be overlooked, however, that in a case of doubt, either of the law or of a fact, the parties may conceivably retain their right to impugn the validity of the marriage.[56]

[53] "Voluntarium directe quidem id in quod voluntas fertur; indirecte autem illud quod voluntas potuit prohibere, sed non prohibet."—St. Thomas, *Summa Theologica*, I-II, q. 77, art. 7, in corp.

[54] Cf. Reh, *ibid.*, pp. 411 f.

[55] Reh remarks that the presence of such ignorance scarcely is possible if the party has a suspicion that the marriage will be invalid: "Ordinarily one would consider it gravely wrong to enter an invalid marriage, and likewise gravely wrong to go ahead with an uncertain conscience ("conscientia practice dubia"). *Ibid.*, p. 415.

[56] "Leges, etiam irritantes et inhabilitantes, in dubio iuris non urgent;

One decision of the Sacred Roman Rota, in particular, seems to confirm the view that, in the event of a mutual pact between the contracting parties, each of the parties usually is to be considered as the malicious and direct cause of the nullity of the marriage:

> Si substantia matrimonii exclusa fuerit positivo voluntatis actu absque pactione, inhabilis ad matrimonium accusandum est coniux, qui substantiam matrimonii exclusit, ideo etiam uterque coniux, si exclusit uterque. Ubi vero substantia matrimonii exclusa fuit aliqua pactione inter contrahentes, inhabilis fit ad matrimonium accusandum non modo coniux qui pactionem proposuit, sed etiam coniux qui eam acceptavit; uterque est enim impedimenti causa.[57]

It is possible, however, that even when there is evidence of a mutual pact in regard to an intention or condition which is contrary to the essence of marriage, one of the parties may not be the malicious cause of the nullity of the marriage. A case decided by the Sacred Roman Rota in 1929 may be cited as an example of such a situation.[58] Although the girl involved in this case married with a *sine qua non* agreement that the conception of children was to be prevented at least temporarily, she apparently was ignorant of the grave and evil consequences of consenting to such a marriage.[59]

Likewise it is possible that one of the parties who agreed to a pact which is contrary to the essence of marriage may be the malicious but not the direct cause of the nullity of the marriage. If one of the parties, although knowing of the grave and evil consequences of such a pact, nevertheless did not intend to co-operate with

in dubio autem facti potest Ordinarius in eis dispensare, dummodo agatur de legibus in quibus Romanus Pontifex dispensare solet."—Canon 15.

[57] S.R.R., *Nullitatis Matrimonii,* 23 iun, 1931, coram R.P.D. Francisco Morano, dec. XXX, n. 7—*Decisiones,* XXIII (1931), 261. Although this decision was issued in 1931, before the responses of the Code Commission in 1933 (July 17) and 1942 (July 27), it indicates the mind of the Sacred Roman Rota in regard to the loss of the right to impugn the validity of a marriage.

[58] S.R.R., *Nullitatis Matrimonii,* 6 aug. 1929, coram R.P.D. Francisco Morano, dec. XLV—*Decisiones,* XXI (1929), 380 ff.

[59] That she was ignorant of the invalidity of such a marriage may be deduced from the fact that she confessed ignorance of the evil of contraception, and when informed of this evil, after marriage, made every effort to stop the abuse of the marriage right. *Ibid.,* 383 (n. 6).

the other party in carrying out the evil stipulation, but hoped to persuade the other party to relinquish all positive opposition to the procreation of children after marriage had been contracted, such a person may be considered merely as an indirect cause of the nullity of the marriage.[60] A decision of the Sacred Roman Rota of the year 1922 offers a possible example of such a situation.[61] The young girl, although opposed to the suggested evil condition expressed by her fiancé, nevertheless consented to marry him, . . . "spe freta ut Renatus [the young man] in melius animum mutaret."[62] The view that such a person would not lose the right to impugn the validity of the marriage, however, is advanced with all due caution and reserve; particularly in view of the fact that the letter of the Apostolic Delegate, quoted previously (p. 96), cannot be cited in confirmation of such a view.[63]

B. The Right to Denounce the Invalidity of a Marriage

(1) The Contracting Parties Are Not Excluded

Even though the parties of a marriage contract have lost the right to protect their own private good by impugning the validity of their marriage, they should, in the interests of the public good, denounce the marriage as invalid to those who have charge of the public good, i. e., to the diocesan promoter of justice. Roberti expresses this thought as follows:

[60] Such is the opinion of Doheny, *op. cit.*, I, 90 and Reh, *ibid.*, p. 413, (A) (c), and p. 415, (A), (c).

[61] S.R.R., *Nullitatis Matrimonii,* 4 aug. 1922, coram R.P.D. Raphaele Chimenti, dec. XXVII, n. 7—*Decisiones,* XIV (1922), 256 f.

[62] *Loc. cit.*

[63] The letter contains the following paragraph: "The innocent consort can impugn the marriage only when this consort is truly innocent, that is, when he or she has not in the least participated—not even only externally or by subterfuge—in the evil intent of the other party; and when, moreover, he or she was ignorant of it before the marriage."—Bouscaren, *Canon Law Digest,* II, 533. It must be remembered, however, that this letter was sent to the bishops of the United States in 1938, four years before the Commission for the Interpretation of the Code declared, in the response of July 27, 1942, that only those who are the direct and malicious cause of the nullity, lose the right to attack the validity of the marriage.

> Coniuges . . . privantur iure accusandi in poenam suae fraudis . . . Attamen omnes tenentur co-operari ut publicae personae recte publicum munus in bonum communitatis exerceant. Quare omnes generatim iubentur huiusmodi facta denunciare. Nec coniuges excluduntur, quia denunciatio dirigatur ad publicum, non ad privatum tuendum bonum.[64]

The right of the married parties to denounce their marriage to the promoter of justice was affirmed again in a response of February 17, 1930.[65]

Non-Catholics, however, even though they are not the direct and malicious cause of the nullity of the marriage, do not enjoy the right to impugn the validity of the marriage.[66] If there are special reasons why they should be admitted as plaintiffs, recourse must be had in each case to the Supreme Sacred Congregation of the Holy Office.[67] This applies also to diocesan tribunals.[68] If a non-Catholic has denounced a marriage to the diocesan promoter of justice, the promoter of justice may impugn the marriage if, in the judgment of the ordinary, the public good is at stake.[69]

(2) The Duty of the Promoter of Justice

If the parties who have lost their right to impugn the validity of their marriage in consequence of an intention or condition contrary to the essence of marriage nevertheless denounce the marriage to the promoter of justice, his first duty is to warn the parties to have

[64] *Apollinaris*, III (1930), 250. The right to impugn the validity of a marriage implies the performance of a judicial act (*accusatio*), whereas to denounce the invalidity of a marriage (*denunciatio*) is not a judicial act. Cf. Roberti, *loc. cit.;* also Vermeersch, *Periodica*, XIX (1930), 269.

[65] "An coniuges qui, iuxta canonem 1971, § 1, 1° et interpretationem diei 12 martii 1929, habiles non sunt ad accusandum matrimonium, vi eiusdem canonis § 2 ius saltem habeant nullitatem matrimonii Ordinario vel promotori iustitiae denuntiandi. R. *Affirmative*."—*AAS*, XXII (1930), 196. Cf. also canon 1971, § 2.

[66] Cf. *Instr.*, S.C. de Sacr., 1936, article 35, § 3—*AAS*, XXVIII (1936), 321.

[67] Cf. the response of the Sacred Congregation of the Holy Office of Jan. 27, 1928, ad. I.—*AAS*, XX (1928), 75.

[68] Cf. the response of the Sacred Congregation of the Holy Office of Jan. 27, 1939, ad. I.—*AAS*, XXXI (1939), 131.

[69] *Ibid.*, ad II.

regard for their consciences and if possible remove the cause of the impediment, for example, by duly making a new act of consent.[70] He has the right and official duty to impugn the validity of the marriage if four factors concur:

(1) If the alleged nullity of the marriage has become public (canon 2197, 1°).

(2) If scandal really exists.[71]

(3) If the person who denounced the marriage has, in the opinion of the Ordinary, given true signs of repentance.

(4) If the alleged ground of nullity is supported by evidence so certain and valid, either in fact or in law, that the nullity of the marriage is altogether probable.[72]

If the four facts as mentioned do not concur in cases which involve the exclusion of the essence of marriage,[73] the common good demands rather that the promoter of justice abstain from impugning

[70] *Instr.* S.C. de Sacr., 1936, article 38, § 1: "Ubi agitur de denuntiatione nullitatis a coniuge vel coniugibus facta, quia alteruter vel ambo (a) positivo voluntatis actu excluserunt matrimonium ipsum, aut omne ius ad coniugalem actum, aut essentialem aliquam matrimonii proprietatem; vel (b) condicionem apposuere contra matrimonii substantiam, promotor iustitiae matrimonium ne accuset, sed coniugem vel coniuges pro viribus moneat ut suae conscientiae consulant, et, si fieri possit, causam impedimenti auferant, e.g. per novum consensum rite praestandum."—*AAS,* XXVIII (1936), 322.

[71] "If the party has secured a legal divorce or has attempted marriage civilly, there can hardly be any doubt about the seriousness and existence of scandal."—Doheny, *Canonical Procedure in Matrimonial Cases,* I, 94.

[72] *Instr.*, S.C. de Sacr., 1936, article 38, § 2: "Si tamen matrimonii adserta nullitas publica evaserit et scandalum revera adsit, denuncians autem resipiscentiae signa, Ordinari iudicio, revera dederit; itemque denunciata nullitatis causa argumentis nitatur, sive in facto sive in iure, ita certis et validis, ut probabilis omnino sit ipsius matrimonii nullitas, tunc promotori iustitiae ius et officium est denunciatum matrimonium rite accusandi."—*AAS,* XXVIII (1936), 322. If these four factors do not concur, and the promoter of justice nevertheless impugns the validity of the marriage, he acts validly but illicitly. Cf. Doheny, *op. cit.*, I, 93.

[73] It is to be noted that article 38 of the Instruction of 1936 applies only to those cases which involve intentions and conditions whereby marriage itself or something which pertains to the essence of marriage is excluded. Article 39 of the same instruction applies to other cases in which the parties have lost their right to attack the validity of the marriage. Cf. Doheny, *op. cit.*, I, 95 f.

the validity of the marriage.[74] This observation leads to the conclusion that the cases in which the promoter of justice may impugn the validity of the marriage which has been denounced to him as invalid because of intentions or conditions contrary to the essence of marriage are rare indeed:

> . . . the case in which the Promoter of Justice can impugn the marriage, when the consorts are disqualified, is very rare indeed, not to say exceptional. The reason is that the Promoter of Justice, under the authority and guidance of the Bishop, can act solely to foster the public. And the public good demands precisely that the culpable parties should not acquire freedom, as if in reward for their fault, but rather, *digna factis recipiant,* that they may receive what is due their evil doing, and in this way serve as a warning to the rest of the faithful not to defile the celebration of Christian marriage with the exclusion of the *bona matrimonii* or with simulations of consent.[75]

[74] Cappello warns that the promoter of justice should not be too quick to impugn the validity of marriages which have been denounced to him: "Porro, cum accusatio sit valde odiosa ideoque quantum fieri potest excludenda, promotor iustitiae, generatim loquendo, difficilem se praebeat in ea admittenda: quo magis severior erit, eo magis laudandus."—*De Sacramentis,* III, n. 881, 3 in fine.

[75] *Apost. Delegate's letter,* 1938—Bouscaren, *Canon Law Digest,* II, 522 f.

CHAPTER IV

PROOF OF THE EXCLUSION OF THE BOON OF OFFSPRING

The present chapter is not intended as a treatise on canonical procedure in matrimonial cases. The following articles will be devoted to a discussion of the principal elements of proof which must be considered when investigating the possible nullity of a marriage on the score of the exclusion of the boon of offspring. Since the invalidating exclusion of the boon of offspring points to a simulated matrimonial consent, the principal elements of proof to be considered are those which must be considered in establishing the nullity of marriages in all cases of simulated consent. These elements may be summed up as follows: the confessions of the parties, the presence of a manifest cause or reason which satisfactorily accounts for simulated consent, and circumstantial evidence which is so clear and convincing, that the ecclesiastical judge can arrive at moral certitude regarding the presence of a simulated matrimonial consent.[1] These three elements of proof are mentioned repeatedly by the Sacred Roman Rota in the decisions which involve the exclusion of the boon of offspring.[2]

[1] "Porro probatio simulationis in foro externo facilis non est. Certe non sufficit affirmatio etiam iurata simulantis, . . . Item nec sufficit assertio iurata utriusque partis, quia, cum simulatio alteram partem lateat, rursus unica simulantis affirmatione simulatio probaretur. Necesse igitur est in primis probare causam simulationis, curnam scilicet Titius ficte contraxerit, ac deinde ipsa simulatio evinci debet coniecturis seu circumstantiis antecedentibus, concomitantibus, subsequentibus, quae adeo praecisae ac urgentes sint, ut certum moraliter reddant iudicem de hoc ficto consensu."—Gasparri, *De Matrimonio,* II, n. 818. Cf. also Wernz-Vidal, *Ius Matrimoniale,* n. 460; Chelodi, *Ius Matrimoniale,* n. 115; Payen, *De Matrimonio,* II, n. 1672; Cappello, *De Sacramentis,* III, n. 603, 2; Ayrinhac-Lydon, *Marriage Legislation,* n. 205.

[2] S.R.R., *Nullitatis Matrimonii,* 23 iun. 1931, coram R.P.D. Francisco Morano, dec. XXX, n. 5: "In iudicio argumenta exclusionis substantiae matrimonii sunt declarationes iudiciales partis cui exclusio adscribitur, declarationes ab ipsa ad rem factae ante matrimonii celebrationem vel in ipsa celebratione, apta causa excludendi matrimonii substantiam, demum ceterae circumstantiae quae exclusionem comprobent, sive sint antecedentes sive concomitantes sive subsequentes celebrationem matrimonii."—*Decisiones,* XXIII (1931), 260.

The importance of circumstantial evidence as an element of proof will be emphasized and illustrated in a review of the actual decisions of the Sacred Roman Rota in the final chapter of this study. The presumptions which must guide the ecclesiastical judge in estimating the probative value of circumstantial evidence in each individual case, however, will be discussed in the present chapter. The order of the discussions in the present chapter, therefore, will be as follows: the confessions of the parties (Article 1); establishing proof of a sufficient motive for simulating consent (Article 2); the importance of presumptions (Article 3).

ARTICLE 1—THE CONFESSIONS OF THE PARTIES

Obviously, it would be impossible to establish whether or not the involved party actually intended to exclude the marriage right itself with reference to the boon of offspring, unless the intention or condition had been manifested to the other party of the marriage contract or to reliable witnesses.[3] Even the judicial confession under oath of both parties, however, does not, of itself, constitute proof against the validity of the marriage.[4] Hence the need of substantiating what the parties themselves asserted by obtaining the testimony of reliable witnesses, by establishing proof of a reason or motive which is sufficient to account for a simulated consent in the individual

Cf. also 6 aug. 1929, coram R.P.D. Francisco Morano, dec. XLV, n. 3—*Decisiones,* XXI (1929), 381; 10 aug. 1929, coram R.P.D. Ubaldo Mannucci, dec. LI, n. 3—*Decisiones,* XXI (1929), 427; 16 iul. 1931, coram R.P.D. Henrico Quattrocolo, dec. XXXIV, n. 3—*Decisiones,* XXIII (1931), 287.

[3] S.R.R., *Nullitatis Matrimonii,* 7 iul. 1926, coram R.P.D. Ubaldo Mannucci, dec. XXVIII, n. 2: ". . . ad probationem in foro externo requiritur ut manifestetur, si non comparti, saltem idoneis testibus, per quos demonstrari possit *expresse* aliquando apposita."—*Decisiones,* XVIII (1926), 222.

[4] *Instr.* S.C. de Sacr., 1936, art. 117: "Depositio indicialis coniugum non est apta ad probationem contra valorem matrimonii constituendam."—*AAS,* XXVIII (1936), 337. Compare also article 93 of the same instruction (*Ibid.,* 333) with canon 1747, 3°. Cf. also S.R.R. *Nullitatis Matrimonii,* 4 maii 1927, coram R.P.D. Iulio Grazioli, dec. XX, n. 9: ". . . coniuges, dum pro matrimonii nullitate decertant, etsi concordes nil ipsi soli probant."—*Decisiones,* XIX (1927), 166; 16 iul. 1931, coram R.P.D. Francisco Guglielmi, dec. XXXV, n. 4—*Decisiones,* XXIII (1931), 293 f.; Gasparri, *De Matrimonio,* II, n. 818; Ayrinhac-Lydon, *Marriage Legislation,* n. 205.

case, and by formulating conjectures on the strength of the circumstantial evidence as furnished in each individual case.

Evidence that one or both of the parties intended to exclude the boon of offspring at the time of the exchange of matrimonial consent may be furnished not only by their own assertions and admissions in the course of the judicial proceedings, but also by written or oral statements which they have made outside of judicial proceedings. If such oral or written statements have been made before or after the marriage was contracted, but at a time and under circumstances which were not open to the suspicion of ulterior sinister motives (*"tempore non suspecto"*),[5] that fact can become an aid in the establishing of proof of the invalidity of the marriage. When evidence that such statements have been made is referred to the ecclesiastical tribunal, it is left to the judge to determine the value of such evidence in the given circumstances of each individual case.[6] In some cases such evidence is furnished in the form of letters or signed statements or promises.[7] More frequently, however, the extra-judicial statements of the parties regarding their opposition to the boon of offspring, take the form of oral statements or assertions before friends, relatives or acquaintances. These come to light when the witnesses are questioned in the course of judicial proceedings.

Other things being equal, however, the extra-judicial assertions or statements of the parties have not the probative force of their judicial confessions. The reason is that a judicial confession, made before the tribunal under oath logically is accepted as a more truth-

[5] S.C. de Sacr., *Regulae Servandae in Processibus super Matrimonio Rato et non Consummato,* 7 maii 1923, n. 70: "Causam enim valde iuvant partium confessiones extraiudiciales tempore non suspecto prolatae; eo nempe tempore, quando de hac quaestione introducenda ne cogitabatur quidem, nec aliae suberant rationes veritatem occultandi aut falsum proferendi."—*AAS,* XV (1923), 406. Cf. also S.R.R., *Nullitatis Matrimonii,* 27 iul. 1931, coram R.P.D. Ubaldo Mannucci, dec. XXXVIII, n. 4—*Decisiones,* XXIII (1931), 327.

[6] *Instr.* S.C. de Sacr., 1936, art. 116: "Confessio extraiudicialis coniugis, quae adversus matrimonii valorem pugnet, prolata ante matrimonium contractum, vel post matrimonium, sed tempore non suspecto, probationis adminiculum constituit a iudice recte aestimandum."—*AAS,* XXVIII (1936), 337.

[7] As examples of the value of such written evidence in actual cases, cf. *infra,* Chapter V, cases nn. 5, 6, 7 and 11.

ful and reliable manifestation of the mind of the party concerned. Hence in case of a divergency or contradiction between an extrajudicial assertion or statement, as brought before the tribunal, and a judicial confession, the latter is to be regarded as having the prevailing force, i.e. other things being equal.[8]

To say that the judicial confession of one or both of the parties does not of itself constitute proof against the validity of a marriage does not detract from its importance as corroborative evidence in many cases. It must be remembered that especially in cases which involve matrimonial consent, the ecclesiastical tribunal must rely principally upon evidence which indicates the actual mind of the parties at the time of the exchange of matrimonial consent. Whereas in marriage cases which involve other impediments, evidence of the validity or nullity of the marriage is furnished, to a greater degree, by external facts.

The value of the judicial confession of the parties in each individual case, will depend upon several factors. Doheny states those factors as follows:

> Its value varies in relation to the trustworthiness of the consorts, the nature of the case under consideration, the time when the statements were made, the very nature of the judicial deposition itself and its agreement with the testimony of witnesses, documents, and the like. The Decisions of the S. Roman Rota indicate the practical norms by which the iudicial depositions may be evaluated.[9]

[8] Cf. S.R.R., *Nullitatis Matrimonii*, 13 ian. 1925, coram R.P.D. Ubaldo Mannucci, dec. V, n. 7: "... praeterquam enim certum est depositiones iudiciales extraiudicialibus actis praevalere debere, . . ."—*Decisiones*, XVII (1925), 35. Cf. also Doheny, *Canonical Procedure in Matrimonial Cases*, I, 213.

[9] *Op. cit.*, I, 214 f. As examples in which the circumstances of the case indicated that the assertions of one or of both of the parties were to be considered as doubtfully true or rejected entirely, cf. S.R.R., *Nullitatis Matrimonii*, 9 iul. 1927, coram Rmo P.D. Maximo Massimi, Decano, dec. XXXV, n. 8—*Decisiones*, XIX (1927), 302 f.; 17 iul. 1929, coram Rmo P.D. Maximo Massimi, Decano, dec. XXXIV, n. 8 f.—*Decisiones*, XXI (1929), 293 f.; 27 iul. 1931, coram R.P.D. Ubaldo Mannucci, dec. XXXVIII, n. 6—*Decisiones*, XXIII (1931), 328 f.; 12 aug. 1931, coram Exc. mo Maximo Massimi, Decano, dec. L, n. 7—*Decisiones*, XXIII (1931), 426.

In matrimonial cases, the parties frequently may discover that it is to their advantage to agree on some points, even at the sacrifice of truth. If there is a basis for suspecting collusion between the parties, the question of establishing the invalidity of the marriage is rendered even more difficult.[10] At other times, the one who is accused of simulation may deny the accusation. In order to arrive at moral certitude regarding the nullity of the marriage in such a case, the ecclesiastical judge must seek evidence of a more weighty reason or motive to account for simulation in the individual case. Furthermore, the case must present more convincing circumstantial evidence.[11] Finally, it would be impossible to pass judgment on the possible invalidating force of an intention or of a condition unless the words which were used when the party expressed the intention or the condition have been brought to light in the course of the judicial proceedings, either by the parties themselves, or through reliable witnesses, or reliable documentary evidence.[12]

It may be well to add a few words in regard to the probative value of the testimony of witnesses. The depositions of at least two witnesses are required in order to constitute full proof of the invalidity of a marriage. There are illustrations among the decisions of the Sacred Roman Rota which reveal that if two absolutely trustworthy witnesses, testifying under oath, speak from a personal knowledge and with strict agreement in their testimony concerning the fact that one of the contracting parties, in effect, excluded the marriage right itself with reference to the boon of offspring, the marriage may be

[10] As an example of collusion between the parties, cf. S.R.R. *Nullitatis Matrimonii,* 12 aug. 1926, coram R.P.D. Francisco Solieri, dec. XLII, n. 8—*Decisiones,* XVIII (1926), 334 f.

[11] S.R.R., *Nullitatis Matrimonii,* 28 febr. 1923, coram R.P.D. Friderico Cattani Amadori, dec. IV, n. 2: "Quid vero si is, qui de simulatione accusatur, se simulasse neget? Tunc simulationis probatio difficilior evadit; oporteret enim quod et causa gravior esset et circumstantiae luculentiores, quae consensus fictionem probarent. Necessaria est enim moralis certitudo, quae independenter a rei confessione, in animum iudicis potest induci."—*Decisiones,* XV (1923), 24.

[12] S.R.R. *Nullitatis Matrimonii,* 17 ian. 1912, coram Rm̃o P.D. Michaele Lega, Decano, dec. V, n. 16: "Conditio autem, ut doctores tenent, debet probari etiam secundum formam verborum quibus concepta fuit, ut de eius vi diiudicari valeat."—*Decisiones,* V (1912), 42.

declared invalid.[13] Thus a case decided in 1919 illustrates the decisive, probative value of the coherent, personal testimony under oath of two unimpeachable witnesses.[14] The proof may always be complemented, however, by presumptions and conjectures based on the circumstances of the case. In fact, if the ecclesiastical judge considers it necessary, he may demand additional proof in view of the serious nature of the case or because of indications which give rise to some doubt about the truth of an assertion.[15]

Of particular interest are those cases in which the main thing lacking for a declaration of nullity was the clear testimony of but one more reliable witness.[16] In other cases the depositions of the witnesses lacked probative value since their testimony was derived mostly from hearsay and not from their own personal knowledge.[17] In yet another group of cases, the value of the depositions of the witnesses was lessened because a tribunal of earlier instance had proposed questions to the witnesses in a suggestive manner.[18]

ARTICLE 2. ESTABLISHING PROOF OF A SUFFICIENT MOTIVE FOR SIMULATING CONSENT

A. Principles as Gleaned from the Jurisprudence of the Sacred Roman Rota

The party who claims, in effect, to have excluded the marriage right with reference to the boon of offspring must adduce a reason which, in the opinion of the ecclesiastical judge, is not only credible,

[13] Cf. canon 1791, § 2 and *Instr.* S.C. de Sacr., 1936, art. 136—*AAS*, XXVIII (1936), 341.

[14] S.R.R. *Nullitatis Matrimonii,* 14 dec. 1919, coram R.P.D. Aloisio Sincèro, dec. XVII, n. 3—*Decisiones,* XI (1919), 147 ff.

[15] Canon 1791, § 2.

[16] For example, cf. S.R.R. *Nullitatis Matrimonii,* 6 aug. 1929, coram R.P.D. Francisco Morano, dec. XLV, n. 10—*Decisiones,* XXI (1929), 384.

[17] Cf. S.R.R. *Nullitatis Matrimonii,* 15 dec. 1915, coram R̃mo P.D. Guilelmo Sebastianelli, Decano, dec. XLI, n. 11—*Decisiones,* VII (1915), 463; 23 iun. 1931, coram R.P.D. Francisco Morano, dec. XXX, n. 10—*Decisiones,* XXIII (1931), 263 f.

[18] Cf. S.R.R., *Querelae Nullitatis et Nullitatis Matrimonii,* 10 aug. 1929, coram R.P.D. Ubaldo Mannucci, dec. LI, n. 4—*Decisiones,* XXI (1929), 427 f.;

but also sufficient to account for the fact of the exclusion of the marriage right in the individual case. It is important to distinguish between the reason for the excluding of the marriage right, that is by the simulating of consent, and the reason for the giving of consent for the marriage. Reasons for the giving of consent for a particular marriage such as a desire to be free of paternal domination, or the ambition to enter into a better class of society are not inconsistent with the full acceptance of all the essential obligations of marriage.[19] The reason which must be sought is the motivating and final reason which led the party to form a positive intention not merely to avoid the dangers or inconveniences which are associated with the procreation of offspring, but to prevent the procreation of offspring as such. Thus in a case decided by the Sacred Roman Rota in 1927, the reasons advanced by the woman in explanation of her opposition to the procreation of offspring indicated not that she was opposed absolutely and irrevocably to having children, but rather that she was anxious to avoid the danger associated with childbirth in her temporary state of poor health.[20]

In order to be accepted as a sufficient explanation of why the party simulated his or her matrimonial consent the reason alleged

19 dec. 1930, coram R.P.D. Iulio Grazioli, dec. LXI, n. 8—*Decisiones,* XXII (1930), 672.

[19] S.R.R., *Nullitatis Matrimonii,* 18 iul. 1923, coram R.P.D. Francisco Parrillo, dec. XIX, n. 4: "Nec confundenda est causa simulationis cum causis sive motivis quae aliquem ad contrahendum induxerunt; haec enim optime stare possunt cum vero matrimonio, imo plerumque dant causam contractui, uti sunt libertatem ope coniugii consequi, statum in societate nuncupare, etc. . . . Causa simulationis, igitur, alio quaerenda est, quam in motivis, quae contrahentem impulerunt ad statum coniugalem deligendum; . . ."—*Decisiones,* XV (1923), 167. Cf. also 16 iul. 1931, coram R.P.D. Francisco Guglielmi, dec. XXXV, n. 4—*Decisiones,* XXIII (1931), 293 f.

[20] S.R.R., *Nullitatis Matrimonii,* 7 iun. 1927, coram R.P.D. Iosepho Florczak, dec. XXVI, n. 7: "Rationes deinde, quibus Margarita ducta fuit ad assertam conditionem apponendam, non exhibent causam motivam et finalem in ordine ad voluntatem prolem non suscipiendi, sed in ordine ad probabilia pericula infirmae suae valetudinis in prolis susceptione avertenda, idque non modo absoluto et in perpetuum, sed modo relativo et ad tempus, seu usquedum Margarita plenam valetudinem ex morbo pulmonum, quo laborabat, consecuta fuisset."—*Decisiones,* XIX (1927), 212. The Rota upheld the validity of the marriage. Cf. *ibid.,* 214 (n. 9).

by that party must be based on a certain element of doubt, of anxiety or of hesitancy, i.e. indicating that the party customarily placed the stipulation regarding the precluding of offspring as a means of assurance or protection against some unwanted or inauspicious event.[21] In other words, if the party who placed the stipulation regarding the preventing of conception appeared to be certain that the conception of offspring would not occur in married life, it is difficult to admit that he or she placed the stipulation as a *true condition.* In such cases, the meaning of the stipulation may well be, "I intend to contract marriage with *because* you are determined to prevent the conception of children," and not, "I intend to contract marriage with you *provided that* you prevent the conception of children."

In some cases, a sufficient explanation for the fact of simulated consent is apparent in the very character of the party who either placed the condition or who expressed the intention which was contrary to the boon of offspring. In a case decided by the Sacred Roman Rota in 1925, for example, the fact that the party who insisted upon an agreement contrary to the boon of offspring was noted for his queer and set ideas regarding procreation and motherhood explained sufficiently why he should have wished to exclude the marriage right itself with reference to the procreation of offspring.[22] In another case as decided in 1922, a sufficient reason for simulated consent with reference to the boon of offspring was furnished by the fact that the man was known as a person who was not only hostile to religion, but as a man without morals and without any sense of responsibility.[23]

[21] S.R.R., *Monacen. Frisingen, Nullitatis Matrimonii,* 25 febr. 1929, coram R.P.D. Ubaldo Mannucci, dec. XV, n. 6, II: "Iuxta enim principium a Rota pluries firmatum, non facile admittitur conditio, nisi constet de quonam *dubio* vel anxietate aut titubantia eam ponentis, qui nempe conditione se tueri solet ab eventu indesiderabili seu nefasto; . . ."—*Decisiones,* XXI (1929), 136 f.

[22] He held that since life itself is evil, it is a crime to propagate new life, and that motherhood connotes an animal act which is unworthy of an intellectual woman. Cf. S.R.R., *Nullitatis Matrimonii,* 13 febr. 1925, coram R.P.D. Francisco Solieri, dec. X, n. 4 ff.—*Decisiones,* XVII (1925), 76 ff. Cf. also 14 mart. 1930, coram R.P.D. Iulio Grazioli, dec. XIV, nn. 8-11—*Decisiones,* XXII (1930), 173 f. In both cases, the marriage was declared invalid (cf. *infra,* Chapter V, cases nn. 7 and 9).

[23] S.R.R., *Nullitatis Matrimonii,* 4 aug. 1922, coram R.P.D. Raphaele

The alleged reason for excluding the procreation of offspring must be a serious one, manifest, and proportionate to warrant the exclusion of the boon of offspring at least in the eyes of the party who expressed the intention or placed the condition.[24] A close examination of the alleged reason for excluding the boon of offspring is of particular importance in cases in which there is no convincing direct evidence of a true condition (*sine qua non*), or of a positive and specific intention to exclude the marriage right itself. For even though there is evidence that the parties expressed their opposition to the procreation of offspring by means of a mutual pact or agreement, it is difficult to conclude that the procreation of offspring was excluded entirely and absolutely unless the alleged reason, all considered, sufficiently explains such an attitude. The fact that one of the parties has a venereal disease, for example, is not of itself a sufficient reason to explain the absolute and perpetual exclusion of children. If, however, there is convincing evidence that the parties believed that the disease would never abate, an argument in favor of the invalidity of the marriage could arise.[25]

B. *Examples of an Insufficient Motive for Simulating Consent*

The question of determining whether or not the alleged reason for excluding the boon of offspring is sufficient to explain the exclusion of the marriage right itself is left to the judge in each individual case. It would be misleading to attempt to determine the reasons which may be considered as sufficient or insufficient in all cases. It may be helpful, however, to mention a few of the decisions of the Sacred Roman Rota in which the alleged reasons were considered to be sufficient to contribute to the proof of an invalid marriage.

Chimenti, dec. XXVII, n. 6—*Decisiones,* XIV (1922), 256. The marriage was declared invalid (cf. *infra,* Chapter V, case n. 6).

[24] Cf. S.R.R., *Querelae Nullitatis et Nullitatis Matrimonii,* 10 aug. 1929, coram R.P.D. Ubaldo Mannucci, dec. LI, n. 3—*Decisiones,* XXI (1929), 427; *Nullitatis Matrimonii,* 16 iul. 1931, coram R.P.D. Francisco Guglielmi, dec. XXXV, n. 4—*Decisiones,* XXIII (1931), 293 f.

[25] Such was the case in a 1926 decision. Cf. S.R.R., *Nullitatis Matrimonii,* 5 iun. 1926. coram R.P.D. Iosepho Florczak, dec. XXIV, n. 9 f.—*Decisiones,* XVIII (1926), 196 ff. The marriage was declared invalid, Cf. *Ibid.,* 199 (n. 11).

In one case, in which the woman claimed to have excluded the boon of offspring, the only feasible reason seemed to be her lack of love for the other party. This reason was not considered an adequate motive or reason for the simulation of the consent.[26] The reason alleged in another case was that the party who placed the stipulation contrary to the boon of offspring was afraid that the children would be born with hereditary diseases stemming from the girl's side of the family. He also added that the girl was too nervous to have children, and that there was a food shortage in the country. The Rota implied that the first reason might have been considered had it not been for the fact that the girl herself was in good health before the marriage. The other two reasons were excluded simply as insufficient.[27] In yet another case, the reason alleged by the man was that he did not wish to take the chance of having weak children brought into the world. The reason was considered as insufficient to account for the simulation of consent.[28]

C. *Examples of a Sufficient Motive for Simulating Consent*

In one case proof of a sufficient motive for excluding the marriage right with reference to the boon of offspring was furnished by the fact that the man wished to marry the girl because of her wealth. Since he feared that the birth of children might prevent him from leaving her when her money was spent, he was opposed to the procreation of offspring.[29] In other cases the reason for excluding the

[26] S.R.R., *Querelae Nullitatis et Nullitatis Matrimonii,* 10 aug. 1929, coram R.P.D. Ubaldo Mannucci, dec. LI, n. 5—*Decisiones,* XXI (1929), 428. The Rota upheld the validity of the marriage. Cf. *Ibid.,* 433 (n. 13). Cf., however, p. 169, footnote, n. 2).

[27] S.R.R., *Viennen Nullitatis Matrimonii,* 11 aug. 1930, coram R.P.D. Francisco Morano, dec. L, n. 9-11—*Decisiones,* XXII (1930), 566 f. The Rota upheld the validity of the marriage. Cf. *Ibid.,* 567 (n. 13).

[28] S.R.R., *Nullitatis Matrimonii,* 23 iun. 1931, coram R.P.D. Francisco Morano, dec. XXX, n. 14—*Decisiones,* XXIII (1931), 266. The reason alleged by the woman in the case likewise was rejected as insufficient, i.e., "quod ille unice ferebatur cupiditate sui." *Loc. cit.* The Rota upheld the validity of the marriage. Cf. *Ibid.,* 266 (n. 16).

[29] S.R.R., *Nullitatis Matrimonii,* 10 maii. 1916, coram Rmo P.D. Guilelmo

boon of offspring was based on the fact that one of the parties was of a lower social scale or of an inferior moral reputation. Hence it was considered a disgrace to the other family to rear children of such a union.[30] Likewise the fact that one of the parties has a complete aversion for the other party of the marriage may be sufficient, in certain cases, to explain the refusal to grant the marriage right with reference to the boon of offspring.[31] In yet another case, the mere fact that the woman who had proposed the agreement contrary to the boon of offspring did so out of a fear of suffering a deformity by having children, and of losing her physical charm, was considered as sufficient to account for the exclusion of the boon of offspring as a *sine qua non* condition for the giving of matrimonial consent.[32] These various examples have been chosen designedly with a view to demonstrating how much the question of the sufficiency of the motive for simulating consent depends upon the particular facts and circumstances of each individual case.

Article 3. The Importance of Presumptions

Presumptions are of great value to the ecclesiastical judge in matrimonial cases. Sometimes adequate natural proof is at hand to dispel the doubt concerning the validity of the marriage in question. At other times, especially in cases which involve defective or simulated consent, the most exacting investigation of the case fails to furnish sufficient grounds to enable the judge to acquire moral certitude concerning the merits of the case. The only solution in such cases is to have recourse to presumptions. The subject of presump-

Sebastianelli, Decano, dec. XIII, n. 4 f.—*Decisiones,* VIII (1916), 141 f. The marriage was declared invalid. Cf. *Ibid.,* 146 (n. 11).

[30] S.R.R., *Nullitatis Matrimonii,* 31 mart. 1922, coram Rm̃o P.D. Ioanne Prior, Decano, dec. X, n. 7 f.—*Decisiones,* XIV (1922), 86 f.; 23 nov. 1923, coram R.P.D. Raphaele Chimenti, dec. XXXII, n. 17—*Decisiones,* XV (1923), 291. In both cases, the marriage was declared invalid.

[31] S.R.R., *Nullitatis Matrimonii,* 18 iul. 1923, coram R.P.D. Francisco Parrillo, dec. XIX, n. 12 ff.—*Decisiones,* XV (1923), 171 ff. The marriage was declared invalid. Cf. *Ibid.,* 174 (n. 15).

[32] S.R.R., *Nullitatis Matrimonii,* 5 dec. 1927, coram R.P.D. Francisco Parrillo, dec. LV, n. 14—*Decisiones,* XIX (1927), 504. The marriage was declared invalid. Cf. *Ibid.,* 506 (n. 18).

tions is too complex to be discussed extensively in a study such as this.[33] A complete discussion, however, of the topic of the present study requires a brief explanation of the principal presumptions employed by the Sacred Roman Rota—both those which favor the validity of the marriage as well as those which militate against the validity of the marriage—in cases which involve the exclusion of the boon of offspring.

A. General Notions Regarding Presumptions

A presumption is defined as a "probable conjecture concerning something which is uncertain."[34] Some presumptions are stated in the law itself (*praesumptiones iuris*); others are formed by the ecclesiastical judge after an investigation of the facts of the case in question (*praesumptiones hominis*).[35] The former are known as legal presumptions; the latter, as natural presumptions. Although all of the legal presumptions involved in the present study admit of both direct and indirect proof to the contrary,[36] it is important to note that all legal presumptions, in effect, constitute full proof of what is stated in the presumption. The mere fact that the law presumes that in a case of doubt the marriage is valid (except for proof to the contrary) means that the full burden of proof rests with the party who alleges that the marriage is invalid. If the party fails to present complete and full proof of the contrary, the judge must pronounce

[33] A thesis on the subject appeared in the Canon Law Studies Series of the Catholic University of America: Manning, *Presumptions of Law in Marriage Cases*, The Catholic University of America Canon Law Studies, n. 94 (Washington, D. C.; The Catholic University of America, 1935).

[34] "Praesumptio est rei incertae probabilis coniectura; . . ."—Canon 1825, § 1.

[35] ". . . eaque alia est iuris, quae ab ipsa lege statuitur; alia hominis, quae a iudice coniicitur."—*Loc. cit.*

[36] The Code of Canon Law in canon 1825, § 2, makes a further distinction between *praesumptiones iuris simpliciter* and *praesumptiones iuris et de iure*, and states that the latter admit only indirect proof to the contrary: ". . . *hoc est contra factum quod est praesumptionis fundamentum*" (canon 1826). The present study involves only those presumptions which are called "*praesumptiones iuris simpliciter.*"

in favor of the one who has the legal presumption on his or her side.[37] In other words, the law is on the side of the one who has the presumption in his favor; and the law must be upheld.

Presumptions which are not stated in the law, however, never share the force of legal presumptions in the sense that the mere fact that the presumption exists indicates immediately that the burden of proof is transferred to the other contending party.[38] In order to estimate the probative value of the personal presumptions of the ecclesiastical judge in comparison with legal presumptions, authors distinguish between light, grave and very grave or vehement personal presumptions.[39] Prudence requires that the judge disregard light or flimsy presumptions in arriving at his decision.[40] But grave or probable presumptions, although insufficient of themselves to furnish full proof of the validity or the invalidity of a marriage, may constitute full proof in concurrence with other supporting proofs and presumptions, thus enabling the judge to arrive at moral certitude concerning the merits of the case.[41] Once a very grave or vehement personal presumption has been established, however, the burden of proof is shifted to the other contending party. Unless that party is able to bring forth convincing proof to the contrary, that which is presumed in the vehement presumption will be accepted as true.[42] The matter of determining just what constitutes a grave or a vehement presumption in each particular case is left to the judge. That which is

[37] "Qui habet pro se iuris praesumptionem, liberatur ab onere probandi, quod recidit in partem adversam; qua non probante, sententia ferri debet in favorem partis pro qua stat praesumptio."—Canon 1827. This does not mean that what is stated in the presumption is evident truth, but that it is regarded as true until proof is adduced to the contrary. Hence it is called proof "in effect." Cf. Manning, *Presumptions of Law in Marriage Cases,* p. 17.

[38] Cf. Wernz-Vidal, *Ius Canonicum,* VI (*De Processibus,* Pars I, 1927), n. 520 (cited hereafter as *De Processibus*).

[39] Cf. Wernz-Vidal, *loc. cit.;* Bachofen [Augustine], *A Commentary,* VII (3. ed., 1931), 272.

[40] Cf. Wernz-Vidal, *loc. cit.*

[41] "Tantus enim potest esse cumulus indiciorum ut sufficienter explicari non possit, nisi supposita veritate facti, de quo quaeritur."—Wernz-Vidal, *loc. cit.*

[42] Cf. Wernz-Vidal, *loc. cit.; Vermeersch Creusen,* Epitome Iuris Canonici, III, n. 206; Wanenmacher, *Canonical Evidence in Marriage Cases,* n. 391. This does not apply, however, in criminal cases. Cf. Wernz-Vidal, *loc. cit.*

a vehement presumption in one case, due to investigated facts and attending circumstances, may be no more than a grave presumption in another case. The formulating of such presumptions, therefore, requires skill and experience.

There is a sense in which certain personal presumptions may be called legal presumptions, i.e., legal presumptions in a wide sense. Those which occur again and again in the jurisprudence of the Sacred Roman Rota, for example, may be called legal presumptions in the sense that if the law does not furnish a guiding norm on a certain point, it is proper to follow the general principles of jurisprudence, the practice of the Roman Curia and the common and constant teaching of authors on the subject.[43] After all, the Code is silent regarding the probative value of personal presumptions. Furthermore, many of the presumptions employed by the Sacred Roman Rota today are based on pre-Code jurisprudence.[44] In fact, the Rota has indicated that the jurisprudence of the pre-Code period still is in effect, even though certain norms followed by the Rota today are not mentioned in the Code.[45]

The danger in forming personal or natural presumptions, however, is that they are sometimes based on the personal views and opinions of the judge instead of on the objective facts and circumstances of the case. Hence the Sacred Congregation of the Sacraments again reminded tribunals in 1936 that the judge may not formulate personal presumptions unless there is question of a *certain* and *specific* fact which has a *direct* bearing upon the controverted point. Otherwise personal presumptions have no probative value in judicial proceedings.[46] The very nature of cases which involve the exclusion of the

[43] This argument, which is based on canon 20 of the Code of Canon Law, is developed by Wanenmacher, *ibid.*, n. 392.

[44] Speaking of the presumption in the earlier law, namely that a ". . . copula libere posita, *pendente conditione,* constituebat *praesumptionem iuris et de iure* revocationis, . . ." Cappello (*De Sacramentis,* III, n. 640, 2.) adds: ". . . num saltem *praesumptionem iuris* constituat, ita distinguendum; praesumptio iuris proprie dicta non constituitur, quia ius positivum nihil statuit; praesumptio lato sensu profecto constituitur."

[45] S.R.R., *Buscoducen, Nullitatis Matrimonii,* 7 ian. 1918, coram Rmo. P.D. Guilelmo Sebastianelli, Decano, dec. I, n. 2—*Decisiones,* X (1918), 2; *AAS,* X (1918), 518.

[46] *Instr.* S.C. de Sacr., 1936, art. 173: "*Praesumptiones, quae non statuuntur*

essence of marriage indicates the practical impossibility of arriving at moral certitude on the merits of the case without recourse to personal presumptions. To formulate them properly the ecclesiastical judge must not only bring out into the open the circumstances which preceded, accompanied and followed the marriage [47] but he should also delve into the decisions of the Sacred Roman Rota "to learn how and wherein presumptions are to be correctly formulated." [48]

It is true that presumptions of law as such prevail over personal or natural presumptions. Likewise presumptions which favor the validity of an act are to receive preference over those which favor the invalidity of the act.[49] This applies in marriage cases, however, only if both presumptions are equally general or specific. If the presumption favoring the nullity of a marriage is specific and the presumption favoring validity is general, the former prevails. This is a logical application of the axiom of Boniface VIII: *"Generi per speciem derogatur."* [50]

B. Presumptions in Favor of the Validity of a Marriage

(1) With Regard to Marriage in General

The key presumption in all marriage cases is that, if there is doubt concerning the validity of the marriage, the marriage is presumed

a iure, iudex ne coniiciat, nisi ex facto certo et determinato, quod cum eo, de quo controversia est, directe cohaereat (can. 1828)."—*AAS*, XXVIII (1936), 346. Cf. also Wernz-Vidal, *De Processibus*, VI, n. 520. There is a distinction to be made between indications (*indicia*) and presumptions. Indications are the facts which form the basis for presumptions. Conjectures, which amount to personal presumptions, are the conclusions drawn from such indications. Cf. Wanenmacher, *Canonical Evidence in Marriage Cases*, n. 385.

[47] *Instr.* S.C. de Sacr., 1936, art. 174: "Praesumptiones *hominis* est potissimum locus in causis, quae spectant ad consensus defectum. Ad eas constabiliendas instructoris est curare, ut circumstantiae proferantur in lucem, quae matrimonium praecesserunt, comitatae vel secutae sunt:"—*AAS*, XXVIII (1936), 346.

[48] Doheny, *Canonical Procedure in Matrimonial Cases*, I, 296.

[49] Cf. Wernz-Vidal, *De Processibus*, n. 521; Bachofen [Augustine], *A Commentary*, VII, 273.

[50] Reg. 34, R. J., in VI°. Cf. also Wanenmacher, *Canonical Evidence in Marriage Cases*, n. 397, and note 59. The same apparently would apply to two equally grave personal presumptions, one in favor of validity and the other in favor of nullity.

as valid until the contrary has been proved.[51] Since this presumption applies in both the internal and the external form[52] and extends to the marriages of Catholics, heretics and the non-baptized,[53] its force is practically universal.[54] The only exception to this general presumption is mentioned in the law itself; the case which involves the "privilege of the faith."[55]

The presumptions stated in canon 1014 should not be applied, however, unless the doubt in favor of the validity of the marriage is based on a probable foundation.[56] All presumptions, whether in favor of validity or of invalidity, are not to be applied unless there is question of a prudent doubt. There is no justification for insisting upon presumptions which favor the validity of a marriage, if proof to the contrary is furnished by the concurrence of "overwhelming evidence and clear facts."[57] Nor does this presumption have any-

[51] "Matrimonium gaudet favore iuris; quare in dubio standum est pro valore matrimonii, donec contrarium probetur, salvo praescripto can. 1127."—Canon 1014.

[52] Cf. Gasparri, *De Matrimonio*, II, n. 817; Cappello, *De Sacramentis*, III, n. 53.

[53] Regarding its application to the marriages of heretics and of the non-baptized, cf. S.C.S. Off. (ad Vic. Ap. Oceaniae Central.), 18 dec., 1872—*Fontes*, n. 1024; S.C.S. Off. (*ad Ep. Nesquallien*), 24 ian. 1877—*Fontes*, n. 1050. In fact the first of these two documents makes it clear that the presumption applies even in cases which involve a doubt as to the *fact* of marriage between two non-baptized persons: ". . . quoties de facto publice apparet et habetur tamquam verum matrimonium; . . ."—Cappello, *loc. cit.*

[54] According to outstanding contemporary authors, the former view of some canonists, namely that in cases of marriage contracted in consequence of the duress of fear, the presumption is reversed in favor of the innocent party, is not tenable today—at least not in practice. Cf. Wernz-Vidal, *Ius Matrimoniale*, n. 44; Cappello, *ibid.*, n. 55.

[55] Cf. canons 1014 and 1127. Even this exception was limited considerably in its potential application through a declaration of the Holy Office on June 10, 1937, wherein it is stated that in case of an insoluble doubt regarding the earlier baptism of the parties one of whom seeks to use the "privilege of the faith," the matter must be referred to the Holy Office. Cf. *AAS*, XIX (1937), 305—Bouscaren, *Canon Law Digest*, II, 343.

[56] *Instr.* S.C. de Sacr., 1936, art. 172: "Dubium sive iuris sive facti, quod faveat matrimonio, debet esse prudens, seu probabili fundamento nixum, ut praesumptioni pro matrimonii valore locus sit."—*AAS*, XXVIII (1936), 346.

[57] Doheny, *Canonical Procedure in Matrimonial Cases*, I, 291.

thing to do with the right of the parties to impugn the validity of their marriage. Obviously, if they have not lost that right, the parties may impugn the validity of their marriage even though they have not a "clear-cut" case.

(2) With Regard to the Validity of Internal Consent

Another strong legal presumption which favors the validity of marriage is that the internal consent of the will always is presumed to be in conformity with the externally manifested consent.[58] This presumption is based on the following dictum of Roman Law: *"Nemo existimandus est dixisse quod non mente agitaverit."* [59] Another Roman Law dictum states that, if a person affirms that he did not mean what he said, he should not be believed.[60] The question of how far these Roman Law notions influenced the views of the early decretalists in regard to total simulation in particular is implied in the course of Chapter II of this study.[61] Applied to cases which involve intentions and conditions which are contrary to the essence of marriage the presumption stated in canon 1086, § 1, is practically the equivalent of the natural presumption mentioned by Benedict XIV, i.e., in the absence of convincing evidence that the parties actually intended to exclude something which pertains to the essence of marriage it is to be presumed that they intended to contract marriage as it was established by Christ, with all of its essential rights and obligations.[62]

(3) With Regard to the Revocation of a Contrary Intention or Condition

As stated in an earlier chapter [63] the commentators on the decretals of Gregory IX held that if the proposal of a condition contrary to one of the three boons of marriage met with the objections

[58] "Internus animi consensus semper praesumitur conformis verbis vel signis in celebrando matrimonio adhibitis."—Canon 1086, § 1.

[59] D. (33. 10) (7. 2).

[60] C. (4. 30), 13.

[61] Cf. *supra*, p. 49 f.

[62] Cf. *De Synodo Dioecesana*, lib. XIII, cap. 22, n. 7.

[63] Cf. *supra*, p. 53.

or silence of the other contracting party, it was to be presumed that the party who proposed the condition revoked it before giving consent to the marriage contract. Although modern authors admit the validity of such a presumption if one of the parties objects to the evil proposal of the other (e.g. a proposed condition contrary to the boon of offspring),[64] some of them clearly deny that the same presumption is to be applied if one of the parties merely maintains silence when the contrary condition is proposed.[65]

It is better to view these presumptions as applying only if, after both parties have given absolute consent to the marriage, there is doubt whether or not the silence or objections of one of the parties may have caused the other to revoke the condition. For, objectively considered, if one of the parties objects to the condition expressly or keeps silent when it is proposed, it appears that the disagreement between the parties would point rather to the invalidity of the contract.[66] Viewed in this light, these presumptions appear as an application of the general presumption that *in a case of doubt* the marriage is to be considered as valid, rather than an application of a presumption in favor of the revocation of the condition. The revocation of an expressed intention or condition is a fact. Facts, however, are not presumed; they must be proved.[67]

There are indications in the decisions of the Sacred Roman Rota

[64] Cf. Gasparri, *De Matrimonio*, II, n. 895; Chelodi, *Ius Matrimoniale*, n. 125; Cappello, *De Sacramentis*, III, 634, 3; Payen, *De Matrimonio*, II, n. 1732, 3); Noldin-Schmitt, *Summa Theologiae Moralis*, III, n. 631, 2, a.

[65] Cf. Payen, *loc. cit.*; Chelodi, *loc. cit.*; Wanenmacher, *Canonical Evidence in Marriage Cases*, n. 474. Gasparri (*loc. cit.*) merely mentions that some authors uphold the validity of such a presumption. Cappello (*loc. cit.*) states: "Est mera praesumptio, quae profecto cedit veritati."

[66] "Quare si *una* pars talem conditionem apponat, et altera pars *expresse contradicat* vel *taceat* per se ob *dissensum* utriusque partis matrimonium ex natura rei est invalidum, . . . nisi ex circumstantiis colligi possit, priorem partem ob contradictionem vel taciturnitatem alterius a sua conditione *recessisse*. Id, quod in casu *dubii* ob favorem matrimonii *praesumendum* est, si *postea* utraque pars *absolute* in matrimonium consensit."—Wernz-Vidal, *Ius Matrimoniale*, n. 518, note (36).

[67] *Versalien, Nullitatis Matrimonii*, Commissio Specialis RR. PP. Cardinalium: ". . . revocatio [conditionis] est factum et facta non praesumuntur sed probantur; . . ."—*AAS*, X (1918), 389.

that the presumptions which are based on the silence or the objections of one of the parties are considered as mere applications of the general presumption that, in case of doubt, the marriage is to be presumed as valid. For, although such presumptions are referred to in some cases,[68] there is ample evidence that once it has been established that one of the parties actually placed a condition which is contrary to one of the boons of marriage, it is to be presumed that the condition was not revoked unless positive proof of its revocation is at hand: "Semel autem apposita conditione, revocatam non fuisse praesumitur, nisi positive id probetur. Siquidem revocatio est factum, et facta non praesumuntur, sed demonstrantur." [69] In other words, if there are no indications in the particular case in question that the contion may have been revoked, then the revocation of the condition is not to be presumed. If there are circumstances which make it doubtful whether or not the party actually revoked the condition before giving consent to the marriage contract, the presumption that the condition was revoked may be employed.

It may suffice to cite a few examples in confirmation of the foregoing statement. In a case decided in 1927, the fact that the man promised, though reluctantly, to prevent the conception of offspring, but at the same time endeavored to make the girl change her mind on the matter, is cited as the basis for a doubt whether he had revoked his promise and hence also his intention to prevent the conception of offspring.[70] The circumstances of another case, decided

[68] Cf., for example, S.R.R., *Nullitatis Matrimonii,* 5 dec. 1927, coram R.P.D. Francisco Parrillo, dec. LV, n. 3—*Decisiones,* XIX (1927), 499.

[69] S.R.R., *Nullitatis Matrimonii,* 4 maii 1927, coram R.P.D. Iulio Grazioli, dec. XX, n. 5—*Decisiones,* XX (1927), 164. Cf. also 10 aug. 1922, coram R.P.D. Francisco Solieri, dec. XXX, n. 4—*Decisiones,* XIV (1922), 275; 23 nov. 1923, coram R.P.D. Raphaele Chimenti, dec. XXXII, n. 2—*Decisiones,* XV (1923), 274; 28 nov. 1928, coram R.P.D. Iulio Grazioli, dec. LIII, n. 3—*Decisiones,* XX (1928), 469.

[70] S.R.R., *Nullitatis Matrimonii,* 7 ian. 1927, coram R.P.D. Iosepho Florczak, dec. XXVI, n. 7—*Decisiones,* XIX (1927), 213. Although the girl insisted upon such a promise from the man, there was no sufficient evidence that she intended to exclude the marriage right itself regarding the boon of offspring (*ibid.,* 211). The Rota upheld the validity of the marriage. Cf. *Ibid.,* 214 (n. 9).

in 1926, led to the personal presumption that, even if the girl, at the alleged time before her marriage, had placed a condition to prevent the conception of offspring, she would have revoked the condition, ". . . nam conditioni propositae viro non assentiente, in suo proposito haud mulier perseveravit, ne nuptiae disperderentur."[71] In another case, decided in 1929, the girl made it very clear by her manner of acting that she was opposed to the condition placed by the man. The circumstances of the case, however, did not warrant the presumption that the man revoked his condition regarding the preventing of the conception of offspring in the marriage.[72]

It seems, therefore, that in the jurisprudence of the Sacred Roman Rota, the silence or the objections of one party to the contrary condition of the other may justify the presumption that the condition was revoked *if* the circumstances of the case point to such a conclusion. The mere fact that the one party is silent or objects when the condition is proposed does not in itself justify such a presumption. In fact, some of the decisions state that the mere fact that one of the parties remained silent when the condition was proposed by the other is an indication of agreement between the parties in regard to the condition. This justifies a presumption in favor of the invalidity of the marriage.[73]

(4) With Regard to Intentions merely to Abuse the Marriage Right

In cases which involve the exclusion of the boon of offspring or the boon of conjugal fidelity, the two major legal presumptions discussed in the first section of the present article usually inspire other

[71] S.R.R., *Nullitatis Matrimonii,* 17 aug. 1926, coram R.P.D. Francisco Guglielmi, dec. XLIV, n. 8—*Decisiones,* XVIII (1926), 357. The Rota upheld the validity of the marriage. Cf. *Ibid.,* 363 (n. 21).

[72] S.R.R., *Nullitatis Matrimonii,* 7 ian. 1929, coram R.P.D. Francisco Parrillo, dec. II, n. 22—*Decisiones,* XXI (1929), 23. The evidence in the case was insufficient to show that the man intended to exclude the right itself in regard to the procreation of offspring. The Rota upheld the validity of the marriage. Cf. *Ibid.,* 24 (n. 24).

[73] " 'Qui tacet, cum loqui debeat, consentire *videtur*', . . ."—*Loc. cit.* (case just cited). Another decision mentions that this is a grave presumption. Cf. S.R.R., *Nullitatis Matrimonii,* 7 iul. 1926, coram R.P.D. Ubaldo Mannucci, dec. XXVIII, n. 2—*Decisiones,* XVIII (1926), 222.

personal or natural presumptions which militate against the exclusion of the marriage right itself or the corresponding obligation. These presumptions are expressed in various ways but have the same meaning. One decision states, for example, that in a case of doubt whether the party intended to deny the obligation itself or merely to neglect the fulfillment of the obligation, it is to be presumed that he simply had an intention of using marriage sinfully, the right inherent in marriage remaining itself intact ("intentio peccandi, salvo iure matrimonii").[74] Another decision may state the presumption as follows: ". . . in dubio, propter favorem matrimonii, praesumitur exclusum fuisse tantum usum et non ius, nisi aliud certo demonstretur."[75] Still another variation of terminology is the following: ". . . generatim in foro externo praesumendum est agi, in similibus adiunctis, de simplici voluntate matrimonii bonis abutendi, integra eius substantia, nisi contrarium probetur." [76]

These presumptions in favor of the validity of a marriage apply with a special force if the contracting parties intend to prevent the conception of offspring only for a time. If, on the other hand, the parties express an intention or place a condition which involves the absolute and perpetual exclusion of the boon of offspring, there is a very grave presumption that they intend to exclude the marriage right itself with reference to the boon of offspring. This important distinction between the temporary and the perpetual and absolute exclusion of the boon of offspring has been discussed sufficiently in an earlier chapter of this study.[77] It must be stressed, however, that all legal presumptions, so also the varying presumptions which are based either on the temporary exclusion of the boon of offspring or on the perpetual and absolute exclusion of the boon of offspring can and must yield to contrary proof. As stated previously in this study,[78] it is readily conceivable that an intention or condition which

[74] S.R.R., *Nullitatis Matrimonii,* 20 maii. 1930, coram R.P.D. Henrico Quattrocolo, dec. XXIV, n. 7—*Decisiones,* XXI (1929), 284 f.

[75] S.R.R., *Nullitatis Matrimonii,* 16 iul. 1931, coram R.P.D. Francisco Guglielmi, dec. XXXV, n. 3—*Decisiones,* XXIII (1931), 293.

[76] S.R.R., *Nullitatis Matrimonii,* 7 ian. 1929, coram R.P.D. Francisco Parrillo, dec. II, n. 5—*Decisiones,* XXI (1929), 14.

[77] Cf. *supra,* p. 62 ff.

[78] Cf. *supra,* p. 63 f.

implies even a temporary exclusion of the boon of offspring can nevertheless suffice to invalidate the marriage. All that is required is this: there must be *proof* (which prevails over the contrary *presumption*) that the party intended, by a positive act of the will, to exclude the *marriage right itself* (not merely the use or proper use of the right). The possibility that the perpetual and absolute exclusion of the boon of offspring may, in the given circumstances of an actual case, indicate merely an intention to abuse the marriage right will be discussed presently.

The reason why even the temporary exclusion of the marriage right affects the validity of the marriage contract is implied in canon 1086, § 2. For if the parties intend, by a positive act of the will, to exclude the *marriage right itself* even temporarily, the marriage right is no longer an *omne ius* (i.e. complete and perpetual).[79] In actual practice, however, it is very unlikely (and very difficult to prove) that the parties who intended to exclude the boon of offspring only for a specified period of time intended to exclude the marriage right itself during that period. It is significant that in all of the cases decided by the Sacred Roman Rota from 1908 to 1931 inclusively which involved intentions or conditions to exclude the boon of offspring temporarily, the decision was in favor of the validity of the marriage.[80]

C. *Presumptions in Favor of the Nullity of a Marriage*

(1) Evidence of the Absolute and Perpetual Exclusion of Offspring

The entire question of proving the invalidity of a marriage on the score of the exclusion of the boon of offspring amounts to a question of proving whether or not the intention to prevent the conception of offspring actually prevailed over the intention (presumed in all marriages) to contract marriage as established by Christ with all of its essential rights and obligations. If the intention or condition to prevent the conception of offspring is expressed or proposed

[79] Cf. *supra*, p. 97.

[80] As an illustration of the *possibility* of a declaration of nullity in such cases, cf. *infra*, Chapter V, case n. 14.

without any limitations (i.e. the absolute and perpetual exclusion of the boon of offspring), there is a very grave presumption that the intention to prevent the conception of offspring prevailed over the intention to contract a true marriage with all of its essential rights and obligations.[81] To say that the intention to prevent the conception of offspring prevails over the intention to contract a true marriage is equivalent to saying, in effect, that the intention or condition to prevent the conception of offspring is introduced into the marriage pact itself as an essential part of the contract.

The fact that the parties intend to prevent the conception of offspring absolutely and during the entire period of their married life does not prove that they intend to exclude the marriage right itself but merely gives rise to a very grave presumption to that effect. The marriage can not be declared invalid in the external forum unless there is *proof* that one or both of the parties excluded the marriage right itself with reference to the boon of offspring. It is necessary, therefore, to establish either that the parties expressed a positive intention to exclude the marriage right itself, or that they expressed a positive intention to prevent the conception of offspring as a *true* condition (*sine qua non*). In either instance it would be clear that the contrary intention or condition entered into the marriage contract itself as an essential part of the contract.

The value of presumptions of the type mentioned above in enabling the ecclesiastical judge to arrive at moral certitude concerning the merits of a case is illustrated clearly in a case as decided in 1926.[82] Although there was no *direct* proof that the girl intended to prevent the conception of offspring as a *sine qua non* condition of her consent to the marriage contract, such an attitude was proved *indirectly* inasmuch as the motives which had induced the girl to

[81] S.R.R., *Nullitatis Matrimonii,* 4 aug. 1922, coram R.P.D. Raphaele Chimenti, dec. XXVII, n. 8: "Ex communi doctrina censetur praevalere intentionem prolis vitandae si absolute et absque ulla limitatione ostendatur."—*Decisiones,* XIV (1922), 258. Cf. also 31 mart. 1922, coram Rm̃o P.D. Ioanne Prior, Decano, dec. X, n. 11—*Decisiones,* XIV (1922), 89.

[82] S.R.R., *Nullitatis Matrimonii,* 7 iul. 1926, coram R.P.D. Ubaldo Mannucci, dec. XXVIII—*Decisiones,* XVIII (1926), 221 ff. The Rota declared the marriage invalid. Cf. *Ibid.,* 228 (n. 12).

place such a condition indicated that she intended to prevent the conception of offspring absolutely and always.[83]

(2) Evidence of a Mutual Pact or Agreement

One Rota decision refers to the difficulty of deciding (in the face of insufficient evidence), whether or not the party intended to prevent the conception of offspring as a *sine qua non* condition, and stresses the value of presumptions in such circumstances as follows:

> In huius generis controversiis, id praecise iudicis animum incertum reddit, an conditio vel positiva voluntas, bono prolis adversans, fuerit uti lex coniugii apposita vel intenta, ita ut non aliter quis contrahere intenderit, quam si dein ius sibi esset prolem vitandi, in quo vere stat boni substantialis exclusio vel consensus restrictio. Et cum plerumque id ex circumstantiis deducere datum non sit, suppetunt iuris praesumptiones, quae matrimonio favent, si res sit de conditione ab una tantum parte, altera inscia vel non acceptante, apposita, vel matrimonio obsistunt, si in pactum conventionemque deducta, . . .[84]

Certainly the presumption in favor of the nullity of marriage which was discussed most by the commentators and early authors was the one which stated that if the contracting parties have entered an agreement or pact concerning the preventing of the conception of offspring in their married life, the marriage was to be considered as invalid. The origin and meaning of this presumption has been discussed at length in an earlier chapter.[85] It may be well, however, to add a few remarks concerning the practical value of this presumption in deciding matrimonial cases.

If the intention to preclude the conception of offspring is reduced to an agreement between the contracting parties or expressed as a true condition, this fact can furnish a very grave argument for the nullity of the marriage.[86] In these two instances the presumption in favor

[83] *Ibid.*, 225 (n. 8). Cf. *infra*, Chapter V, case n. 3 for the final decision of this case.

[84] S.R.R., *Nullitatis Matrimonii*, 5 dec. 1927, coram R.P.D. Francisco Parrillo, dec. LV, n. 13—*Decisiones*, XIX (1927), 504.

[85] Cf. *supra*, p. 44 ff.

[86] S.R.R., *Nullitatis Matrimonii*, 26 iun. 1925, coram R.P.D. Andrea Jullien,

of the validity of the marriage gives way to a contrary presumption in favor of its invalidity.[87] This is mentioned in the decisions of the Sacred Roman Rota especially in regard to a pact or agreement between the contracting parties concerning the contrary condition.[88] This presumption applies, however, only if the condition concerns the absolute and perpetual exclusion of the boon of offspring. For if the condition is placed with limitations, as frequently happens, it is to be presumed that the parties intend merely to abuse the marriage right. Hence the presumption in favor of the validity of the marriage prevails in such cases.[89]

The fact that the one party accepted the contrary condition of the other party indicates that the party who proposed the condition intended the condition as a matter of obligation between them.[90]

dec. XXXIII, n. 2: ". . . ex deductione in pactum aut ex conditione apposita desumi possit argumentum gravissimum ad probationem in foro externo pravae intentionis et consequenter nullitatis matrimonii."—*Decisiones,* XVII (1925), 263.

[87] "S.R.R., *Nullitatis Matrimonii,* 19 apr. 1926, coram R.P.D. Iulio Grazioli, dec. XVIII, n. 11: ". . . ea vis conditioni sine qua non aut pacto inter coniuges inito inest, ut cesset favor iuris quo matrimonium gaudet et illud praesumatur nullum."—*Decisiones,* XVIII (1926), 144.

[88] S.R.R., *Nullitatis Matrimonii,* 5 dec. 1927, coram R.P.D. Francisco Parrillo, dec. LV, n. 3: "Iuxta diversum modum quo apponitur conditio, diversa est in foro externo praesumptio circa actus valorem, nam si una pars illam apponat et altera acceptet, tunc habetur *pactum,* seu stipulatio matrimonio adiecta, quo statuitur aliquid contrarium essentiae illius, quo in casu, ex aperta Pontificis declaratione, modo relata, cessat praesumptio matrimonio favens, et subintrat contraria praesumptio de consensu essentialiter corrupto: 'Matrimonialis consensus *quantumcumque sit favorabilis, caret effectu*'."—*Decisiones,* XIX (1929), 499. Cf. also 10 febr. 1931, coram R.P.D. Arcturo Wynen, dec. VII, n. 9—*Decisiones,* XXIII (1931), 49. Cf. also *infra,* Chapter V, cases n. 1-5 inclusively.

[89] S.R.R., *Nullitatis Matrimonii,* 5 dec. 1927, coram R.P.D. Francisco Parrillo, dec. LV, n. 8: "Conditio autem vel propositum, etsi in pactum deductum, tunc solum praesumptionem favore matrimonii excludit, iuxta dicta, cum absolute et absque temporis limitatione fuerit elicitum; secus contraria militat praesumptio de simplici matrimonii abusu, . . ."—*Decisiones,* XIX (1927), 502. Cf. also 23 mart. 1925, coram R.P.D. Andrea Jullien, dec. XVIII, n. 2—*Decisiones,* XVII (1925), 131; 30 iun. 1925, coram R.P.D. Francisco Parrillo, dec. XXXIV, n. 3—*Decisiones,* XVII (1925), 270; 7 ian. 1929, coram R.P.D. Francisco Parrillo, dec. II, n. 6—*Decisiones,* XXI (1929), 15.

[90] S.R.R., *Nullitatis Matrimonii,* 7 ian. 1929, coram R.P.D. Francisco

This furnishes the basis for a strong argument that at least the party who proposed the contrary condition may have intended to exclude the marriage right itself with reference to the boon of offspring.[91] There is always the possibility, however, that in proposing the contrary condition, the one party intended to impose upon the other merely a post-contractual obligation, i.e. not an intention to exclude the marriage right itself, but merely an intention to abuse the right.[92] Although the presence of a pact or agreement justifies the *presumption* that one of the parties intended to exclude the marriage right itself with reference to the boon of offspring, it is necessary in each individual case to seek convincing evidence that one of the parties actually intended to exclude the marriage right itself or actually intended the contrary condition as an essential part of the marriage contract itself. This will be illustrated clearly in a review of the actual decisions of the Sacred Roman Rota in the final chapter of this study.[93]

(3) Evidence of a *sine qua non* Condition

If the contrary condition is placed clearly as a *sine qua non* condition, a very grave presumption arises that the marriage right

Parrillo, dec. II, n. 22: ". . . quodque [i.e. pactum] propositione unius et acceptatione alterius conficitur, et ex quo obligatio ultro citroque servanda enascitur."—*Decisiones,* XXI (1929), 22. Cf. also 5 dec. 1927, coram R.P.D. Francisco Parrillo, dec. LV, n. 16—*Decisiones,* XIX (1927), 505; 7 iul. 1926, coram R.P.D. Ubaldo Mannucci, dec. XXVIII, n. 2—*Decisiones,* XVIII (1926). 222.

91 Cf. S.R.R., *Nullitatis Matrimonii,* 9 aug. 1929, coram Rmo P.D. Maximo Massimi, Decano, dec. L, n. 10—*Decisiones,* XXI (1929), 423; 5 dec. 1927, coram R.P.D. Francisco Parrillo, dec. LV, n. 16—*Decisiones,* XIX (1927), 505.

92 S.R.R., *Nullitatis Matrimonii,* 11 feb. 1929 coram R.P.D. Francisco Guglielmi, dec. XI, n. 18: 'Verum etiamsi ut probatum admitteretur aliquod pactum vel intentionem de vitandis liberis exstitisse, tenuerunt Patres minime constare omne ius ad actum coniugalem exclusum fuisse, et non potius iuris exercitium et obligationis implementum; quae postrema exclusio, . . . matrimonii validitati non officit, et in dubio praesumitur."—*Decisiones,* XXI (1929), 102 f.

93 Cf., for example S.R.R., *Nullitatis Matrimonii,* 15 dec. 1915, coram Rmo P.D. Guilelmo Sebastianelli, Decano, dec. XLI, n. 12—*Decisiones,* VII (1915),

itself is excluded in regard to the procreation of offspring.[94] If the contracting parties intend to contract marriage *only* on condition that the conception of offspring will be precluded throughout their married life, it is clear that they want a childless union more than they want marriage itself.[95] In such a case there is no need to investigate whether or not the contracting parties intended to exclude the marriage right with reference to the procreation of offspring, for it is clear that consent to the marriage contract as such is withheld if it is to entail the giving of any rights or the accepting of any obligations in regard to the boon of offspring. Once the ecclesiastical tribunal has ascertained that such a condition proceeds not from an error on the part of the intellect but from a positive act of the will, a declaration of nullity is entirely justified (Can. 1092, 2°).[96]

Every *true* condition is a *sine qua non* condition at least implicitly and in effect. If one of the contracting parties makes his or her consent dependent upon the stipulation that the conception of offspring will be precluded in conjugal life, there is no reason to doubt that the intention to prevent the conception of offspring prevails over the otherwise presumed intention to contract marriage as established by Christ with all of its essential rights and obligations. In other words, the most secure way of verifying the presence of a positive intention to exclude one of the essential obligations flowing from the contract of marriage is to establish the presence of an intention not

464; 31 iul. 1928, coram R.P.D. Iosepho Florczak, dec. XXXVI, n. 9—*Decisiones*, XX (1928), 341. Cf. *infra*, Chapter V, cases nn. 1-10 inclusively.

[94] Flieszer, "Ehewille und *bonum prolis*": "Die Präesumption für die *exclusio iuris radicalis* ist zweifellos bei der *conditio sine qua non* viel gröszer als bei der *fictio*, auch schon bei der teilweisen *exclusio prolis*, um so mehr bei der *exclusio prolis absoluta*, namentlich, wenn die Bedingung von beiden Seiten gestellt und angenommen wurde."—*Quartalschrift*, XC (1937), 441.

[95] S.R.R., *Nullitatis Matrimonii*, 7 iul. 1926, coram R.P.D. Ubaldo Mannucci, dec. XXVIII, n. 2: ". . . nam conditio subingredi debet ipsum consensum, qui ideo in casu excluditur, quia contrahens magis vult quod in conditio ponit, quam matrimonium ipsum: . . . hinc dici solet conditionem esse debere *sine qua non*."—*Decisiones*, XVIII (1926), 222.

[96] As examples of such cases in which only one of the parties expressed a condition contrary to the boon of offspring but as a *sine qua non* condition, cf. *infra*, Chapter V, cases n. 6 f.

to contract marriage at all except on condition that the essential obligation in question is excluded from the contract. If, then, in exact or equivalent terms, the party places the contrary condition clearly as a *sine qua non* condition, there is no reason to doubt the presence of an intention not to contract marriage as established by Christ, and, in consequence, no reason to doubt the invalidity of the marriage.

CHAPTER V

A REVIEW OF ACTUAL CASES AS DECIDED BY THE SACRED ROMAN ROTA

FROM 1909 to 1931 inclusively, the Sacred Roman Rota decided fifty-nine cases which involved the exclusion of the boon of offspring. Since this number includes sixteen instances in which a case, which previously had been decided by the Rota, was reviewed by that tribunal for a second or third time, the number of distinct cases is reduced to forty-three. In twenty of these cases, the ultimate decision was a declaration of nullity. In the remaining twenty-three cases, the final decision, as issued by the Rota, was in favor of the validity of the marriage.

For the purpose of illustrating the various types of cases which may confront a diocesan tribunal, twenty of the cases referred to above will be classified and reviewed in the following chapter. Each one of the remaining cases will be classified in the proper footnote after the last case of one or the other group of cases. The forty-three cases have been classified as follows:

A. Ten cases which furnished sufficient evidence of a mutual pact contrary to the boon of offspring. A study of these ten cases justifies a further classification:

   (1) The marriage was declared invalid in nine cases because of a *sine qua non condition* on the part of at least one of the contracting parties (Case No. 1 ff).

   (2) The marriage was declared invalid in one case apparently because of a positive *intention* to exclude the marriage right itself with reference to the boon of offspring (Case No. 5).

B. Thirty-three cases which furnished no evidence or insufficient evidence of a mutual pact contrary to the boon of offspring. All but ten of these cases resulted in a declaration in favor of the validity of the marriage. A study of these thirty-three cases likewise justifies a further classification:

(1) The marriage was declared invalid in four cases because of a *sine qua non* condition on the part of one of the contracting parties (Case No. 6 f).

(2) The marriage was declared invalid in six cases because of a positive intention on the part of at least one of the contracting parties, to exclude the marriage right itself with reference to the boon of off spring (Case No. 8 ff).

(3) The validity of the marriage was upheld in twenty-three cases. These cases furnished evidence of merely an intention or condition to *abuse* the marriage right or to neglect the *fulfillment* of the corresponding essential obligation (Case No. 11 ff).

A. Cases Which Furnished Sufficient Evidence of a Pact

It will be noted that each of the cases in the present group (as well as in the following group) which resulted in a declaration of nullity involved the absolute and perpetual exclusion of the boon of offspring. One case, which resulted in a declaration of nullity (Case No. 5), involved an agreement to prevent the conception of offspring temporarily. The declaration of nullity, however, apparently was based on evidence of a positive intention to exclude the boon of offspring altogether. The following cases demonstrate that, even though a case may furnish evidence of a pact contrary to the boon of offspring, the marriage cannot be declared invalid unless there is evidence either of a *sine qua non* condition (Can. 1092, 2°) or of a positive intention to exclude the marriage right itself with reference to the boon of offspring (Can. 1086, § 2).

(1) *Evidence of a Pact and of an Underlying* "sine qua non" *Condition* (*Can.* 1092, 2°)

Case No. 1—Nullity Declared

Due particularly to the persuasive arguments of a priest (Pantaleon), Patroclus wished to satisfy his conscience concerning his illicit relations with Felicitas and to legitimatize the two children born of those relations, by contracting marriage with her. They contracted marriage in the private chapel of the priest, Pantaleon. Later on, wishing to contract marriage duly with another woman, Patroclus proposed to impugn the validity of his marriage to Felicitas. Both the tribunal of first instance and the tribunal of second instance (the Sacred Congregation of the Council) upheld the validity of the marriage. By the will of the Holy Father, the case was sent to the Sacred Roman Rota with the stipulation that it be reviewed before seven auditors of that tribunal. The case presented two points of doubt which were stated as follows: *An constet de celebratione matrimonii in casu; et posita celebratione matrimonii an constet de eius nullitate?* [1]

With regard to the question whether or not the marriage between Patroclus and Felicitas had been celebrated, the Rota answered in the affirmative. The first argument which Patroclus and his advocate brought forth to prove the second point of doubt (i. e., that the marriage was invalid) was based on the alleged fact that, since the priest, Pantaleon, had informed him that he had been the true spouse of Felicitas ever since the day when he had first performed the conjugal act in a manner suitable to lead to the conception of offspring, he (Patroclus) consented to marry Felicitas only on condition that the marriage already had existed before. The argument was considered as inacceptable, however, for two reasons; it was considered altogether unlikely that the priest, Pantaleon, actually had given Patroclus the alleged information, and the argument was not confirmed by a single witness. The second argument of Patroclus and his advocate, which was based on Patroclus' repeated assertion that he had placed a condition contrary to the boon of offspring, was not supported sufficiently by the testimonies of the witnesses. Furthermore, there was no sufficient evidence whether the alleged condition had been a mere proposal, or a true condition, properly so-called. The decision was in favor of the validity of the marriage.[2]

The case was appealed to the Sacred Tribunal of the Apostolic Signatura, which ordered a *restitutio in integrum*: "quoad eam tantum partem sententiae quae respicit appositionem conditionis de vitanda

[1] S.R.R., *Nullitatis Matrimonii,* 6 dec. 1909, coram R.P.D. Gustavo Persiani, dec. XVIII—*Decisiones,* I (1909), 155 ff.

[2] *Ibid.,* 163 (n. 17).

prole."[3] Since, however, by the will of the Holy Father, all of the auditors of the Rota (who had not been impeded by law from doing so) had reviewed the case, the question of what tribunal should examine the case again was presented to the Holy Father for solution. The Holy Father ordered that the case be sent again to the Sacred Roman Rota.[4] A detailed review of the case, however, failed to produce evidence that Patroclus, when placing the alleged condition, had intended to exclude the essential obligation with regard to the conception of offspring:

> . . . dum ex una parte constat de matrimonii celebratione, et ex alia parte non satis constat neque de certa forma verborum quibus conditio concepta fuit, neque quaenam fuit Patrocli intentio, cum testes videantur conditionem referre tum ad fornicarios amores, cum ad statum coniugalem; hinc in dubio nedum praesumendum est de matrimonii valore, sed de intentione ipsa Actoris praesumi debet, ipsum non obligationem sed etiam exequutionem impedire intendisse iuxta regulas praestitutas.[5]

Again, the decision was in favor of the validity of the marriage.[6]

In 1923, by the authority of the Holy Father, the case was examined again, this time by all of the auditors of the Sacred Roman Rota.[7] The Rota concentrated its attention especially on two points: (1) the attitude of Patroclus towards Felicitas during the entire period which had preceded the marriage, and (2) especially, the particular reason or consideration with which Patroclus had accepted marriage with Felicitas. Patroclus had fallen in love with Felicitas in 1886. A child was born in 1887. Soon after, having tired of his relationship with Felicitas, he went to Lybia and joined the army at war. From letters which he had written to Felicitas and to others during his stay in Lybia, it was clear that, ever since his stay in Lybia, marriage with Felicitas had been proposed to him, but that

[3] S.R.R., *Nullitatis Matrimonii,* 17 ian. 1912, coram Rmo P.D. Michaele Lega, Decano, dec. V—*Decisiones,* IV (1912), 33 ff.

[4] *Loc. cit.*

[5] *Ibid.,* 54 f. (n. 33).

[6] *Ibid.,* 55 f. (n. 35). "Sententia facta est exsecutiva."—*Loc. cit.*

[7] S.R.R., *Nullitatis Matrimonii,* 23 nov. 1923, coram R.P.D. Raphaele Chimenti, dec. XXXII—*Decisiones,* XV (1923), 273 ff.

he had been entirely averse to marriage at that time, either because of the shameful life of Felicitas, or because of the opposition of his family. He had maintained, in a letter to his brother, Maurice, that he was prepared to act according to the wishes of his family in the matter: "Credi, sono pronto a far tutto, purchè sappia mammà e papà e voi tutti tranquilli: sopratutto mammà." [8]

About eight months later, Patroclus returned home and resumed his illicit relations with Felicitas. Another child was born in 1890. Felicitas renewed her attempts to have Patroclus marry her. There was no trace in the acts of the case that Patroclus wished to desert her after his return from Lybia. To all indications, he intended to remain with her in that illicit union. Due to his financial condition, however, a condition to prevent the conception of offspring in the future was placed to their illicit union by both parties. That was after the second child had been conceived. The Rota made the following observation:

> Ex tunc, ut planum est, concubinatus versus est in meram societatem turpitudinis, a qua nullus erat ad legitimum matrimonium transitus, nisi a conditione vel turpi pacto voluntas penitus recederet. Contrarium tamen constat contigisse. Nimirum ad matrimonium quidem, et singulari sane ratione, Patroclus adducitur, sed omnino firma manente conditione concubinatui apposita.[9]

The mother of Patroclus, seeing that he and Felicitas were inseparable, began to insist upon his duty to marry her. Since Patroclus had maintained that he was prepared to give in especially to the will of his mother, only one obstacle to the marriage seemed to remain, namely, the disgrace which would come to himself and to his family as a result of such a marriage. This obstacle was noted to have vanished, however, when the priest, Pantaleon, had confronted him with an accomplished fact in telling him that, before God, he already was joined to Felicitas. In using this argument to persuade Patroclus to marry Felicitas, it was considered not improbable that the priest could have exaggerated the obligation to marry her, which arose from Patroclus' illicit relations with Felicitas:

[8] *Ibid.*, 276 (n. 4).
[9] *Ibid.*, 278 (n. 5).

> Ita expressis verbis agendi rationem sacerdotis Pantaleonis interpretatus est testis coram S.C. Concilii [i. e., which, as the tribunal of second instance, had upheld the validity of the marriage], Revm̃us S., . . . : "Dato il carattere franco del sac. Pantaleone, non credo improbabile che abbia potuto esagerare a Patroclo l'obbligazione che aveva di sposare la Felicetta . . . usando espressioni equivoche, dicendogli p.e.—Tu hai difficoltà di sposare questa donna; ma bada che davanti a Dio sei vincolato, fin da quando l'hai trattata maritalmente e ne hai avuto figli;—le quali espressioni potrebbero intendersi o del vincolo matrimoniale o dell'obbligo di sposare." [10]

The Rota noted, however, that, in entering the marriage contract with Felicitas, Patroclus undoubtedly had accepted, not a substantial modification of his relationship with regard to Felicitas (especially concerning the procreation of offspring), but merely a formal manifestation of that relationship in the eyes of the Church. It was noted likewise that, during the preparations which had preceded the marriage, there had been no trace of the obstacle which formerly had deterred Patroclus very much from contracting marriage with Felicitas, i. e., his financial condition. The reason was that he thought that, by previously having placed the condition to not beget offspring, he had taken care of the situation sufficiently.

The facts which preceded and accompanied the marriage gave rise to a grave presumption or at least to a very strong suspicion that the marriage had not been contracted except with the firm retention of the condition which indisputably already had been placed to their illicit union, i. e., the condition of preventing offspring from the union with Felicitas in the future. The suspicion was confirmed by the circumstances which followed the marriage: during the six following years (1891-1896), no other children had been born of the union (although, during the ten subsequent years, seven children had been born of his illicit relations with two other women); he had indicated that he fostered an aversion for the children which already had been born of his union with Felicitas. The Rota judged that at least the beginning of proof (*"inchoatio probationis"*) or even a half-full proof could be deduced from such presumptions and indications. The depositions of the witnesses, however, furnished the prin-

[10] *Ibid.*, 278 f. (n. 7).

cipal weight of the proof. After a review of the testimonies of the witnesses, the Rota made the following statement:

> Iamvero, ad iuridicam aestimationem horum testimoniorum quod est, ea quippe *directe* non probant, nec intendunt, inter Patroclum et Felicitatem pactum intercessisse de vitanda prole, . . . sed nescimus quomodo negari possit . . . ex eis plene probari, quod Patroclus, sive ante matrimonium sive tempore immediate sequenti, pluribus patefecerit suam firmam deliberatam voluntatem non aliter contrahendi, nisi sub conditione vitandi prolem, immo etiam notificaverit, alteram partem seu Felicitatem talem conditionem acceptasse.[11]

The fact that Patroclus had placed his condition as a *sine qua non* condition followed not only from the explicit assertions of Patroclus and the witnesses, but it was demonstrated likewise by the following circumstance; to those who reprehended him for having married Felicitas (as bringing disgrace to his family and as reducing his already scanty funds), Patroclus used to, as it were, defend himself, by mentioning the shameful condition which had been placed to the marriage contract, as if that had been the *entire reason* which sustained the marriage itself (". . . quasi ea esset *tota ratio* quae matrimonium ipsum sustineret"). The reasons which had deterred Patroclus from contracting marriage with Felicitas were based on Felicitas' shameful morals and upon the difference in social status between her and Patroclus. Hence the marriage itself and especially having children of such a marriage represented a disgrace to Patroclus' family. Moral or social considerations of such a nature pointed to the simple, absolute and perpetual exclusion of offspring from Patroclus' union with Felicitas. The marriage was declared invalid.[12]

Case No. 2—Nullity Declared

Margaret was already planning on contracting marriage with Aemilian when, having been examined by two doctors of the place where she was staying, she learned that she had such a serious heart

[11] *Ibid.*, 289 (n. 15).

[12] *Ibid.*, 292 (n. 19). "Adversus sententiam rursus provocatum est ad Apostolicam Signaturam, quae conformiter censuit in peculiari coetu Emorum Patrum, die 30 Iulii, 1924."—*Loc. cit.*

ailment that, in order to avoid being drawn into a proximate danger to her life, she had to either refrain absolutely from contracting marriage, or at least from having children. Since she did not want to marry Aemilian, she willingly took that occasion to free herself from his entreaties for marriage. She indicated to him that she did not wish to contract marriage except with the condition of preventing the conception of offspring. Aemilian rejected the condition entirely.

Later Margaret met Robert and immediately fell in love with him. She resolved to marry him. Through the intermediary of a third person, she took it upon herself to warn Robert regarding the state of her health and at the same time offered to marry him, with an added stipulation, however, against the procreation of offspring. Robert gave in to her wishes, and they contracted marriage in 1921. Scarcely eight months later, they separated. Margaret was granted a civil divorce and contracted a civil marriage with another man. Urged on by her conscience, however, she thought of obtaining freedom also in the eyes of the Church. Her petition for a declaration of nullity in 1922 resulted in favorable decisions from the tribunals of first and second instance. The defender of the bond of the tribunal of second instance nevertheless appealed the case to the Sacred Roman Rota. The judges of the Rota observed, however, that further investigations should be carried out, namely, the questioning of the two doctors who had examined Margaret and the questioning of Aemilian. After such investigations had been completed, the case was again proposed to the Rota for a decision.[18]

Although Margaret and Robert differed in their statements as to the time before marriage when the *sine qua non* condition of preventing the conception of offspring had been placed, the judges of the Rota thought that there could be no doubt that the parties actually entered the marriage contract with the condition of preventing the conception of offspring. The parties added that, at various times (also during the days which immediately preceded the marriage), they concerned themselves with the question of what means might be used to prevent the conception of offspring, and that they procured means to prevent conception. Robert stated that Margaret

[18] S.R.R., *Nullitatis Matrimonii,* 4 maii. 1927, coram R.P.D. Iulio Grazioli, dec. XX—*Decisiones,* XIX (1927), 161 ff.

and her mother bought preservatives for his use, and showed them to him eight days before the marriage, and that he found them placed on the night table the evening of the marriage. Both of the parties likewise asserted that they never receded from their agreement to prevent conception.

The two doctors who had been consulted by Margaret before the marriage testified that, as a matter of fact, they did examine Margaret before her engagement, and that they found that she was afflicted so seriously with a heart ailment that they warned her that the birth of a child could be dangerous for her ("Qu'une maternité pourrait être dangereuse pour ellé"). Aemilian stated (outside of judicial proceedings; however) that the proposed marriage between himself and Margaret did not take place because he was unwilling to approve of the condition of having no children, with which she wished to enter the contract. Almost all of the witnesses gave testimony from personal knowledge of that which was the foundation of the whole case, i. e., that Margaret placed the condition of preventing the conception of offspring and that Robert accepted that condition. Two of the witnesses stated explicitly that Margaret and her mother placed the condition in question as a *sine qua non* condition for the marriage. Witnesses also testified to the fact that the parties concerned persevered in adhering to that condition up until the time of the marriage and also after the celebration of the marriage.

The fact that Margaret, scarcely having obtained a civil divorce, entered a civil marriage with another man, might seem to indicate that she was not to be believed in her contention that she placed the condition of preventing conception to her first marriage lest the birth of a child might place her in a proximate danger to her life (". . . ne mater effecta in proximo vitae periculo constitueretur"). There was the fact, however, that the two doctors who had examined Margaret before her marriage to Robert had asserted under oath that she was in such a state of health due to a heart ailment, that the birth of a child could be dangerous for her. In referring to these facts, the Rota made the following observation:

> . . . obiective saltem loquendo denegari nequit, legitimam adfuisse causam, ob quam Margarita debuisset non quidem matrimonium inire cum conditione devitandi prolem, sed a matrimonio

> contrahendo omnino se abstinere, prouti reapse duo medici Bruno et Felicianus eidem se dixisse declararunt. Aliter proinde explicanda agendi ratio Margaritae videtur, quod nempe ipsa, temporis progressu ex una parte experientia edocta prioris coniugii, haud utile putaverit matrimonium iterum inire sub conditione prolem devitandi, et ex altera minoris fecerit periculum, de quo loquuti sunt ei medici, humanae quippe naturae consentaneum est, pericula quae praevidentur magis tunc metuere, cum primo mentem percellunt, quam postea.[14]

The Rota declared the marriage invalid.[15]

Case No. 3—Nullity Declared

Marcella married Stephen in 1911. In 1913, they moved from France to America, and their married life seemed to have been peaceful in both places. After their return to France, when Stephen had been called into military service in 1914, an aversion on the part of Stephen with regard to his wife manifested itself, and became more serious day by day. They separated in 1916. At Marcella's insistence, the separation was sanctioned in 1918, and at Stephen's insistence, the separation became a decree of divorce after the lapse of three years. When Stephen attempted a civil marriage in 1923, Marcella, who had learned only then that a declaration of nullity could be obtained, petitioned the ecclesiastical tribunal for a declaration of nullity on the grounds that, when entering the marriage contract, she had harbored an intention or condition contrary to the boon of offspring. The decision in 1925 was in favor of the validity of the marriage. Marcella appealed to the Sacred Roman Rota.[16]

Marcella asserted that, before the marriage, she had expressed her will to not have children and that Stephen had accepted the condition immediately and without any discussion. She added that she had told her two sisters, her two sisters-in-law and her nursemaid about the conversation with Stephen and about the condition in question. Stephen asserted that when he proposed to Marcella, she said that if her family consented, she would accept his proposal, but with

[14] *Ibid.*, 168 (n. 12).

[15] *Ibid.*, 169 (n. 13). "Sententia facta est exsecutiva."—*Loc. cit.*

[16] S.R.R., *Nullitatis Matrimonii*, 7 iul. 1926, coram R.P.D. Ubaldo Mannucci, dec. XXVIII—*Decisiones*, XVIII (1927), 221 ff.

the formal condition that there would be no children. He added that he gave in to her demand immediately. The Rota accepted the testimonies of the witnesses mentioned by Marcella as truthfully spoken, and noted that there was no doubt that the preventing of the conception of offspring had been proposed between the parties and that a promise had been made in return with regard to the proposal.

There was no direct proof, however, that the proposal in question had been based on a true *sine qua non* condition. For, according to the assertions of the parties themselves, Stephen had given in to Marcella's demand immediately. Hence, there had been no reference to the hypothesis, "if Stephen had not accepted." Stephen had accepted Marcella's proposal, but he likewise had asserted that if Marcella had desired to have children, he would have married her anyhow. The assertions of Marcella and a few of the witnesses which did refer to a *sina qua non* condition were considered by the Rota as lacking probative value. Indirect proof of a *sine qua non* condition, however, was deduced sufficiently from the fact that Marcella had intended to exclude the procreation of offspring absolutely and always. This was indicated, first of all, by the vain and evil reasons for excluding the boon of offspring as stated by Marcella: that children were the cause of disagreements in the home; that she wished to conserve her physical qualities, fearing that motherhood would deform her; that, in accordance with her false view of life (she considered life as evil), she considered it a shame to give existence to another; that she shrunk from the pains of childbirth.

Stephen likewise mentioned that men often leave their women after childbirth, because they have not the same physical admiration for them. Each of the witnesses (Marcella's nursemaid, her sister-in-law and her sister) also referred to one or more of the reasons which Marcella had mentioned. Since those reasons or motives were, of themselves, perpetual, it was easy to understand why the witnesses who had heard Marcella mention those reasons, had pointed out that she had intended to exclude the procreation of offspring always and absolutely. This was indicated also by Marcella's great tenacity and perseverance in manifesting her intention to Stephen and in demanding an altogether secure promise from him (". . . cui, velut 'lex coniugii' ipse post matrimonium teneretur, ***restrictis*** itaque iuribus quae sunt contractus obiectum: . . ."). The witnesses confirmed what the parties themselves indicated in their assertions with regard to their perseverance in adhering to their agreement up to the time of the marriage. They had not revoked the condition before the marriage. This was confirmed again by the disgraceful manner in which both Marcella and Stephen (perhaps at Marcella's suggestion) had informed their mothers, after the marriage, of their view regarding children in marriage. Formerly, they had carefully hidden their intention from their mothers, lest the affair may have been broken up immediately. The Rota made the following concluding remarks:

> Itaque mulier quae tantam aversionem fovet in prolem tamquam sibi abominandam, cum in uxorem petita viro ante omnia suam voluntatem de re pandit, eumque promissione obstringit, cum, durantibus sponsalibus, iterum atque iterum suam pravam intentionem manifestat, saepiusque factam promissionem viro in mentem revocat, cum post matrimonium *legem* coniugio impositam urget seque a viro edocendam curat, ut, mediis etiam turpibus, quae antea se ignorasse obtendit, hunc *finem* obtineat, dicenda prorsus est *finem* matrimonii primarium exclusisse, *iura* ad rem marito tradere noluisse, deque his conditionem sine qua non consensui suo apposuisse, quo, vel nescia, matrimonii valorem penitus sustulit.[17]

The marriage was declared invalid.[18]

In 1927, the case was reviewed by another panel of the Sacred Roman Rota.[19] In a review of the principles involved in the case, due stress was concentrated on the fact that, even though the *use* of the marriage right may have been taken away by an agreement and *perpetually*, the marriage is not invalid unless the obligation itself or the right to conjugal acts has been excluded in a positive manner.[20]

[17] *Ibid.*, 227 f. (n. 11).

[18] *Ibid.*, 228 (n. 12).

[19] S.R.R., *Nullitatis Matrimonii*, 5 dec. 1927, coram R.P.D. Francisco Parrillo, dec. LV—*Decisiones*, XIX (1927), 497 ff.

[20] *Ibid.*, 501 (n. 7). The text was cited in Chapter II of this study (cf. p. 97). Immediately following this text, the Rota made the following observation in regard to an expression which had appeared in the former review of

It was the opinion of the judges who reviewed the case as the tribunal of third instance, that the acts of the case furnished sufficient evidence that Marcella had placed a *sine qua non* condition (i. e., to not have children), which, by Stephen's acceptance, had been reduced to a pact or agreement. It was observed, furthermore, that the tribunal of former instance justly had maintained that the acts of the case did not furnish *direct* evidence that Marcella had placed her condition as a *sine qua non* condition. The acts of the case did furnish evidence that there was an agreement between Marcella and Stephen. This fact, joined to the fact that the agreement was absolute and that it had retained its force at the time of the exchange of matrimonial consent, justified the presumption that, at least on the part of Marcella, the condition had been placed as a *sine qua non* condition.

The Rota admitted that more than sufficient evidence that the condition as placed by Marcella was an absolute condition, and that it had retained its force at the time of the marriage, was furnished by the fact that the motives which had led Marcella to prevent the conception of offspring were motives which, subjectively considered, made the condition absolute and limitless. It was noted, likewise, that the agreement which the parties had entered into before the marriage had been recalled to mind more than once during the days which preceded the wedding day, and also after the marriage had been contracted. The concluding remarks concerning the case were stated as follows:

the case by another panel of the Rota: "Ex his patet, minus recte videri, quae appellata sententia docet circa viam indirectam ad deducendum conditionem vel propositum exclusivisse ipsum ius ad prolem, nempe, '*si exercitium iuris absolute* et in perpetuum excludatur, quia practice non intelligitur vera traditio iuris, cuius nullus debeat esse actus'. Praeter enim modo dicta, conditioni turpi contra bonum prolis, aptius distinctio congruit inter obligationem et huius implementum, vel obligationem et propositum peccandi, quod utique, *iuxta omnes,* stare potest cum vero coniugio. Conditio autem vel propositum, etsi in pactum deductum, tunc solum praesumptionem favore matrimonii excludit, iuxta dicta, cum absolute et absque temporis limitatione fuerit elicitum; secus contraria militat praesumptio de simplici matrimonii abusu, . . ."—*Ibid.,* 501 f. (n. 8).

Diximus autem, quod saltem ex Marcellae parte conditio revera fuit *sine qua non,* nam Stephanus aperte fassus est, se morem sponsae suae gessisse in conditione ab ea posita acceptanda, paratus contrarium velle si illa voluisset. . . . Sed id non officit quominus habeatur pactum seu conventio matrimonii substantiae repugnans, et consequenter praesumptio, quod mutua iura fuerint restricta: sufficit enim, quod unus conditione vel positiva voluntate aliquod substantiale bonum excludat, ut consensus nullitas habeatur, nam matrimonium duorum voluntate regitur; acceptatio autem alterius efficit, quod conditio vel voluntas in pactum seu conventionem convertatur, et exinde praesumptio matrimonio favens submoveatur. Ad cuius effectum satis est, quod alter acceptet, nec requiritur repromissio, ut in sponsalibus, et generatim in contractibus onerosis, nam acceptatio, vel passiva, satis est ad mutua iura obligationesque determinanda.[21]

The decision confirmed the previous decision of the Rota which was in favor of the nullity of the marriage.[22]

Case No. 4—Nullity Declared

Domitilla fell in love with Alfred, her music teacher. In an effort to prevent her from marrying him, Domitilla's parents sent her to Europe. Five years after their engagement, Domitilla, having returned from Europe and having overcome the opposition of her parents, contracted marriage with Alfred in 1918. Less than five years later, they separated, and Domitilla petitioned the ecclesiastical tribunal for a declaration of nullity on the grounds that Alfred, in entering the marriage contract, had excluded the procreation of offspring, and that he had rejected the sacramental dignity of marriage. In its decision in 1926, however, the tribunal upheld the validity of the marriage. The case was appealed to the Sacred Roman Rota.[23]

Alfred had been imbued with the principles of the philosophy of Nietzsche. Although he had been baptized, he denied the existence of God, he practiced no religion, and he considered marriage as dissoluble and as a mere formality to avoid social annoyances. He re-

[21] *Ibid.,* 505 (n. 16).

[22] *Ibid.,* 506 (n. 18). "Sententia facta est exsecutiva."—*Loc. cit.*

[23] S.R.R., *Nullitatis Matrimonii,* 31 iul. 1928, coram R.P.D. Iosepho Florczak, dec. XXXVI—*Decisiones,* XX (1928), 333 ff.

jected marriage as such inasmuch as, through marriage, life is propagated among men (which, according to the foul theory of Nietzsche, is something evil). He also rejected marriage for a private reason of his own, i. e., inasmuch as, on account of children, a man's cares and attention are diverted from the exercise of his musical art and from teaching his pupils. According to Domitilla's testimony, Alfred thought of their union merely as an *"artist's union,"* for she was a singer and they could have gone on the stage. There was ample testimony regarding his views on marriage and children. One witness testified that Alfred always said that to marry and to have children was the act of a fool.

While Domitilla was in Europe, Alfred tried in vain to dissuade her from marrying him. He said that, after her return from Europe, she nevertheless had reminded him of his promises, so that, as a man of honor, he had felt obliged to fulfill his promise and marry her. He added that, in entering into the marriage contract, he had placed conditions. Domitilla indicated that Alfred had permitted a religious marriage ceremony only because of a concession which he had made to her when she was sick, but that he had agreed to go through with the religious ceremony only on condition that such a ceremony would not oblige him to change his views, i. e., the total exclusion of children, and a divorce if all did not go according to his convenience. She added that she had accepted the marriage, hoping that, through her love, she might be able to change his ideas and his character. According to Domitilla's deposition, Alfred had expressed his condition regarding the exclusion of offspring approximately as follows: *"Il est bien entendu que nous n'aurons pas d'enfants et que tu n'en demanderas pas, et cela pour toujours."* [24] Alfred asserted that he had given a full and free consent to the marriage *on condition that there would be no children* (*". . . à condition que je n'aie pas d'enfants"*), and that he would not have married without that condition.

From the testimonies of the witnesses, it was clear that Alfred had not merely been imbued with a theoretical error contrary to the procreation of offspring but that, in consequence of such an error, he had manifested a clear and positive intention of excluding the

[24] *Ibid.*, 337 (n. 5).

marriage right itself with reference to the procreation of offspring ("... positivam voluntatem ... excludendi omne ius in ordine ad filios generandos, ..."), so that in his case, not only the use of the marriage right had been excluded [with reference to the procreation of offspring], but the obligation itself. With his perverse ideas, it seemed that he possessed such a strong will in the matter, that he could not be induced by any means to use the marriage right in the proper manner. When he was asked what he would have done if his wife had conceived a child, he answered simply that he would have made her induce an abortion. Both Domitilla and Alfred asserted that they never had performed the conjugal act in a complete manner. Domitilla asserted that Alfred had not only used means to prevent the conception of offspring, but that he had forced her to do likewise.

The judges of the Rota who reviewed the case were of the opinion that the case did not furnish evidence that Alfred had placed the stipulation to prevent the conception of offspring as a true condition:

> Infrascripti Patres de turno tamen censuerunt non constare in casu de propria conditione consensui matrimoniali adiecta, cui ipse consensus alligatus fuisset. Quamvis enim Alaphridus testetur, se hanc conditionem posuisse, cum spe, ne acceptaretur, ... et quamvis Domitilla declaret, sua ex parte, se illam specie tenus acceptasse, cum spe, ne ad ipsam implendam obligaretur ..., tamen hac apparenti Domitillae acceptatione efficiebatur, ut in momento matrimonii Alaphridi mens in consentiendo non esset identica cum momento quo conditionem proponebat: unde deest quaelibet probatio Alaphridum tempore matrimonii suum consensum alligasse appositae conditioni.[25]

The case furnished sufficient evidence, however, that Alfred had manifested and had persevered in a positive intention to exclude the marriage right itself with regard to the boon of offspring (can. 1086, § 2). The Rota declared the marriage invalid.[26]

In the appeal instance of the same case in 1929, however, another

[25] *Ibid.,* 341 (n. 9).

[26] *Ibid.,* 341 (n. 10).

panel of the Sacred Roman Rota stated that there was sufficient evidence not only that Alfred had intended to exclude the procreation of offspring, but that he had introduced that intention into the marriage contract itself as a true condition.

> Omnibus igitur attentis, visum est PP. satis constare non tantum in genere de voluntate Alaphridi matrimonium contrahentis bono prolis contraria, sed in specie de eadem voluntate in pactum deducta, seu de matrimonio sub huiusmodi conditione contracto. . . . Neque obstare videtur ratio qua appellata sententia appositam consensui matrimoniali conditionem non admisit in casu, quod nempe "in momento matrimonii Alaphridi mens in consentiendo non esset identica cum momento quo conditionem proponebat" cum spe vitandi nuptias, quae in irritum cessit propter assensum Domitillae. Praesumendum enim est, cum contrarium non constet, voluntatem Alaphridi non fuisse mutatam a momento propositae conditionis ad celebratas nuptias.[27]

The marriage was declared invalid.[28]

[27] S.R.R., *Nullitatis Matrimonii,* 9 aug. 1929, coram Rmo P.D. Maximo Massimi, Decano, dec. L, n. 10—*Decisiones,* XXI (1929), 423.

[28] *Ibid.,* 424 (n. 12). "Sententia facta est exsecutiva."—*Loc. cit.* There were five other cases which furnished sufficient evidence of a pact contrary to the boon of offspring and of an underlying *sine qua non* condition. They were the following: (1) S.R.R., *Nullitatis Matrimonii,* 10 maii. 1916, coram Rmo P.D. Guilelmo Sebastianelli, Decano, dec. XIII—*Decisiones,* VIII (1916), 139 ff. (second instance—nullity declared—"Sententia facta est exsecutiva."); (2) 31 mart. 1922, coram Rmo P.D. Ioanne Prior, Decano, dec. X—*Decisiones,* XIV (1922), 83 ff. (second instance—nullity declared)—"Sententia facta est exsecutiva."); (3) 10 iun. 1922, coram Rmo P.D. Ioanne Prior, Decano, dec. XVIII—*Decisiones,* XIV (1922), 179 (second instance—nullity declared—"Sententia facta est exsecutiva."); (4) 10 febr. 1926, coram R.P.D. Andrea Jullien, dec. V—*Decisiones,* XVIII (1926), 22 ff. (first instance—nullity declared); 12 aug. 1926, coram R.P.D. Francisco Solieri, dec. XLII—*Decisiones,* XVIII (1926), 331 ff. (second instance—validity upheld); 9 maii. 1928, coram Rmo P.D. Maximo Massimi, Decano, dec. XVIII—*Decisiones,* XX (1928), 177 ff. (third instance—nullity declared—"Sententia facta est exsecutiva."); (5) 5 iun. 1926, coram R.P.D. Iosepho Florczak, dec. XXIV—*Decisiones,* XVIII (1926), 190 ff. (first instance—nullity declared); 28 nov. 1928, coram R.P.D. Iulio Grazioli, dec. LIII—*Decisiones,* XX (1928), 466 ff. (second instance—nullity declared—"Sententia facta est exsecutiva.").

(2) *Evidence of a Pact and of an Underlying Positive Intention* (Can. 1086, § 2)

Since the final decision in the following case was issued by the Sacred Tribunal of the Apostolic Signatura, it is not possible to state precisely what arguments formed the basis for the declaration of nullity as issued by that supreme tribunal. It seems, however, that the arguments upon which the Apostolic Signatura based its decision would have been similar to the arguments which formed the basis for a declaration of nullity in the same case by one panel of the Sacred Roman Rota (Cf. *infra*). Although the case involved an agreement or pact to exclude the procreation of offspring temporarily, the one decision of the Rota which favored the nullity of the marriage was based on evidence that the marriage right had been excluded altogether, and not merely for the period as stipulated in the agreement.

Case No. 5—Nullity Declared

In 1900, Francis, a wealthy Hollander of about thirty years of age proposed to Elisabeth, a Belgian woman of moderate means. Since Elisabeth's parents were dead and she had been living with one or the other of her married sisters or with a certain Julius B., she accepted Francis' proposal of marriage immediately. About eight days before the wedding day, however, she unexpectedly changed her mind about marrying Francis, and informed the family of Francis of her decision. By more or less specious arguments the mother of Francis persuaded Elisabeth to go through with the marriage. The marriage took place in 1901. Due to disagreements in their conjugal life Elisabeth left the home of her husband five months after the marriage had been contracted. The following year (1902) she obtained a civil divorce. Both Francis and Elisabeth contracted a second marriage. Ten years after his marriage to Elisabeth Francis requested the Holy See for a dispensation from the marriage. He thought that because of the perverse manner in which conjugal relations with Elisabeth had taken place the marriage had not been consummated.

The Sacred Congregation for the Discipline of the Sacraments accepted the case after the process had been drawn up both on the score of non-consummation and on the score of the alleged defective consent on the part of Elisabeth. In 1913 the same congregation denied the dispensation which Francis had requested but commissioned the bishop of the diocese in question to settle the case under the aspect of nullity. In 1914 the ecclesiastical judge who had been delegated by the bishop to draw up the process and decide the case issued a decision in favor of the validity of the marriage. Through the Sacred Congregation for the Discipline of the Sacraments the case was then sent to the Sacred Roman Rota. Before the case was submitted to the Rota for a decision, however, new acts of the case had been gathered, and Elisabeth had been heard (since her place of domicile was unknown at the time when the case was investigated for the first time, she had not been heard previously).[29]

Francis said that fourteen days before the marriage Elisabeth had spoken of having children as if to say that it depended upon her happiness in married life and hence, as if she excluded the conception of offspring for the first period of their marriage. Later, however, after the acts had been made public, and at the instigation of his advocate, he spoke much differently of Elisabeth's proposal, i.e. he said that already before the marriage Elisabeth had told him categorically that she wished not to have children, and that otherwise she would not go through with the marriage. He added that he had acquiesced to her design. Elisabeth asserted that they had agreed before the marriage to not have children, at least for a time, but that there never had been question of renouncing the strict and radical right to procreate children. She added that no period had been determined with regard to the procreation of children, but that she had wished to wait until she had felt a true love for her husband. In two letters which she had written to Francis after the marriage, however (one in 1901 and the other in 1913), she had stated that in accepting Francis as her husband, she had the firm intention never to be his wife, and that she did not want any children. In the course of a new examination (as requested by Francis' advocate), she admitted the authenticity of the letters and attempted to translate her former disposition in the sense of the ideas as expressed in the letters.

[29] S.R.R., *Nullitatis Matrimonii,* 29 apr. 1922, coram R.P.D. Francisco Parrillo, dec. XIV—*Decisiones,* XIV (1922), 119 ff.

The testimonies of the witnesses, considered together, indicated that Elisabeth truly had married Francis with the evil proposal to abuse the marriage, lest children may have been born, and that the proposal had been limited to the first period of conjugal life either because she had not as yet appeared to love her husband, or, more likely, because she had wished not to have children right away. Especially Elisabeth's own assertions indicated, however, that she had not renounced the strict and radical right to procreate offspring. The Rota implied that in view of those clear assertions of Elisabeth her first deposition was to be accepted as the truth, and the subsequent investigation in the matter was to be set aside: ". . . nam si ille, cuius animus est indagandus, absque fraude vel fraudis suspicione fatetur aperte, se iuri radicali et stricto procreandi filios nuncium non misisse, ulteriore indagine seposita, ipsi credendum est; . . ."[80] Furthermore, as stated by one of the witnesses, a Redemptorist priest, Francis had understood Elisabeth's proposal with regard to the procreation of offspring in the sense that it appeared to him that he could hope that the matter would take a turn for the better later on. The Rota inferred that Francis would not have conceived such a hope if there had been question of the denial of the marriage right.

It was likewise noted by the Rota that there was no adequate reason why the truth of Elisabeth's first deposition should be denied in favor of placing credence in the letters in question. First of all, the fact that the letters had been shown without the customary envelope (bearing the postmark) gave rise to a considerable suspicion that they had been written later than was claimed. The first letter (1901) allegedly had been written a few days after Elisabeth had deserted Francis, and at a time when she already had been planning on obtaining a divorce by bringing him before the civil judge and accusing him of adultery. It appeared scarcely credible that she would have wished, at that time, to ascribe the unhappy ending of the marriage to herself, on account of her simulated consent to the marriage. There were also reasons for looking upon the other letter (1913) with very great suspicion. Furthermore, the letters pointed rather to total simulation, which was not at issue in the case. Finally, in the letters, Elisabeth had indicated the motive for her

[80] *Ibid.*, 128 (n. 26).

simulation of consent by saying that she had married Francis because of the repeated insistence of her family, whereas the acts of the case indicated rather the contrary.

With the letters rejected and the first testimony of Elisabeth restored to its integrity, it was noted that the latter deposition of Francis (inasmuch as it contradicted his former deposition), was without value. There was no reliable testimony or indication to strengthen Francis' latter deposition (i.e. that Elisabeth had told him categorically before the marriage that she wished not to have children, and that otherwise she would not go through with the marriage). In fact, the first deposition of Francis was not only consistent with Elisabeth's statements (i.e. that they had agreed before the marriage to not have children at least for a time,—that she wished to wait until she had felt a true love for her husband), but it was confirmed by the testimonies of Julius and of the Redemptorist priest (Francis' advisor). With regard to the circumstantial evidence in the case, it may suffice to say that none of the circumstances which had been adduced as favoring Francis' latter contention (as stated above) were considered by the Rota as militating in favor of the invalidity of the marriage. The decision was in favor of the validity of the marriage.[31]

After another appeal, the case was examined by another panel of the Sacred Roman Rota.[32] It was admitted that there were serious arguments to indicate that Elisabeth did not have an intention to accept the obligations of marriage. As to her character and disposition, the acts of the case showed that she was a woman without religion and without shame. The letters which she had written to Francis were considered as constituting a very strong argument that Elisabeth had excluded the obligations of marriage. In one of those letters, she declared boldly as follows: "En vous acceptant comme époux, j'avais *la volonté ferme* de n'être jamais votre femme."[33] The Rota maintained that those words of Elisabeth, which had been written during the sixth month after the marriage, brought out the

[31] *Ibid.*, 132 (n. 34).

[32] S.R.R., *Nullitatis Matrimonii*, 14 mart. 1924, coram R.P.D. Raphaele Chimenti, dec. XIV—*Decisiones*, XVI (1924), 105 ff.

[33] *Ibid.*, 109 (n. 5).

true mind of Elisabeth when she contracted the marriage, so that they were to be believed also in the external forum. Between the time of the marriage and the date when she had written the letter in question, she was noted never to have acted as Francis' wife, not even on the wedding day. Her manner of acting on the wedding day and during the period of conjugal life with Francis indicated that she safely could be believed in her assertion that she had the firm will never to be Francis' wife.

The fact that Elisabeth had simulated her matrimonial consent with regard to the boon of offspring in particular was evident not only inasmuch as she had denied the conjugal act in a manner suitable for the procreation of offspring, but also inasmuch as she had proposed an agreement, which had been accepted by Francis (although dejectedly) to exclude the procreation of offspring at least during the first period of the marriage. The following observations were made by the Rota to explain why, in Elisabeth's case, the presumption stood in favor of the exclusion of the marriage right: (1) there was no doubt about her general intention contrary to the accepting of the obligations of marriage; (2) it was clear that the limitation as to the procreation of offspring (i.e. to not have children until she felt a true love for her husband) was only apparent and deceitful. It was a question of Elisabeth waiting for a feeling of love to arise towards Francis, and of finding happiness in the marriage. In view of her disposition, the Rota considered such things absurd: "Nam si amor exsulaverat a die matrimonii, in quo animi motus vehementiores sunt, quomodo sperari poterat ut in posterum esset obventurus?;"[84] (3) Elisabeth had indicated that the exclusion of offspring was but temporary only as a means of deceiving Francis, and of thereby enabling herself to continue her shameful conduct with her lover:

> . . . cum ius matrimoniale perpetuo concedendum sit, asseri potest Elisabeth hoc ius concessisse, quando in praesens illud viro suo denegavit, et in posterum in indefinitum et pro suo lubitu coarctavit? Potius dicatur Elisabeth obligationes suscipere noluisse, et cum ex alia parte non intenderet simplicem spem adimere Francisco, ea formula usam esse, qua et virum fallaci quadam spe deciperet, et suis inhonestis moribus provideret. Quod confir-

[84] *Ibid.,* 110 (n. 6).

> matur per illud *saltem* "au moins," quo Elisabeth tegebatur, cum semper opponere posset Francisco, sua iura petenti, reservationem illam. Duo igitur sibi praestitit Elisabeth, retinere scilicet amasium propter carnale opus, et simul habere Franciscum, qui opes suppeditaret et turpem eius agendi rationem umbraculo obtegeret.[85]

With regard to the first judicial deposition of Elisabeth, when she had stated that there never had been question of renouncing the radical and strict right to procreate children, the Rota made the following observations: (1) that deposition was outweighed by the statements and deeds of Elisabeth as considered above; (2) Elisabeth herself had revoked that deposition when she had stated that it was to be explained in the light of the ideas concerning marriage which she had expressed in her two letters to Francis; (3) Elisabeth's intention stood out more clearly when viewed in the light of certain statements and deeds (of Elisabeth) and the circumstances of the case as related by Francis and by the witnesses. The brother of Francis said that Elisabeth had told him personally that she considered children "ut *suburam,*" [86] and that she therefore rejected children altogether. The same witness added that Elisabeth did not love Francis, but rather despised him. The Rota noted likewise that, since the Redemptorist priest had stated that he had told Francis that there was some founded hope for a declaration of nullity, his words [i.e. the priest's] were not to be interpreted as referring only to the exclusion of the use of the marriage right. There were other testimonies in regard to Elisabeth's attitude towards Francis in conjugal life and with regard to her shameful relations with her lover. The decisions was a declaration of nullity.[87]

Again, the case was appealed to another panel of the Sacred Roman Rota.[88] It was noted that both Elisabeth and Francis had referred to the exclusion of the procreation of offspring during the first period of the marriage, and that the Redemptorist priest and

[85] *Ibid.*, 110 f. (n. 6).

[86] *Subura* was a street in Rome where prostitutes lived.

[87] *Ibid.*, 113 (n. 10).

[88] S.R.R., *Nullitatis Matrimonii,* 23 mart. 1925, coram R.P.D. Andrea Jullien, dec. XVIII—*Decisiones,* XVII (1925), 129 ff.

another witness had confirmed the statements of the parties. Since those assertions referred to the temporary exclusion of offspring, it was easier to apply the presumption that Elisabeth had not refused the marriage right. The argument as advanced by the tribunal of former instance with regard to Elisabeth's ulterior motives in proposing the temporary exclusion of offspring, was not accepted in the instance of the case which, at present, is under discussion:

> Neque ut evincatur intentio actoris, fas est eadem verba, tam manifesta, interpretari eo sensu, ut facit sententia appellata, quatenus limitatio posita fuerit nonnisi subdola, apparens ut excogitatio artificiosa, a muliere, quae revera iuris exclusionem in perpetuum intenderet. Elisabeth enim, quae firma voluntate perpetuo se coniunxit cum Francisco, huius contractus obligationes suscepit, quamquam eas statim adimplere noluit et iure matrimoniali abuti voluit, donec certa fieret de mutuo amore, quem ut impossibilem minime excludebat, et patet ex propria eius confessione.[39]

The Rota noted that the arguments as furnished by the circumstances of the case, by Elisabeth's letters to Francis, and by the depositions of Francis and of the witnesses as given in the suppletory investigation of the case, were not sufficient to overthrow the presumption whereby a person who contracts marriage seriously is presumed to accept the obligations of marriage. After having reviewed the various circumstances of the case, the Rota made the following statement:

> Siquidem intentio contrahentis desumenda est ex circumstantiis; verum ad declarandam matrimonii validitatem, satis non est ex circumstantiis aequivocis inferre generalem aliquam veri similitudinem, qua penitus non excludantur dubia contraria; sed iure meritoque requiritur ut moralis certitudo invaliditatis desumatur ex circumstantiis illis quae, habita ratione personarum et temporis, concordes sint et directe concludentissimeque cohaereant cum capite invaliditatis, seu in casu cum iuris exclusione positiva, et non tantum interpretativa.[40]

With regard to the letters which Elisabeth had written to Francis after the marriage, it was noted that the things asserted in those

[39] *Ibid.*, 135 f. (n. 6).
[40] *Ibid.*, 137 f. (n. 7).

letters did not agree with what Elisabeth had affirmed most clearly and under oath before the ecclesiastical judge, and that the latter assertions agreed fully with the depositions of Francis and of two witnesses. With regard to the depositions which had been given by Francis, his father and the Redemptorist priest in the suppletory investigation (". . . post primam instantiam peracto, . . ."), it was noted that both of the witnesses had asserted only what they had heard from Francis, and that their testimonies did not indicate that Elisabeth had placed her proposal contrary to the boon of offspring as a *sine qua non* condition. The Rota observed that, even in the supposition that Elisabeth had told Francis before the marriage that she excluded children altogether, and that she intended to contract marriage only with such a condition, the question would arise as to how such an absolute exclusion of the right to conjugal union could stand with her other clear and confirmed proposal to not have children only during the first period of the marriage. For her own words indicated that she had not excluded children absolutely for the future (" 'il n'avait jamais été question de renoncer au droit radical et strict de procréer des enfants',"). It was noted also that Elisabeth's conduct during the wedding trip did not militate against the validity of the marriage. The decision was in favor of the validity of the marriage.[41]

The case was proposed to the Sacred Tribunal of the Apostolic Signatura. On July 26, 1926, that tribunal issued a decision in favor of the nullity of the marriage.[42]

B. Cases Which Furnished No Evidence or only Insufficient Evidence of a Pact

The following cases have been divided into three groups: (1) those which furnished sufficient evidence of a *sine qua non* condition contrary to the boon of offspring and consequently resulted in a declaration of nullity, (2) those which furnished evidence of a positive intention to exclude the marriage right with reference to the boon of offspring and consequently resulted in a declaration of

[41] *Ibid.*, 141 (n. 11).
[42] *Loc. cit.*

nullity, and (3) those which did not furnish sufficient evidence either of a *sine qua non* condition or of a positive intention as explained above. The first two groups of cases demonstrate that a declaration of nullity is possible in cases which involve the exclusion of the boon of offspring, even though there is no evidence or insufficient evidence of a pact between the contracting parties with regard to the exclusion of the boon of offspring. The third group of cases demonstrates that intentions or conditions contrary to the boon of offspring, as alleged by the contracting parties, usually amount to a mere intention or proposal to *abuse* the marriage or to *neglect* the *fulfillment* of the corresponding essential obligation.

(1) *Insufficient Evidence of a Pact (if any), but Evidence of a* "sine qua non" *Condition (Can.* 1092, 2°)

Case No. 6—Nullity Declared

Alice, who already had reached the age of thirty, became engaged to René, a man of thirty-five. Although she wished to marry him, she broke the engagement when he made it clear to her, openly and without shame, that he did not wish ever to have children. Alice was eager to have children. Casimir, a relative of Alice, in an effort to promote the marriage of Alice and René, advised Alice to cast aside the intention or plan of René, since men often desist from their way of thinking after marriage, and comply with the wishes of the wife. With reliance on that hope, she contracted marriage with René in 1914. After some weeks, their marital life was interrupted by the war. During the war, they were together only at rare and brief intervals. Tired of the shameful behavior of René, who remained firm in his intention to prevent the conception of offspring and indulged in adulterous love-affairs, Alice obtained a civil divorce (1920), and impugned the validity of her marriage with René on the ground that a condition had been placed (to the marriage) to prevent the conception of offspring. The same year (1920), the tribunal declared the marriage invalid. The case was appealed to the Sacred Roman Rota.[48]

[48] S.R.R., *Nullitatis Matrimonii,* 4 aug. 1922, coram R.P.D. Raphaele Chimenti, dec. XXVII—*Decisiones,* XIV (1922), 252 ff.

René was unwilling to appear before the tribunal and was declared contumacious. There were letters which he had written to Alice, however, which manifested his mind in the matter under discussion, and which did not contradict the depositions of Alice and the witnesses. The evidence as furnished by the acts of the case easily proved that René had contracted marriage with the explicit intention of precluding the conception of offspring. The things which Alice related were proved by the testimonies of the witnesses. Six witnesses were mentioned as agreeing in their testimonies that René wished absolutely not to have children. A priest testified that René had not hesitated to tell Casimir that if he (René) saw his wife pregnant, he would say without hesitation that it was not on his account. In letters which he had sent to his wife after the marriage, he forcibly declared his contrary will with regard to the exclusion of offspring: "Pour la question des enfants, j'ai solutionné la question; il n'y a plus à revenir, rien . . . rien à faire. . . ."[44]

In order to determine whether René had wished to accept the obligation with regard to the procreation of offspring without, however, intending to fulfill the obligation, or whether he had rejected the obligation itself, the Rota noted, first of all, the immoral character of René. After having reviewed the testimonies of the witnesses with regard to the anti-religious character of René, his immoral behavior, his infidelity towards his wife and his interest in marriage with Alice because of her money, the Rota made the following observation:

> Iam vero attentis indole, educatione, dictis, gestis et animo quo nuptias contraxit, prolis generationi contrario, suasio in animo iudicis insinuatur, Renatum parvi pendisse dignitatem Sacramenti matrimonii et obligationes et onera substantialia reiecisse praesertim relate ad prolis bonum.[45]

Witnesses likewise testified with regard to René's tenacity in his ideas. One witness commented on the seriousness with which René had spoken to him concerning his views on marriage and children. The Rota noted that if the engagement had been broken off because of

[44] *Ibid.*, 255 (n. 5).
[45] *Ibid.*, 256 (n. 6).

René's intention contrary to the procreation of offspring, that fact furnished an argument to indicate the prevailing intention of René, who was prepared to put off the marriage altogether rather than reform his intention. He not only intended to prevent the conception of offspring, but he was convinced, in principle, that offspring should be excluded in marriage.

René had resisted the admonitions of relatives and the pleadings and tears of Alice, and remained firm in his intention to prevent the conception of offspring. The Rota made the following remark:

> Iam vero ex firmitate propositi arguitur ad praevalentiam voluntatis, . . . Non agitur ergo in casu, de proposito abutendi matrimonio, sed de voluntate positiva et expressa respuendi obligationem substantialem generationis prolis contrariam turpissimae agendi rationi Renati.[46]

The fact that René's intention contrary to the boon of offspring was not limited, but absolute and extended to the entire period of life, was considered as an indication that the intention to preclude the procreation of offspring prevailed over the intention to contract a true marriage, and hence an indication that René had intended to exclude the marriage right itself. The Rota declared the marriage invalid.[47]

Case No. 7—Nullity Declared

After almost four years of conjugal life, the marriage of Ida and Maevius ended in a civil divorce in 1909. In 1921, Ida petitioned the ecclesiastical tribunal for a declaration of nullity on three scores: (1) that, before marriage, Maevius had placed a condition contrary to the boon of offspring; (2) that she had consented to the marriage under the duress of fear; (3) that she had entered the marriage contract with a condition contrary to the boon of conjugal fidelity and contrary to the boon of sacramental stability. The declaration of nullity, issued in 1922, was based only on the first of the three scores of nullity as alleged by Ida. The case was appealed to the Sacred Roman Rota.[48]

[46] *Ibid.*, 257 f. (n. 8).

[47] *Ibid.*, 258 (n. 9). "Sententia facta est exsecutiva."—*Loc. cit.*

[48] S.R.R., *Nullitatis Matrimonii,* 13 febr. 1925, coram. R.P.D. Francisco Solieri, dec. X—*Decisiones,* XVII (1925), 74 ff.

The acts of the case indicated that both the pretended aversion of Ida to the marriage with Maevius, as well as her conditions contrary to the boon of conjugal fidelity and the boon of sacramental stability, had been merely hypothetical, and that the necessary supposition or basis for such an aversion and such contrary conditions had been the proposal or condition contrary to the boon of offspring which Maevius had added to the marriage contract. The assertions of both of the parties with regard to Maevius' condition contrary to the boon of offspring were explicit. Authenticated portions of letters which Ida had written to Maevius a little before the marriage also stood out in the acts of the case; letters which indicated that Maevius, *in principle,* always had refused to consent to have a child, that he had spoken of an abortion if, *despite his precautions,* a child was conceived, and that Ida was eager to have children. Letters which Maevius had written to Ida before the marriage were not among the acts of the case, but the contents of those letters were indicated, under oath, by the pastor to whom Ida had given them. The pastor had judged that the letters contained nothing to establish a matrimonial case on the score of force and fear, and had advised Ida to burn them. He testified that Maevius had left no doubt in those letters as to his express will to not have children. Witnesses confirmed the same view with regard to Maevius' attitude concerning the procreation of offspring.

The testimonies, as furnished in the acts of the case, made it clear that Maevius had excluded offspring altogether, "in principle," that is, the obligation itself; and that he had excluded them "eternally," that is, perpetually, absolutely, not hypothetically. The judges of the Rota who reviewed the case were of the opinion that the acts of the case furnished abundant evidence that Maevius had placed a true condition to prevent the conception of offspring, a condition without which he would not have contracted the marriage. Hence it was clear that he had rejected entirely from his consent not only the use of the right, but the right itself ("ius omne"), which is the object of the marriage contract. This was confirmed by the facts which indicated how firmly Maevius had observed and insisted upon his proposal or pact after the marriage had been contracted. Ida asserted that when, to Maevius' surprise, she had conceived a child, he had endeavored to bring about an abortion, and that after she had conceived a second time, she left Maevius (and went to live with her parents) for fear of assaults, injuries and rude deeds on his part. He added that when Ida had conceived a second time, he had taken legal action to disavow that he was the father of the child. Conception occurred in both instances because Ida had failed to take certain post-coital lotions which Maevius had prescribed for her. Reliable witnesses confirmed the assertions of both Ida and Maevius. The evil intention of Maevius to exclude offspring had remained the same after the marriage as it had been from the beginning; an intention which was incompatible with true matrimonial consent. The Rota declared the marriage invalid.[49]

(2) *Insufficient Evidence of a Pact (if any), but Evidence of a Positive Intention (Can.* 1086, § 2)

Case No. 8—Nullity Declared

Inez married Roman in 1912. They lived together up until the beginning of the great war, and occasionally, during the war. No children were born of the union. After the war, due to the perverted morals of Roman, the marriage resulted first in a separation, and then in a civil divorce (1924). Then Inez went to the ecclesiastical tribunal with the contention that the marriage was invalid inasmuch as both she and Roman had, by a positive act of the will, excluded all right to the conjugal act. The decision of the tribunal, issued

[49] *Ibid.*, 89 (n. 9). "Sententia facta est exsecutiva."—*Loc. cit.* There were two other cases which did not involve a pact to exclude the boon of offspring, but which furnished sufficient evidence of a *sine qua non* condition to that effect on the part of one of the contracting parties. They were the following: (1) S.R.R., *Nullitatis Matrimonii,* 7 febr. 1914, coram R.P.D. Guilelmo Sebastianelli, dec. V—*Decisiones,* VI (1914), 56 ff. (second instance—nullity declared—"Sententia facta est exsecutiva."); (2) 10 dec. 1914, coram R.P.D. Ioanne Prior, dec. XXXIII—*Decisiones,* VI (1914), 339 ff. (second instance—validity upheld); 31 oct. 1919, coram R.P.D. Aloisio Sincero, dec. XVII—*Decisiones,* XI (1919), 145 ff. (third instance—nullity declared—"Sententia facta est exsecutiva.").

in 1926, was in favor of the validity of the marriage. The case was appealed to the Sacred Roman Rota.[50]

Inez related that Roman had harbored an intention contrary to the boon of offspring, which he had manifested to her at the time of their engagement, and that he had retained that intention firmly and had remained faithful to the same during the entire period of their conjugal life. This was confirmed by the testimonies of a sister of Inez, a sister of Roman and three other witnesses. Inez stated that at first, when Roman had manifested his contrary intention to her, she had intended otherwise, and had hoped that he would change his deliberate purpose later on. Later, according to Inez's own assertion, she had been so frightened on the occasion of the death of an intimate friend in childbirth, that she adhered to the intention of Roman and entered marriage with that intention. She added that later on, a few months after the marriage, when she had heard from her sister-in-law that it was wrong to prevent the conception of offspring, she changed her mind and wished to observe the laws of Christian morality, but that her husband never had wished to do so. The witnesses likewise confirmed those assertions of Inez.

Roman, however, contradicted Inez openly. He stated that he had meant to give to his wife all of the rights of a Christian spouse, and that there never had been question of doing anything whatsoever to prevent the birth and the procreation of children. The Rota considered his assertions as lies, for they were inconsistent with the testimonies of trustworthy witnesses (among them his own sister). He also had sent a letter to Inez before he had made the assertions in question. In that letter, he had offered to co-operate with her in obtaining a declaration of nullity: "Si vous voulez m'accorder une entrevue . . . je vous ferai connaître une procédure canonique présentant toutes les chances d'aboutir le plus rapidement qu'il est possible." [51] Such a letter necessarily rendered his deposition gravely suspicious. In view of such facts, the judges of the Rota who examined the case maintained that, since the parties (due to their intention contrary to the boon of offspring) had not wished to accept

[50] S.R.R., *Nullitatis Matrimonii,* 9 iul. 1927, coram Rmo P.D. Maximo Massimi, Decano, dec. XXXV—*Decisiones,* XIX (1927), 299 ff.

[51] *Ibid.,* 303 (n. 8).

the necessary obligations with regard to the boon of offspring, matrimonial consent had been lacking in the marriage. All of the accessory circumstances of the case indicated that Roman had intended to exclude the obligation itself with regard to the boon of offspring: he had intended to preclude the conception of offspring without any limitation ("simpliciter"); being a tenacious person, he never had withdrawn his contrary intention, nor had he taken any account of Inez' change of mind in the matter. The fact that he was alien to religion, and that he had entered into the marriage contract out of a desire for money rather than with the proper intention, likewise made it more easily admissible that he had simulated his matrimonial consent.

The fact that Inez praiseworthily had revoked her contrary intention later on, indicated that she was not tenacious in her intention. Furthermore, she was not without religion and a love for her husband. Nevertheless, her own words indicated that she had entered into the marriage contract with a simple intention contrary to the boon of offspring [simple, i.e. without any limitation] i.e. her words indicated that, since the death of her friend, she had excluded the procreation of offspring without any limitation. Hence the first of the arguments which had been adduced to prove that Roman had excluded the obligation itself with reference to the boon of offspring applied to Inez as well. The Rota added the following significant observation:

> Cum vero sponsalium tempore intentioni viri bono prolis contrariae accesserit simul mulieris intentio, factus est utriusque in idem placitum consensus. Atqui cum res deducitur in pactum, grave argumentum exsistit pro exclusione obligationis. Pacto enim solent mutua iura restringi.[52]

The marriage was declared invalid.[53]

The case was reviewed by another panel of the Sacred Roman Rota in 1928.[54] It was noted that the acts of the case failed to

[52] *Ibid.*, 304 (n. 9).

[53] *Ibid.*, 304 (n. 10).

[54] S.R.R., *Nullitatis Matrimonii,* 11 febr. 1928, coram R.P.D. Francisco Guglielmi, dec. V—*Decisiones,* XX (1928), 48 ff.

furnish sufficient evidence that the intention of the parties regarding the preventing of the conception of offspring had been either placed as a true condition or reduced to a pact. It was admitted, however, that each of the parties, by a positive act of the will, had excluded the marriage right itself with reference to the procreation of offspring:

> . . . Testes autem de adiecta conditione nihil se scire aiunt; . . . Nec de propria dicta pactione testes expresse locuti sunt, sed nonnisi potius de proposito in una et altera parte, scilicet de uniformi sponsorum voluntate vitandi prolem.
>
> Verum de positiva contrahentium intentione se non obligandi, seu positive excludendi non tantummodo iuris exercitium, sed omne ius ad coniugalem actum, ob quam intentionem, iuxta can. 1086, §2, nullum est matrimonium, ex perpensis omnibus adiunctis constare dixerunt Patres.[55]

The marriage was declared invalid.[56]

Case No. 9—Nullity Declared

In order to show his appreciation to Elvira for her kindness to him in time of sickness, Cassian promised her that if he recovered, he would marry her. In time, however, his former love for her grew cold and he regretted his promise. In 1917, he nevertheless kept his promise and married her. Immediately after the marriage he treated Elvira in such a manner that she doubted whether he had intended seriously to marry her. During the few times that they lived together, Cassian practiced onanism. After having tried in vain to persuade him to give up the practice of onanism, Elvira left him (1920). Later, having heard that the marriage might be invalid, she petitioned the ecclesiastical tribunal for a declaration of nullity (1926), and received a favorable decision in 1927. The Rota examined the case for the first time in 1930. Since, however, no witness from the city where the marriage took place had been heard, the Rota postponed the deciding of the case until the acts of the case

[55] *Ibid.*, 54 (n. 11).

[56] *Ibid.*, 56 (n. 16). "Sententia facta est exsecutiva."—*Loc. cit.*

had been completed in accordance with its instruction. When this had been done, the Rota reviewed the case.[57]

Certain circumstances of the case lent strong support to Elvira's contention that Cassian had married her with the intention of preventing the conception of offspring altogether. First of all, there was the fact that Cassian had not even wished ever to establish a life in common with Elvira. This was indicated by the assertions of the parties themselves and by the testimonies of witnesses. Elvira's contention likewise was supported by the fact that she had declared that she was prepared to live with Cassian, provided that he would withdraw his intention to prevent the conception of offspring. Finally, there was positive evidence that Cassian married Elvira with the intention of neither having children by her nor of living with her. This was indicated not only by his manner of acting (as pointed out by Elvira), but also by his own assertions, whereby he also indicated reasons for his manner of acting. It was clear from his assertions that he did not love Elvira, but that he married her only to keep his promise, and hence wanted no children of his union with her. This was confirmed by the testimonies of witnesses who heard him express his views to this effect before his marriage to Elvira. The judges of the Rota who reviewed the case were of the opinion that there was no doubt that when Cassian entered into the marriage contract with Elvira, he excluded the marriage right itself with regard to the procreation of offspring:

> Equidem haud de eo esse ambigendum censuerunt Patres quod ius ipsum ad prolem excluserit Cassianus dum matrimonium iniit. Nam non modo nullis limitibus vel temporis . . . vel numeri filiorum circumscriptum suum propositum prolem devitandi ipse expressit, sed hac una de causa, ne filios ex sua uxore susciperet, nunquam cum ea stabili modo cohabitavit ab eaque discessit, ubi primum ipsa institit, ut copula iuxta naturae leges perageretur.[58]

The marriage was declared invalid.[59]

[57] S.R.R., *Westmonasterien., Nullitatis Matrimonii,* 14 mart. 1930, coram R.P.D. Iulio Grazioli, dec. XIV—*Decisiones,* XXII (1930), 169 ff.

[58] *Ibid.,* 175 (n. 11).

[59] *Ibid.,* 175 (n. 13). "Sententia facta est exsecutiva."—*Loc. cit.*

Case No. 10—Nullity Declared

James discovered that Regina would not yield to his lustful advances unless he could persuade her to marry him. Claiming that he would kill himself if she refused his proposal of marriage, he succeeded in winning her consent to marry him. His cruelty and infidelity after the marriage led Regina to leave him and return to her mother. In 1927, she impugned the validity of the marriage before the ecclesiastical tribunal on the grounds that James had simulated his consent to the marriage. The decision of the tribunal in favor of the nullity of the marriage was reversed by the tribunal of second instance. The case was appealed to the Sacred Roman Rota.[60]

Regina stated that James had told her many times before their marriage that he would have no children because they were a source of embarrassment in case of a divorce. James asserted, under oath, that he strongly had insisted that Regina accept the marriage in his sense, i. e., in the sense that they would be free to resume their freedom when they so desired. He added that, in desiring the marriage, he had not wished to establish a home in the strict sense of the word, but that he saw in the marriage merely a legal means to enjoy having a woman (". . . 'le moyen légal de jouir d'une femme' . . ."). The assertions of James indicated that he was determined not to enter a true marriage contract.[61] The testimonies of witnesses who, either before or after the marriage had heard James manifest his intention regarding marriage, indicated that Regina's action in impugning the validity of the marriage on the grounds that James had simulated his consent, truly was well founded.

The motive for simulating consent was indicated by the fact that James saw that he could not overcome Regina's modesty and possess her for his lustful purposes except by simulating to contract marriage with her. Although such a motive could be consistent with an

[60] S.R.R., *Nicien.*, *Nullitatis Matrimonii,* 16 iul. 1931, coram R.P.D. Henrico Quattrocolo, dec. XXXIV—*Decisiones,* XXIII (1931), 286 ff.

[61] His conception of marriage was indicated quite clearly when he stated: "Je lui répondais toujours que notre amour n'avait rien à voir avec le mariage indissoluble et avec les obligations qui pourraient cesser quand nous le voudrions." *Ibid.,* n. 5. This attitude on the part of James was brought out also by the witnesses (*Ibid.,* n. 6) and stressed by the Sacred Roman Rota (*Ibid.,* n. 7).

intention to contract a true marriage, it indicated an exclusion of juridical matrimonial consent in James's case; for in his case such a motive was joined to a positive act of the will contrary to the essential properties and the essential obligations of marriage, i.e. contrary to the indissolubility of the marriage and contrary to the procreation of offspring.

The fact that James had simulated his consent to the marriage contract was indicated likewise by his manner of acting after the marriage. One witness said that, as they were leaving the church after the wedding ceremony, James said to him: "The comedy is over" ("*Finita la commedia*"). Furthermore, as brought out by the depositions of Regina and of several witnesses, James continually had endeavored by artificial means, to prevent the conception of offspring; he had kept up sexual relations with other women during the marriage (having given Regina permission to commit adultery), and he had done all that he could to induce Regina to request a divorce. The Rota declared the marriage invalid.[62]

(3) *Insufficient Evidence of a Pact (if any), and Insufficient Evidence of Nullity*

The following cases constitute over one-half of the cases which involved the exclusion of the boon of offspring, as decided by the Sacred Roman Rota from 1909 to 1931 inclusively. The evidence as furnished in these cases was insufficient to establish that the

[62] *Ibid.*, 292 (n. 10). "Sententia facta est exsecutiva."—*Loc. cit.* There were three other cases which did not involve a pact contrary to the boon of offspring, but which furnished sufficient evidence of a positive intention to exclude the marriage right itself. They were the following: (1) S.R.R., *Nullitatis Matrimonii,* 18 iul. 1923, coram R.P.D. Francisco Parrillo, dec. XIX—*Decisiones,* XV (1923), 165 ff. (second instance—nullity declared—"Sententia facta est exsecutiva."); (2) *Querelae Nullitatis et Nullitatis Matrimonii,* 10 aug. 1929, coram R.P.D. Ubaldo Mannucci, dec. LI—*Decisiones,* XXI (1929), 425 ff. (second instance—validity upheld—decision reversed, May 16, 1933 "ex capite defectus consensus" [*AAS,* XXVI (1934), 117(dec. XXXVI)]); (3) *Luganen, Nullitatis Matrimonii,* 16 ian. 1930, coram R.P.D. Andrea Jullien, dec. V—*Decisiones,* XXII (1930), 55 ff. (second instance—validity upheld—decision reversed, Feb. 16, 1932 "ex capite defectus consensus atque intentionis contra bonum sacramenti et prolis" [*AAS,* XXV (1933), 86 (dec. VIII)]).

intention to exclude the boon of offspring prevailed over the intention (presumed in all marriages) to contract marriage as established by Christ, with all of its essential obligations. The evidence as furnished in these cases indicated not a positive intention to exclude the marriage right or to reject the corresponding essential obligation with regard to the boon of offspring, but merely an intention to abuse the marriage right or to neglect the fulfillment of the corresponding essential obligation. It will be noted that some of the following cases involved merely the temporary exclusion of the boon of offspring.

Case No. 11—Validity Upheld

Anna's parents were divorced when she was less than seven years old. After several changes of fortune, she was taken in by her grandmother, who saw to it that the girl was reared in an unrestrained manner ("liberali modo"). Leocard, a cousin of Anna's who was living with the same grandmother, soon fell in love with Anna, and they planned to get married. Due to the fact that their families were opposed to the union, however, they had to renounce their plans for marriage. In the meantime, the grandmother, because of diminished funds, wished to get rid of Anna, and insisted that she accept Mark, who had asked to marry her. They contracted marriage in 1910. Although two children were born of the union, their conjugal life, already disturbed by disagreements, was broken up on account of the war. Thereafter, in order to escape the disgrace which Mark's evil deeds brought upon her and the family, Anna discontinued conjugal life with him definitively. Having obtained a civil divorce, she petitioned the ecclesiastical tribunal for a declaration of nullity on a double score; that she had married Mark under the duress of the fear inflicted upon her by her grandmother, and that she had placed a condition contrary to the procreation of offspring, to which Mark had given his approval. The decision in 1924 stated: *"Non satis constare de nullitate matrimonii, in casu."* The case was appealed to the Sacred Roman Rota.[63]

The acts of the case did not furnish sufficient evidence to establish

[63] S.R.R., *Nullitatis Matrimonii*, 15 iun. 1925, coram R.P.D. Andrea Jullien, dec. XXX—*Decisiones*, XVII (1925), 239 ff.

the nullity of the marriage on the grounds of the fear inflicted by Anna's grandmother. The judicial confession of Anna and the depositions of witnesses as well as the facts of the case indicated, however, that Anna had placed a condition contrary to the boon of offspring. Anna stated before the ecclesiastical judge that, at various times, and in the presence of her cousin, her grandmother and Mark, she had placed a condition contrary to the boon of offspring ("Oui, j'ai posé expressément à Marc la condition de ne jamais être physiquement sa femme."), and that Mark had approved of the condition in writing (". . . la condition était si nette que Marc en a signé la promesse écrite sur ma demande. . . ."). When Mark had been asked whether he had promised Anna that he would not consummate the marriage with her, however, he had replied in the negative.

Leocard (Anna's cousin) expressed the opinion that Anna had placed a condition contrary to marriage, but he could not remember whether or not Mark may have accepted the condition. The grandmother said that, several days after the marriage, she found a paper whereon Mark had declared in writing (bearing his signature) that he would make no demands upon Anna until the day that she wished to be truly his wife. The grandmother added that she blushed when she read the declaration and immediately tore it up. It appeared, therefore, that she did not know about the alleged condition until, to her shame and surprise, she found the signed paper. This indicated that, if the grandmother had known about the condition before the marriage, she would have reproved Anna very violently, or at least that she would have thought that the condition had not been placed seriously. Nevertheless, her deposition furnished an argument to prove that Anna had placed a condition, and that Mark had subscribed his name thereto. Especially the argument that Anna had placed the condition was strengthened by the assertions of her father and another witness. Other witnesses testified that they had heard about the condition from Anna, but after the marriage had been contracted. Furthermore, there was the fact, as revealed by the grandmother, that the consummation of the marriage had been delayed due to Anna's unwillingness. That fact likewise furnished corroborative proof (*"adminiculum"*) in Anna's favor.

Although Anna had asserted that she had expressed explicitly to

Mark the condition that she would never be his wife physically ("Oui, j'ai posé expressément à Marc la condition de ne jamais être physiquement sa femme."), the two witnesses who, from personal knowledge, referred to the purport of the condition placed by Anna, described the condition only in general terms.[63a] Although the grandmother had referred to the condition in more specific terms, the Rota noted that she was the only witness who testified concerning the approximate wording of the condition, and that her testimony alone in a matter of such importance did not seem to be sufficient to enable the ecclesiastical judge to arrive at moral certitude in the matter. Furthermore, the wording of the condition as indicated by the grandmother was not considered as indicative of the exclusion of the right itself with reference to conjugal acts. Finally, there was a doubt whether the intention, as expressed in the declaration signed by Mark, was made seriously, not only on the part of Mark (who wished to use his marriage right very soon after the marriage), but also on the part of Anna, who was said to be a woman with a natural inclination for thinking up fabulous things ("esprit très romanesque"). As a matter of fact, after Anna had been reproved by her grandmother, she did consummate the marriage and, as Anna herself testified, she accepted the son and daughter contentedly. The Rota upheld the validity of the marriage.[64] The Supreme Tribunal of the Apostolic Signatura, however, granted the kindness of a new hearing of the case by the Sacred Roman Rota.[65] Again, the decision was in favor of the validity of the marriage.[66]

Case No. 12—Validity Upheld

In 1920, Mario, who was then thirty-six years old, married Rita, a girl of twenty-two. In 1921, due to disagreements with Mario,

[63a] Anna's father merely said: "Anne avait posé comme condition que son mari ne la toucherait pas." Another witness said: "Anne m'a dit quelques jours avant le mariage, qu'elle avait posé comme condition qu'elle n'aurait pas d'enfants et que même il y avait un écrit, ou cette condition était consignée." *Ibid.*, 249 (n. 12).

[64] *Ibid.*, 250 (n. 13).

[65] *Loc. cit.*

[66] The decision was given on August 4, 1932, "ex capite defectus consensus et conditionis appositae"—*AAS,* XXV (1933), 93 (dec. XLII).

Rita returned to the home of her parents. Mario opposed her efforts to obtain a civil divorce, and the divorce was not granted. In 1923, Mario requested the ecclesiastical tribunal for a declaration of nullity on the ground that Rita had harbored an intention contrary to the indissolubility of marriage. The tribunal upheld the validity of the marriage (1923). Although Mario had requested the metropolitan tribunal for a *restitutio in integrum,* and had been granted his request in part, the same tribunal which had upheld the validity of the marriage in 1923, issued the same decision in 1925. Mario appealed to the Sacred Roman Rota. In 1926, at the instance of his advocate, he petitioned the Holy Father for the faculty to have the Sacred Roman Rota examine the case also on the score of an intention, on the part of his wife, contrary to the boon of offspring.[67]

The acts of the case did not furnish sufficient evidence to establish that Rita had harbored a positive intention contrary to the indissolubility of marriage. With regard to the alleged exclusion of the boon of offspring, Mario asserted that he thought that he could say that Rita had placed to the marriage at least the condition to not have children right away, and he added that she once had told him that she did not want more than one child. "Surtout pas plus d'un enfant, parceque après cela, ça fait de petits malheureux." [68] Before the tribunal of first instance, Mario likewise had asserted that if he spoke of a condition, he referred only to Rita's will to not have children more or less during the first period of the marriage, and he had added that he had known well that such a condition was not sufficient to nullify a marriage. Rita stated that, after the marriage, she had expressed to Mario her desire and her intention to not have children before a year had passed, but that she had been convinced at the time that, before a year had passed, she would no longer be with him. She added: "J'étais bien décidée de ne pas avoir d'enfants avec lui, toujours dans l'intention de pouvoir m'en aller." [69] In the course of the judicial proceedings she had explained that the proposal to not have children, which in appearance was lim-

[67] S.R.R., *Nullitatis Matrimonii,* 18 dec. 1926, coram R.P.D. Francisco Guglielmi, dec. L—*Decisiones,* XVIII (1926), 416 ff.

[68] *Ibid.,* 427 (n. 20).

[69] *Ibid.,* 427 (n. 21).

ited as to time, actually was perpetual. The acts of the case, however, did not furnish confirmation of such a contention. Neither did the acts of the case demonstrate the pretended motive for Rita's proposal to exclude children, namely that she might not remain permanently bound to Mario (". . . intentio scilicet ne vinculum perpetuaretur").

The testimonies of the witnesses did not indicate that Rita had intended to exclude the marriage right itself. Her parents had learned only after the marriage that she (Rita) refused to have children. The testimonies of the witnesses who had learned of Rita's intention before the marriage seemed to indicate either that she intended to exclude children only for a time, or that, when revealing her mind on the subject, Rita had intended to speak only of a will to abuse the marriage right. The fact that she had taken means to prevent the conception of offspring along with her on the wedding trip, and that she had used them at that time and thereafter, confirmed the view that she had intended to abuse the marriage right, so as to avoid a pregnancy for the time being. Such a fact did not indicate that she had intended positively to exclude the right itself to the conjugal act (". . . omne ius ad coniugalem actum . . ."). The Rota upheld the validity of the marriage.[70]

Case No. 13—Validity Upheld

Paul and Germaine were engaged before the great war. During the war, however, it was noted that Paul's love for Germaine gradually disappeared. Nevertheless, they contracted marriage after the war had ended (1919). From the beginning, Paul sensed a repugnance to conjugal relations. Although he had declared to Germaine soon after the marriage that he no longer wished to grant the marriage debt, Germaine remained with him in the hope that he might revoke his declaration. Finally, in 1925, she returned to her own people. After having obtained a civil divorce in 1925, she petitioned the ecclesiastical tribunal for a declaration of nullity on the ground that Paul had excluded the boon of offspring when entering the marriage contract. The decision was in favor of the nullity

[70] *Ibid.,* 428 (n. 25). "Sententia facta est exsecutiva."—*Loc. cit.*

of the marriage (1926). In 1927 the tribunal of second instance upheld the validity of the marriage. The case was appealed to the Sacred Roman Rota.[71]

Although Paul vehemently opposed the accusation of Germaine, he nevertheless admitted that his former love for her had vanished during the period of their engagement, but that he nevertheless had married her upon the advice of his family and of friends. Three witnesses—two of his sisters and his paramour—testified that, before the marriage, Paul had expressed doubts and hesitancy about marrying Germaine. The fact that, after the marriage, he had shunned Germaine more and more as time went on, likewise fully confirmed the assertion that he had married her unwillingly. After bearing with him patiently for almost six years, Germaine finally was driven to return to her own people.

The Rota conceded Germaine's contention that Paul had prevented the conception of offspring of his own accord during the entire period of their life together. She asserted that he had also made her use contraceptive injections each time that they had conjugal relations. Paul admitted that he had done what was necessary to prevent the conception of offspring, without, however, taking extraordinary precautions, and added: "Et puis le dégoût physique est venu. *En fait, il ne pouvait pas y avoir d'enfant.*" Germaine's mother and another woman testified that Germaine had confided to them, soon after the marriage, that Paul made her take precautions to prevent the conception of offspring. The mother added that Paul also took all necessary precautions. A sister of Paul likewise expressed the opinion that Germaine took precautions to prevent the conception of offspring. On the other hand, Paul himself and four reliable witnesses asserted that Germaine was anxious to have children. Apparently Paul had harbored an intention to prevent the conception of offspring already at the time of the marriage.

The judges of the Rota stated, however, that the evidence was not sufficient to establish that Paul had intended to exclude the obligation itself with regard to the procreation of offspring. Paul explained his intention by saying that, in accordance with the advice

[71] S.R.R., *Nullitatis Matrimonii,* 17 iul. 1929, coram Rmo P.D. Maximo Massimi, Decano, dec. XXXIV—*Decisiones,* XXI (1929), 289 ff.

of Germaine's mother, he had married with the intention to avoid having children during the first two years of married life, but that after the marriage, when he sensed a repugnance to conjugal relations with Germaine, he had determined to have no children by her. Since this contradicted Germaine's accusation, however, and since the acts of the case showed that Paul was a dishonest person, the Rota was doubtful about the truth of his assertions. Furthermore, Germaine's mother vehemently denied Paul's assertion that she had advised him to exclude the procreation of offspring during the first two years of married life [i. e., so as to have more freedom].

Undoubtedly, something new and altogether serious came about after the marriage which made Paul averse to his conjugal duties: "Patuit scilicet summa difficultas perfectae copulae cum uxore habendae." [72] There were declarations of doctors to indicate that, even after the entire period of her conjugal life, Germaine retained some signs of virginity (". . . declarationes medicorum de Germana servante ex parte virginitatis signa . . ."). Germaine advanced the opinion that Paul was impotent, and furthermore that he wanted no children, since a child would keep her always at home. Germaine's mother expressed a similar opinion with regard to the possibility of Paul's impotency. This, however, weakened the accusation of Germaine. From the fact that Paul tenaciously had retained an intention contrary to the boon of offspring and that he had observed or lived according to such an intention until the end, it may have been argued that he had excluded the right itself with reference to the boon of offspring. His discovery of his impotence after marriage, however, was considered sufficient to explain very well both his aversion to and his discontinuance of conjugal life with Germaine, without pointing to an intention to not accept the essential obligation with reference to the boon of offspring. The Rota upheld the validity of the marriage.[73]

Case No. 14—Validity Upheld

Ernest, a non-Catholic, married Bernardine, a Catholic, in 1920. A few months after the marriage, due to disagreements with Ernest,

[72] *Ibid.*, 294 (n. 9).

[73] *Ibid.*, 294 (n. 11). "Sententia facta est executiva."—*Loc. cit.*

Bernardine separated from him. She petitioned the ecclesiastical tribunal for a declaration of nullity on the score of a condition contrary to the essence of marriage (Can. 1092, 2°). In 1927, the tribunal declared the marriage invalid. The case was appealed to the Sacred Roman Rota.[74]

Bernardine asserted that, before the marriage, Ernest had placed a condition that the procreation of offspring be prevented for at least one year, and that she had agreed to the condition. She asserted likewise that she had understood the condition as a part of the marriage contract, and that Ernest would not have contracted the marriage except with such a condition. Ernest confirmed all this under oath, but outside of judicial proceedings. He declared that he had entered into a mutual and explicit pact with Bernardine, before the marriage, to not have children and to practice onanism at least for one year. He added that if Bernardine had not accepted that condition, he would not have married her. The Rota stated that those declarations were expressive of a true condition to preclude offspring from the marriage contract.

The principal witness in the case, Ernest's father, confirmed the assertions of both Ernest and Bernardine as to the presence of a *true* condition. There was no other testimony, however, to confirm the assertions of Ernest's father. The declaration which Ernest had made before a notary public was not accepted as a confirming testimony, for such a document did not prove that the things declared therein were in conformity with the truth, but merely confirmed that Ernest actually had made the declaration. The motive or reason for placing the condition in question, according to Bernardine, was that Ernest had told her that he had no home and that he lacked sufficient funds to support children. The Rota remarked that such a motive might well be consonant with a simple proposal to preclude the right use of marriage for one year. The motive as indicated in the testimony of Ernest's father, however, seemed to point to the presence of a true condition; for according to his testimony, the motive for simulating consent consisted in the fact that, since Bernardine had been born and reared in a religion which prohibited onanism

[74] S.R.R., *Nullitatis Matrimonii,* 6 aug. 1929, coram R.P.D. Francisco Morano, dec. XLV—*Decisiones,* XXI (1929), 380 ff.

very severely, the parents of Ernest (who did not want to have children around them in their old age, to disturb the peace of the house) wanted Ernest to forewarn Bernardine concerning their desires and his own desires [i. e., Ernest's] with regard to the procreation of children, and thus avoid a disagreement in the matter. This indicated that Bernardine had been informed of Ernest's intention in the matter so that she could not request the right use of marriage during the first year. This, however, was based on the testimony of but one witness. The Rota concluded the case as follows:

> In actis igitur non asseritur simplex modus, sed vera conditio vitandi prolem saltem per annum, et ideo contra matrimonii substantiam. At cum declarationes partium confirmentur solummodo depositione unius testis, ob can. 1791, § 1, dicenda est deesse iuridica probatio assertae conditionis. Concedendum quidem actricem esse fide dignam, . . . Nihilominus ob tenuitatem actorum concludendum est non constare de appositione conditionis contra matrimonii substantiam, et ideo neque de nullitate matrimonii.[75]

The decision was in favor of the validity of the marriage.[76]

Case No. 15—Validity Upheld

Tiburtius, a Catholic doctor, fell in love with Rebecca, a young Jewish girl. After a period of engagement during which they had, for a time, lived together and even slept together, they were married before a civil magistrate. They were reported to have claimed that their marriage would be a so-called "Josephitic marriage." Later, at the insistence of Tiburtius, Rebecca became a Catholic. In 1917, three days after her baptism, they were joined in marriage according to the laws of the Catholic Church. The marriage was consummated soon and frequently but no children were born. But since Rebecca perceived that she had been deceived in her ideas by Tiburtius (who had told her that he was interested only in her spiritual progress and had suggested to her that she would find in the Catholic Church the response to her idealistic proclivity), and since she was in love with

[75] *Ibid.*, 384 f. (n. 10).

[76] *Ibid.*, 385 (n. 11). "Sententia facta est exsecutiva."—*Loc. cit.*

another young man, she left Tiburtius less than two years after the marriage and remained with her other lover. The marriage ended in a civil divorce. Tiburtius' petition to the ecclesiastical tribunal for a declaration of nullity resulted in a decision in favor of the validity of the marriage (1924). In 1926, however, the tribunal of second instance declared the marriage invalid. The case was appealed to the Sacred Roman Rota.[77]

Tiburtius stated that, although he did not formally invite Rebecca to marry him, she did not reject the inclination towards marriage which he had revealed to her. He added that, close to the time of the marriage and even before that time, she told him at various times that she excluded having conjugal union with him and having children by him, and that, in sexual matters, she submitted rather to a certain Tobias. It was noted, however, that such an intention, attributed by Tiburtius to Rebecca, could be interpreted as a mere proposal to abstain from the use of the marriage right, and not an exclusion of the marriage right itself. There was no indication that Tiburtius himself had an intention contrary to the procreation of offspring. He asserted that he was interested only in promoting the spiritual progress of Rebecca. This was confirmed by the fact that Tiburtius had spoken to Rebecca about entering a "Josephitic marriage" with him (i. e., a marriage celebrated with the intention of abstaining from conjugal acts). He even mentioned that they had agreed before the marriage to abstain from conjugal union. He also asserted that later on, when he had revealed his sexual propensities to Rebecca, she took the occasion to remind him of her declaration that all sexual union was to be excluded in the marriage [Rebecca, however, made no mention of this before the tribunal]. The Rota noted that if Tiburtius had manifested his sexual propensities to Rebecca (thereby indicating that his previous intention and agreement was not very firm), the new declaration of Rebecca [i. e., reminding him of the agreement] likewise could be understood as referring not to the exclusion of the marriage right itself, but to abstinence from conjugal union.

In several declarations before the tribunal, Rebecca indicated that

[77] S.R.R., *Harlemen., Nullitatis Matrimonii,* 26 mart. 1930, coram R.P.D. Francisco Guglielmi, dec. XV—*Decisiones,* XXII (1930), 176 ff.

she married Tiburtius with the intention of excluding the right to conjugal acts. One statement was worded as follows:

> "Prolis generatio in mea intentione absolute exclusa erat, immo huius viri ipsum ius ad actum coniugalem. Ego solummodo intendebam societatem amicalem. . . . Volebam esse eius uxor idque perpetuo; non tamen relate ad matrimonii finem primarium, in quaestione descriptum"; . . .[78]

There were indications, however, that they had intended to enter a true marriage as established by God. She had said repeatedly that she was led to the marriage by a spirit of mortification. Later on, she explained this as follows:

> "Is [i. e., Tiburtius], quamvis a me didicisset meum amorem femineum in alium virum, me perduxit ut nihilominus secum nuptias inirem, scilicet spiritu mortificationis: per hanc enim ille intendebat exsecutioni practicae mandare idealisticum pessimismum, quo probe sciebat me esse repletam. . . . Volebam solummodo coniunctionem destructivam, ad quam, ut aiebat ille, sacramentum matrimonii esset medium necessarium"; . . .[79]

In a letter to the tribunal, she explained that, when she was falling in love with another man, Tiburtius persuaded her to mortify herself and give herself to a man whom she did not love, namely, to Tiburtius himself. Tiburtius, however, said little or nothing about such ideas of mortification allegedly suggested by him.

Rebecca's clear assertions, considered in the light of the fact that Tiburtius ardently desired to possess the girl (to whom he had even made known his sexual propensities), indicated that both in conceiving and in suggesting the perverse theory of mortification to Rebecca and in accepting her intention to abstain from conjugal acts, Tiburtius wished only to deceive her. It was difficult to admit that Tiburtius actually entertained an intention of abstaining from conjugal acts, and much less, of excluding positively the right itself with regard to conjugal acts.

The parties claimed that they had informed the priest who had

[78] *Ibid.*, 181 (n. 9).

[79] *Ibid.*, 183 (n. 11).

blessed their marriage of the intention or condition in question. In his testimony, Cornelius, the priest in question, admitted that Rebecca had told him that she and Tiburtius had agreed to a condition to exclude offspring, and that she intended to enter merely a mystical marriage with Tiburtius. The priest likewise stated that he thought that he had succeeded in having her change her condition regarding offspring into a mere proposal, and that he was convinced that Tiburtius and Rebecca had given valid consent to the marriage contract. With regard to the testimonies of the other witnesses, the Rota made the following observation:

> Verum circa etiam hos testes, praeter quod non directe quidquam a rea didicerunt, est animadvertendum quod asserta conditio vel saltem propositum de sobole vitanda, ipso iure denegato, exinde minime corrivatur; de simplici enim abstinentia ab unione sexuali et, proinde, implicite et necessario, a suscipienda prole, sermo ab hisce testibus instituitur, qui saltem aequivoce intelligi potest, scilicet tum de iuris exclusione, tum de abstinentia a iuris exercitio.[80]

An argument against the contention of the plaintiff likewise was furnished by the fact that the parties had consummated the marriage very soon after the marriage had been celebrated. Rebecca explained that she later gave in to conjugal union with Tiburtius for reasons of *true mortification*: ". . . ut ita actum coniugalem exercere pergerem, contra meam propriam ideam, ad augendam destructionem pessimisticam: . . ."[81] The Rota considered that such an explanation could not be sustained. In view of the prudent doubt regarding the existence of a condition or positive act of the will to exclude the marriage right itself, the Rota upheld the validity of the marriage.[82]

Case No. 16—Validity Upheld

In 1924, Anna married Alphonse, a painter by profession. Alphonse, however, lacked the means with which to support himself and his wife. Before the end of their first year of married life, he

[80] *Ibid.*, 189 (n. 21).
[81] *Ibid.*, 190 (n. 23).
[82] *Ibid.*, 190 (n. 24). "Sententia facta est exsecutiva."—*Loc. cit.*

left Anna under the pretext of going to visit his parents, and no longer wished to return to her. In 1928, Anna petitioned the ecclesiastical tribunal for a declaration of nullity on the score of defective consent, i. e., that the marriage had been contracted with a condition or agreement to prevent the conception of offspring. In the course of the judicial proceedings, however, she added that Alphonse likewise had married with the proposal of asking for a divorce in so far as disagreements may have arisen or the means of livelihood may have been lacking. In 1929, the tribunal declared the marriage invalid. The same year, this decision was reversed by the tribunal of second instance. The case was appealed to the Sacred Roman Rota.[83]

Both of the parties asserted that the marriage had been contracted with a condition that both the boon of offspring and the boon of sacramental stability be excluded absolutely and forever. Alphonse's statement was especially precise: "Nous eussions préféré ne pas nous marier que de nous engager dans des liens indissolubles, et pour ce motif nous excluions les enfants que nous considérions comme un lien que lie les époux, ce dont nous ne voulions pas." [84] Whereas Alphonse included Anna as having agreed to exclude the boon of sacramental stability, however, Anna attributed the exclusion of the boon of sacramental stability to Alphonse alone. They likewise differed in assigning motives or reasons for simulating consent to the marriage contract. Alphonse explained the reason for the agreement or pact to prevent the conception of offspring by referring to his intention to separate from Anna later on. According to Anna, however, the principal reason for the pact was an economic one; Alphonse did not make very much money. Furthermore, the tribunal of first instance had not heard a single witness in Alphonse's behalf, and had proposed altogether suggestive questions to the parties and to the witnesses.

Only one of the witnesses, Anna's sister, confirmed the assertions of Anna and Alphonse, but only in regard to their exclusion of an intention of procreating offspring. Another witness knew about the exclusion of the procreation of offspring, but she had learned about

[83] S.R.R., *Nullitatis Matrimonii,* 19 dec. 1930, coram R.P.D. Iulio Grazioli, dec. LXI—*Decisiones,* XXII (1930), 669 ff.

[84] *Ibid.,* 672 (n. 7).

it from Anna after the marriage. In her testimony, she expressed her own opinion, rather than the intention of the contracting parties. The testimonies of another sister and a brother of Anna did not indicate that Anna and Alphonse had entered into the marriage contract with a positive intention to exclude either the procreation of offspring or the indissolubility of the marriage bond. The Rota observed that, although Anna and Alphonse undoubtedly had entered into the marriage contract very carelessly and unwisely, the evidence nevertheless was insufficient to establish that they actually had entered into the marriage contract with the conditions alleged by them. The Rota considered as futile the argument of the advocate of Anna that the testimony of Anna's brother indicated that the parties had excluded the procreation of offspring absolutely and without limitation. For, according to the same witness, the sole reason for which both of the parties had excluded the procreation of offspring was based on their economic condition, which, in time, could have become better. The decision was in favor of the validity of the marriage.[85]

Case No. 17—Validity Upheld

After seventeen years of married life, Lucy obtained a legal separation from Henry in 1928. The following year, she requested the ecclesiastical tribunal for a declaration of nullity on the score of the exclusion of the essence of marriage. In 1930, the tribunal declared the marriage invalid. The case was appealed to the Sacred Roman Rota.[86]

The words which (according to Lucy's deposition) Henry had used to express his opposition to the boon of offspring (*"Ti avverto che non dovremo aver figliuoli"*) were considered, by the Rota, as easily consistent with a simple intention to abstain from the use of the marriage right, or to abuse the marriage right, or to violate conjugal obligations. Lucy indicated that, at her insistence, Henry had retracted his condition to preclude the conception of offspring

[85] *Ibid.*, 675 (n. 16). "Sententia facta est exsecutiva."—*Loc. cit.*

[86] S.R.R., *Nulllitatis Matrimonii*, 23 iun. 1931, coram R.P.D. Francisco Morano, dec. XXX—*Decisiones*, XXIII (1931), 258 ff.

always, and that he had accepted her counter-proposal to exclude the conception of offspring for two years only. She contended, however, that his retraction of the former condition was insincere, for, after the two years had elapsed, he continued to prevent the procreation of offspring. The Rota observed, however, that Henry could have revoked the condition sincerely and later, having changed his mind, he could have rejected the procreation of offspring again. Hence Lucy's narrative did not offer sufficient arguments for the nullity of the marriage.

The five witnesses introduced by Lucy testified not from what they had heard from Henry himself, but from what they had heard from Lucy (four of the witnesses) or from another one of the witnesses (the fifth witness). Furthermore their testimonies, in general, were equivocal. In view of the fact that these witnesses relied only on their memories to recall words which had been spoken twenty years previously, there was little hope of finding a certain proof of a contrary condition in their declarations. There was no sufficient evidence to prove the assertion of Lucy that Henry had not sincerely revoked his original condition (i. e., in the mere supposition that he had placed such a condition as alleged by Lucy).

In a judicial declaration before the tribunal of first instance in 1929, Henry had stated that he had entered into the marriage contract with the firm proposal to preclude offspring (to which Lucy agreed), and that he could not recall having revoked that intention: "Non ricordo di una sua controproposta nel senso che io derogassi dalla mia ferma intenzione al suo consenso matrimoniale." [87] Furthermore, there was no evidence of a suitable and urgent motive for precluding the procreation of offspring. His reason was that there was a danger that the children of the union might be weak. Lucy indicated that his reason was based on personal egoism (". . . quod ille unice ferebatur cupiditate sui"). In regard to Lucy's contention that they both had agreed to exclude the procreation of offspring for two years, the Rota observed that, in the event that such a stipulation actually had been reduced to a true condition, Lucy was to be considered as incapable of impugning the validity of the marriage

[87] *Ibid.*, 265 (n. 12).

(interpretation of the Code Commission, March 12, 1929). The decision was in favor of the validity of the marriage.[88]

Case No. 18—Validity Upheld

Louis contracted marriage with Yvonne in 1908. Already during the period of their engagement, Yvonne, imbued with improper reading, had manifested, even to Louis, her complete aversion to having children. She had even drawn him into her counsels on the subject. After about ten years of married life, the marriage was broken up because of the corrupted morals of Louis. Having obtained a divorce, Louis attempted a marriage with another woman. In 1929, he petitioned the ecclesiastical tribunal for a declaration of nullity on the ground that Yvonne had entered into the marriage with a positive intention to not have children. In 1930, the marriage was declared invalid. The case was appealed to the Sacred Roman Rota.[89]

The Rota indicated that, since the tribunal of first instance had attached too much importance to the simple, affirmative assertions of the parties and of the witnesses, the statements of both the parties and the witnesses had to be sifted seriously in order to distinguish that which was spoken from personal knowledge and truthfully from that which rather was suggested by the questions which had been proposed to them. The Rota likewise observed that both of the parties in the case had prepared their case very studiously, and that the splendid affirmations of the witnesses with regard to the veracity and the religious character of the parties did not fit in with the testimonies given with regard to the evil deeds of the parties, i. e., that they had been given to the disgraceful practice of onanism for several years ("et quidem conscii tantae pravitatis . . ."); that Yvonne deliberately had imposed that practice upon Louis, and that he had accepted it readily. Furthermore, Louis, although married to Yvonne, had entered a civil union with another woman and had a child by her. Although Yvonne, by her own confession, had most insistently demanded from Louis a promise to prevent the

88 *Ibid.*, 266 (n. 16).

89 S.R.R., *Nullitatis Matrimonii*, 27 iul. 1931, coram R.P.D. Ubaldo Mannucci, dec. XXXVIII—*Decisiones*, XXIII (1931), 326 ff.

conception of offspring absolutely, she nevertheless admitted that she had been aware of the evil of onanism. In view of other circumstances of the case—the natural sense of shame in such matters as onanism, the youthfulness of Yvonne and her education by nuns, the fact that Louis and his people ardently desired that children be born of the union—the shameful things asserted by Yvonne and by others concerning her seemed to contain unlikely and even contradictory statements.

There were also grounds for suspecting the evidence offered because, already before their examination, the principal witnesses had given written declarations to Louis and to his advocate concerning the points upon which they were to be questioned. The Rota remarked that such a circumstance should make the ecclesiastical judge doubtful whether the witnesses, in testifying, were free, or whether they felt obliged not to contradict what they almost had promised to the plaintiff. Some of the witnesses testified that they had heard about Yvonne's contrary intention long after the parties had been married, even after they had been separated. Although Louis had asserted that he had spoken to no one in the matter, two witnesses testified that he had informed them, before the marriage, of Yvonne's perverse intention with regard to the procreation of offspring. The testimony of two other witnesses who claimed to have learned, before the marriage, of Yvonne's intention or condition contrary to the boon of offspring, were considered as insufficient to establish proof that the marriage right itself had been excluded with regard to the boon of offspring (i. e., insufficient especially because of deficiency in their testimony as to accompanying circumstances under which they had obtained their knowledge). The decision was in favor of the validity of the marriage.[90]

Case No. 19—Validity Upheld

Immediately after Julia's marriage to Andrew in 1926, she was so shocked by the manner in which he proposed to perform the act of conjugal union that she separated from him within a month and

[90] *Ibid.*, 333 (n. 13). The decision was confirmed by the Sacred Roman Rota on June 6, 1935, after a final review of the case, "ob exclusum bonum prolis"—*AAS*, XXVIII (1936), 132 (dec. XLIII).

returned to her own people. After having obtained a civil divorce, she requested the ecclesiastical tribunal for a declaration of nullity on the ground that Andrew had excluded the boon of offspring. In its decision in 1929, the tribunal upheld the validity of the marriage. Julia appealed to the Sacred Roman Rota.[91]

Andrew admitted that the marriage had not been consummated in a manner suitable to lead to the conception of offspring. The fact that Julia, indignant at his perversion of the sexual act, had left him without delay, indicated that the conception of offspring had been prevented by his will and against the will of his wife. Both of her parents testified that she had returned from the wedding trip unhappy because of Andrew's manner in conjugal relations. Although Andrew asserted that he had endeavored to perform the act of conjugal union in a normal way but that Julia objected, his former statements contradicted such an assertion.

Julia admitted that Andrew had not manifested his intention (contrary to the procreation of offspring) to her before the marriage except in very vague terms. Five witnesses testified, however, that, before the marriage, Andrew had told them that he wanted no children of his marriage. At first Andrew denied having told this to anyone except to Julia, but, speaking with one of the witnesses later on, he was forced to admit that he may have said that he wanted no children, but in a joking way. By order of the Sacred Roman Rota, the five witnesses who had testified previously were questioned again. Three of them asserted that Andrew had manifested his contrary intention to them on the wedding day itself. The other two witnesses said that it was shortly before the wedding day that they heard Andrew say that he wanted no children of the marriage. The Rota stated that the value of such declarations of Andrew's will had to be determined in the light of his moral character and the attitude of mind with which he entered the marriage contract.

Witnesses confirmed the statements of Julia and her parents with regard to Andrew's depraved morals. Their testimonies revealed that before the marriage he had associated shamefully with the woman with whom he later (i. e., after his civil divorce from Julia) renewed

[91] S.R.R., *Nullitatis Matrimonii,* 12 aug. 1931, coram Exc. mo P.D. Maximo Massimi, Decano, dec. L—*Decisiones,* XXIII (1931), 423 ff.

concubinage under the appearance of a civil marriage, and that he had married Julia not because he loved her, but because he wanted her money. The Rota made the following observations:

> Perpendentes igitur Patres Andreae facta, dicta, mores atque animum ab uxore alienum atque ad concubinam propensum, putarunt eam fuisse Andreae nuptias contrahenti intentionem, ut saltem circa bonum prolis obligationem ipsam respueret. Facta enim ostendunt serio, non ioco, Andream locutum fuisse contra bonum prolis, in ordine ad matrimonium cum Iulia ineundum vel initum. Dicta autem, nulli limitationi obnoxia, exclusionem ipsius iuris suadent, attentis praesertim iis quae supra exposita sunt de moribus et animo Andreae, affectione erga aliam mulierem devincti atque per nuptias cum Iulia huius pecuniam unice persequentis.[92]

The Rota noted that Andrew could not be believed in his contention that he was only joking when he expressed the intention to exclude offspring from the marriage, and this in spite of the fact, as contended by Andrew, that he had offspring in his concubinage. Regarding his assertion that he had intended to prevent the conception of offspring only for a time, the Rota noted that the witnesses had said nothing about such a limitation, and that, considering the income of Julia, the reason alleged by Andrew for the temporary exclusion of offspring (i. e.: "pour stabiliser la situation du foyer, . . .") was to be considered as false. The marriage was declared invalid.[93] On July 17, 1933, however, another panel of the Sacred Roman Rota reversed this decision and upheld the validity of the marriage.[94]

Case No. 20—Validity Upheld

In 1924, Ida impugned the validity of her marriage before the ecclesiastical tribunal on the basis of an alleged agreement to prevent the procreation of offspring. The tribunal declared the marriage invalid. The case was appealed to the Sacred Roman Rota.[95]

[92] *Ibid.,* 428 f. (n. 12).

[93] *Ibid.,* 429 (n. 13).

[94] ". . . ob exclusum prolis et ob simulatum consensum,"—*AAS,* XXVI (1934), 121 (dec. LVI).

[95] S.R.R., *Nullitatis Matrimonii,* 16 apr. 1928, coram R.P.D. Henrico Quattrocolo, dec. XI—*Decisiones,* XX (1928), 113 f.

Although the acts of the case indicated that Ida and perhaps also Carl had harbored an intention, before marriage, to prevent the procreation of offspring, the evidence was insufficient to indicate that the right itself to conjugal acts had been excluded. From the assertions of Ida and almost all of the witnesses it appeared that neither a pact nor a true condition was involved in the case but only the simple proposal or purpose (*propositum*) of the consorts to frustrate the procreation of offspring. The fact that Ida later on apparently spoke of a pact was ascribed to the fact that the ecclesiastical judge, completely unmindful of Ida's former assertions, had asked her imprudent and suggestive questions. The witnesses who did speak of a pact between the parties either expressed merely an opinion or judgment in the matter, or they testified that they had learned about such a pact and a condition only after the marriage had been celebrated, or they spoke of a condition in general without recalling any circumstance in which they had heard the parties speak of a condition.

The case furnished numerous testimonies which indicated that Ida and Carl, when entering the marriage contract, in reality had intended to enter a true marriage as established by Christ. There was certain evidence that: (1) Ida and Carl had been very deeply in love with one another; (2) they had hastened the celebration of the marriage before the date designated to them by their parents and relatives; (3) By entering marriage with Carl, Ida had wished to procure for herself a permanent status; (4) the proposal of preventing conception had been conceived by Ida and Carl as applying only for a time. Both Ida and the witnesses indicated only a temporary and accidental reason for preventing the conception of offspring, i. e., the lack of funds, and the fact that their dwelling place was liable to be changed on short notice (for Carl was engaged in military service). The Rota made the following observation:

> Porro commemorata et probata magni momenti huiusmodi adiuncta, . . . grave argumentum profecto suppeditant intendisse Idam, Carolo nubendo, sese vere obligare ex parte contractus, seu verum matrimonium inire ac perpetuo cum viro sacro foedere copulari; . . . Quod magis magisque in praesenti est tenendum si consideretur quod recensitae rationes, quibus prolem detrecta-

runt coniuges, nedum necessario sponsis haud suadent matrimonialia iura sibi invicem denegare . . . sed optime componuntur cum eorumdem iurium abusu, per quem et proles fraudatur et iura servantur.[96]

Ida stated that, after about one year and a half of conjugal life, Carl relaxed his onanistic practice for a time, fearing its detrimental effect upon his nervous system, and that she accordingly intensified the strength of the post-coital lotions employed by her in such a manner that they endangered her health. It was in consequence of these circumstances that a child was conceived and born despite the precautions taken by Ida to frustrate the natural effects of conjugal union. The Rota drew the following conclusion:

> Igitur certissime constat in casu haud exclusisse actricem eiusque maritum in matrimonii celebratione ius ipsum ad coniugales actus implendos et ideo obligationem ad hos actus admittendos; et per propositum vitandi prolem eos intellexisse dumtaxat propositum impediendi prolis conceptionem et procreationem sive per iuris matrimonialis abusum, sive remediis adhibitis post copulam naturali modo completam; quod matrimonii validitati profecto non officit.[97]

The decision was in favor of the validity of the marriage.[98]

In a review of the case in 1931, another panel of the Sacred Roman Rota noted that the same witnesses who formerly had testified that there was no pact or agreement between Ida and Carl with regard to the preventing of conception, tried to change their former testimonies when they were questioned again. The argument that the parties had excluded marriage as such, which was later added by the illustrious advocate in the case, lacked even the beginning of proof. The decision was in favor of the validity of the marriage.[99]

[96] *Ibid.*, 120 (n. 10).

[97] *Ibid.*, 120 f. (n. 11).

[98] *Ibid.*, 121 (n. 12).

[99] S.R.R., *Nullitatis Matrimonii*, 20 nov. 1931, coram R.P.D. Ubaldo Mannucci, dec. LIII—*Decisiones*, XXIII (1931), 456 ff. "Sententia facta est executiva."—*Ibid.*, 462. There were thirteen other cases which did not furnish sufficient evidence (if any) of a pact, and which, furthermore, did not indicate sufficiently either the presence of a *sine qua non* condition or of a positive intention to exclude the marriage right with regard to the boon of offspring.

They were the following: (1) S.R.R., *Nullitatis Matrimonii,* 30 mart. 1926, coram R.P.D. Andrea Jullien, dec. XIII—*Decisiones,* XVIII (1926), 102 ff. (second instance—validity upheld—"Sententia facta est exsecutiva."); (2) 7 iun. 1927, coram R.P.D. Iosepho Florczak, dec. XXVI—*Decisiones,* XIX (1927), 208 ff. (third instance—validity upheld—"Sententia facta est exsecutiva."); (3) 3 dec. 1927, coram R.P.D. Francisco Guglielmi, dec. LIV—*Decisiones,* XIX (1927), 487 ff. (fourth instance [the case had not been examined on the score of the exclusion of the boon of offspring in the tribunals of second and third instance]—validity upheld—"Sententia facta est exsecutiva."); (4) 15 dec. 1915, coram Rm̃o P.D. Guilelmo Sebastianelli, Decano, dec. XLI—*Decisiones,* VII (1915), 452 ff. (third instance [the case had not been examined on the score of the exclusion of the boon of offspring in the tribunals of first and second instance]—validity upheld); 3 apr. 1917, coram R.P.D. Friderico Cattani Amadori, dec. VIII—*Decisiones,* IX (1917), 67 ff. (fourth instance—validity upheld); 11 febr. 1929, coram R.P.D. Francisco Guglielmi, dec. XI—*Decisiones,* XXI (1929), 91 ff. (fifth instance—validity upheld—"Sententia facta est exsecutiva."); (5) 17 aug. 1926, coram R.P.D. Francisco Guglielmi, dec. XLIV—*Decisiones,* XVIII (1926), 353 ff. (first instance—validity upheld—"Sententia facta est exsecutiva."); (6) 9 febr. 1927, coram R.P.D. Iulio Grazioli, dec. VI—*Decisiones,* XIX (1927), 42 ff. (third instance—validity upheld—"Sententia facta est exsecutiva."); (7) *Constantinopolitana. Nullitatis Matrimonii,* 30 iun. 1925, coram R.P.D. Francisco Parrillo, dec. XXXIV—*Decisiones,* XVII (1925), 268 ff. (first instance—validity upheld); 5 iun. 1928, coram Rm̃o P.D. Maximo Massimi, Decano, dec. XXIV—*Decisiones,* XX (1928), 230 ff. (second instance—validity upheld—"Sententia facta est exsecutiva."); (8) *Nullitatis Matrimonii,* 7 ian. 1929, coram R.P.D. Francisco Parrillo, dec. II—*Decisiones,* XXI (1929), 12 ff. (first instance—validity upheld—"Cum actrix appellationem, a se interpositam, prosecuta non sit, sententia facta est exsecutiva."); (9) 29 dec. 1928, coram R.P.D. Ubaldo Mannucci, dec. LVIII—*Decisiones,* XX (1928), 506 ff. (second instance [the case had not been decided on the score of the exclusion of the boon of offspring in the tribunal of first instance]—validity upheld); 14 ian. 1930, coram Rm̃o P.D. Maximo Massimi, Decano, dec. IV—*Decisiones,* XXII (1930), 45 ff. (third instance—validity upheld—"Sententia facta est exsecutiva."); (10) *Parisien., Nullitatis Matrimonii,* 31 iul. 1930, coram R.P.D. Henrico Quattrocolo, dec. XLV—*Decisiones,* XXII (1930), 505 ff. (third instance—validity upheld—"Sententia facta est exsecutiva."); (11) *Viennen., Nullitatis Matrimonii,* 11 aug. 1930, coram R.P.D. Francisco Morano, dec. L—*Decisiones,* XXII (1930), 563 ff. (third instance—validity upheld—decision confirmed, Jan. 11, 1932 "ob intentionem contra bonum prolis" [*AAS,* XXV (1933), 85 (dec. II)]); (12) *Nullitatis Matrimonii,* 15 ian. 1931, coram R.P.D. Henrico Quattrocolo, dec. I—*Decisiones,* XXIII (1931), 1 ff. (third instance—validity upheld—"Sententia facta est exsecutiva."); (13) 10 febr. 1931, coram R.P.D. Arcturo Wynen, dec. VII—*Decisiones,* XXIII (1931), 45 ff. (first instance—validity upheld—"Deficiente appellatione, sententia facta est exsecutiva.")

CONCLUSIONS TO SECTION II

I. The expression *"deducta in pactum"* usually is referred to in the decisions of the Sacred Roman Rota as indicating an agreement between the contracting parties, whereby it is manifested that one of the parties intends to obligate the other party to something which is contrary to one of the boons of marriage. As such, it is a most suitable *means of proving* the presence of a vitiated consent—not, however, the only means. Irrespective, however, of what means of proof is available in the individual case, the marriage is not invalid unless the contrary intention or condition was introduced into the marriage contract itself as a part of the contract—*"deducta in pactum matrimoniale."*

II. An external pact or agreement between the parties is suitable evidence not only of an intention on the part of one of the contracting parties to obligate the other party to something which is contrary to one of the boons of marriage, but also, particularly in cases which involve the exclusion of the boon of sacramental stability (*bonum sacramenti*), a suitable indication that the intention or condition proceeds not from an error on the part of the intellect, but from a positive act of the will.

III. In the event of a pact between the parties, or of evidence that the condition was placed as a *sine qua non* condition for the matrimonial consent, a strong presumption arises that the party concerned intended to exclude the marriage right itself with reference to the boon of offspring. This presumption applies, however, only if the condition or intention involves the absolute and perpetual exclusion of the boon of offspring. If an intention is expressed or if a condition is placed, but with limitations with regard to time or with regard to the number of children desired, the presumption is that the party intends merely to abuse the marriage right, or to neglect the fulfillment of the corresponding essential obligation.

IV. Of the twenty cases reviewed by the Sacred Roman Rota between the years 1909 and 1931 inclusively which resulted ultimately in a declaration of nullity, ten cases furnished sufficient evidence of a mutual pact contrary to the boon of offspring. Thirteen of these twenty cases were declared invalid because of the presence of a *sine qua non* condition contrary to the boon of offspring, whereas the remaining seven cases were declared invalid because of the presence of a positive intention to exclude the marriage right itself with reference to the boon of offspring.

BIBLIOGRAPHY

Sources

Acta Apostolicae Sedis, Commentarium Officiale, Romae, 1909—

Acta Sanctae Sedis, 41 vols., Romae, 1865-1908.

Bouscaren, T. Lincoln, *The Canon Law Digest,* 2 vols., Milwaukee: Bruce, 1934—

Catechismus Romanus ex Decreto Concilii Tridentini ad Parochos Pii V. Pontificis Maximi iussu editus, 4. ed., 4 vols., Ratisbonae, Romae, Neo Eboraci et Cincinnati: Sumptibus et typis Friderici Pustet, 1907.

Codex Iuris Canonici Pii X Pontificis Maximi jussu digestus, Benedicti Papae XV auctoritate promulgatus, Romae: Typis Polyglottis Vaticanis, 1917, Reimpressio, 1933.

Codicis Iuris Canonici Fontes cura Emi Petri Card. Gasparri editi, 9 vols., Romae (postea Civitate Vaticana): Typis Polyglottis Vaticanis, 1923-1939 (Vols. VII, VIII et IX ed. cura et studio Emi Iustiniani Card. Serédi).

Corpus Iuris Canonici, ed. Lipsiensis secunda post Aemilii Ludovici Richteri curas . . . instruxit Aemilius Friedberg, 2 vols., Lipsiae, 1879-1881.

Corpus Iuris Civilis, 3 vols., Vol. I, ed. stereotypa quinta decima, *Institutiones* recognovit Paulus Kreuger, *Digesta* recognovit Theodorus Mommsen, retractavit Paulus Kreuger, Berolini: Apud Weidmannos, 1928.

Corpus Iuris Civilis, Vol. II, ed. stereotypa nona, *Codex Iustinianus* recognovit et retractavit Paulus Kreuger, Berolini: Apud Weidmannos, 1915.

Corpus Scriptorum Ecclesiasticorum Latinorum, 68 vols., Vindobonae, 1866—

Decretales D. Gregorii Papae, una cum Glossis Restitutae, Romae, 1582.

Decretum Gratiani Emendatum et Notationibus illustratum una cum Glossis, Romae, 1582.

Denzinger, Henricus et Bannwart, Clemens et Umberg, Ioannes, *Enchiridion Symbolorum Definitionum et Declarationum de Rebus Fidei et Morum,* 21.-23. ed., Friburgi Brisgoviae: Herder, 1937.

Potthast, Augustus, *Regesta Pontificum Romanorum inde ab anno post Christum natum MCXCVIII ad annum MCCCIV,* 2 vols., Berolini, 1874-1875.

Sacrae Romanae Rotae Decisiones seu Sententiae quae iuxta Legem Propriam et Constitutionem "Sapienti Consilio" Pii PP. X prodierunt, cura eiusdem S. Tribunalis editae, 23 vols., Romae, 1912—

Thesaurus Resolutionum Sacrae Congregationis Concilii, 167 vols., Romae, 1718-1908.

Authors

Alphonsus Liguori, St., *Theologia Moralis,* 11. ed., Gaudé, 4 vols., Romae, 1905-1912.

Arregui, Antonius, *Summarium Theologiae Moralis ad Recentem Codicem Iuris Canonici Accomodatum,* 13. ed., Westminster, Maryland: The Newman Bookshop, 1944.

Ayrinhac, H. A., and Lydon, P. J., *Marriage Legislation in the New Code of Canon Law,* new, revised edition, New York: Benziger Brothers, 1943.

Bachofen [Charles Augustine], *A Commentary on the New Code of Canon Law,* 8 vols., Vol. V, 4. ed., 1929; Vol. VII, 3. ed., 1931, St. Louis: B. Herder Book Co.

Benedictus XIV, *De Synodo Dioecesana,* 2 vols., Ex Typographia Sacrae Congregationis de Propaganda Fide, Romae, 1806.

Blat, Albertus, *Commentarium Textus Codicis Iuris Canonici,* 5 vols. in 6, Vol. III (*De Rebus*), Pars I, Romae, 1924.

Böckhn, Placidus, *Commentarium in Ius Canonicum Universum,* Salisburgi, 1776.

Bohic, Henricus, *In Quinque Decretalium Libros Commentaria,* Venetiis, 1576.

Cappello, Felix, *Tractatus Canonico-Moralis de Sacramentis,* 3 vols. in 6, Vol. III, *De Matrimonio,* 4. ed., Romae: Marietti, 1939.

Cerato, P., *Matrimonium a Codice Iuris Canonici Integre Desumptum,* editio altera locupletior, Patavii: Typis Seminarii, 1919.

Chelodi, Ioannes, *Ius Matrimoniale iuxta Codicem Iuris Canonici,* 3. ed., Tridenti: Libr. Edit. Tridentum, 1921.

Claeys Bouuaert, F.-Simenon, G., *Manuale Iuris Canonici,* 3 vols., Vol. II, *De Sacramentis,* Gandae et Leodii, 1931.

Coscius, Christophorus, *De Separatione Tori Coniugalis,* Florentiae, 1856.

Craisson, D., *Manuale Totius Iuris Canonici,* 5. ed., 4 vols., Pictavii: Ex Typis H. Oudin, 1877.

D'Annibale, J., *Summula Theologiae Moralis,* 5. ed., 4 vols., Romae, 1908.

Davis, Henry, *Moral and Pastoral Theology,* 4. ed., 4 vols., New York: Sheed & Ward, 1943.

De Angelis, Phillipus, *Praelectiones Iuris Canonici ad methodum Decretalium Gregorii IX exactae,* 5 vols., Vol. III, Romae, 1880.

De Becker, Julius, *De Matrimonio Praelectiones Canonicae,* nova ed., Louvain: Ceuterick, 1931.

De Camillis, J., *Institutiones Iuris Canonici,* 3 vols., Parisiis: apud Ludovicum Vivès, 1889.

De Smet, Aloysius, *Tractatus Theologico-Canonicum de Sponsalibus et Matrimonio,* 4. ed., Brugis: Beyaert, 1927.

Doheny, William, *Canonical Procedure in Matrimonial Cases,* 2 vols., Vol. I, Milwaukee: Bruce, 1938.

Esmein, A.-Génestal, R.-Dauvillier, J., *Le Mariage en Droit Canonique,* 2. ed., 2 vols., Paris, 1929-1935.

Fagnanus, Prosper, *Ius Canonicum seu Commentaria Absolutissima in Quinque Libros Decretalium,* Romae, 1661.

Feije, Henricus, *De Impedimentis et Dispensationibus Matrimonialibus,* 4. ed., Lovanii: Typis Caroli Peeters, 1893.

Ferraris, Lucius, *Prompta Bibliotheca Canonica Iuridica Moralis Theologica nec non Ascetica Polemica Rubricistica Historica,* 9 vols., Romae, 1885-1899.

Ford, John C., *The Validity of Virginal Marriage*, A Doctoral Dissertation Presented in the Theological Faculty of the Pontifical Gregorian University, Worcester, Mass.: Harrigan Press, 1938.

Freisen, J., *Geschichte des Canonischen Eherechts bis zum Verfall der Glassenliteratur*, 2. ed., Paderborn: Ferdinand Schöningh, 1893.

Gasparri, Petrus, *Tractatus Canonicus de Matrimonio*, editio nova ad mentem Codicis I. C., 2 vols., Romae: Typis Polyglottis Vaticanis, 1932.

Genicot, E.-Salsmans, J., *Institutiones Theologiae Moralis*; 14. ed., 2 vols., Buenos Aires: Dedebec, 1942.

Gonzalez-Tellez, Emmanuel, *Commentaria Perpetua in Singulos Textus Quinque Libros Decretalium Gregorii IX*, 5 vols. in 4, Venetiis, 1699.

Gougnard, Armandus, *Tractatus de Matrimonio*, 7. ed., Mechliniae: H. Dessain, 1931.

Gury, J.-Ballerini, A., *Compendium Theologiae Moralis*, 7. ed., 2 vols., Romae, 1887.

Heneghan, John J., *The Marriages of Unworthy Catholics*, The Catholic University of America Canon Law Studies, n. 188, Washington, D. C.: The Catholic University of America Press, 1944.

Hostiensis, Cardinalis (Henricus de Segusio), *Commentaria in Quinque Decretalium Libros*, 5 vols. in 3, Venetiis, 1581.

Ioannes Andreae, *Commentaria in Quinque Decretalium Libros*, Venetiis, 1581.

Joyce, George H., *Christian Marriage: An Historical and Doctrinal Study*, London and New York: Sheed & Ward, 1933.

Knecht, August, *Handbuch des katholischen Eherechts*, Freiburg im Breisgau: Herder, 1928.

Konings, A., *Theologia Moralis, Novissimi Ecclesiae Doctoris S. Alphonsi, in Compendium Redacta, et Usui Venerabilis Cleri Americani Accomodata*, 4. ed., 2 vols., Neo Eboraci: Benziger Fratres, 1880.

Lancelotti, Giovanni, *Institutiones Iuris Canonici*, Lugduni, 1579.

Laymann, Paul, *Theologia Moralis*, 5 vols., Venetiis, 1630.

Lavaud, Benoit, *Le Monde Moderne et le Mariage*, Paris: Desclée de Brouwer, 1935.

Lehmkuhl, Augustinus, *Theologia Moralis*, 6. ed., 2 vols., Friburgi Brisgoviae: Herder, 1890.

Manning, John J., *Presumptions of Law in Marriage Cases*, The Catholic University of America Canon Law Studies, n. 94, Washington, D. C.: The Catholic University of America, 1935.

Merklebach, Benedictus H., *Summa Theologiae Moralis*, editio altera aucta et emendata, 3 vols., Parisiis: Typis Desclée de Brouwer et Soc., 1936.

Noldin, H.-Schmitt, A.; *Summa Theologiae Moralis iuxta Codicem Iuris Canonici*, 26. ed., 3 vols., Oeniponte-Lipsiae: Rauch, 1940.

Panormitanus, Abbas (Nicolaus de Tudeschis), *Commentaria in Quinque Libros Decretalium*, 5 vols. in 7, Venetiis, 1588.

Payen, G., *De Matrimonio in Missionibus ac Potissimum in Sinis, Tractatus et Casus*, 3 vols., Zi-ka-wei: in typographia T'ou-sè-wè, 1929.

Petrovitz, Joseph J. C., *The New Church Law on Matrimony* (second amplified and revised edition), Philadelphia: John Joseph McVey, 1926.

Petrus Lombardus, *Petri Lombardi Libri IV Sententiarum*, 2. ed., 2 vols., Quaracchi: Ex Typographia Collegii S. Bonaventurae, 1916.

Pichler, V., *Candidatus Iurisprudentiae Sacrae*, Ingolstadii, 1724-1728.

Pirhing, Enricus, *Ius Canonicum Nova Methodo Explicatum*, 5 vols. in 4, Dilingae, 1674-1678.

Raus, P. J., *Institutiones Canonicae iuxta Novum Codicem Iuris pro Scholis vel ad Usum Privatum Synthetice Redactae*, altera editio aucta atque emendata, Lugduni-Parisiis: Typis Emmanuelis Vitte, 1931.

Reiffenstuel, Anacletus, *Ius Canonicum Universum*, 5 vols. in 7, Paris, 1864-1870.

Salmanticenses, *Cursus Theologiae Moralis*, 6 vols., Venetiis, 1714.

Sanchez, Thomas, *Disputationum de Sancto Matrimonii Sacramento Tomi Tres*, Antverpiae, 1626.

Santi, Franciscus-Leitner, Martinus, *Praelectiones Iuris Canonici*, 4. ed., 5 vols. in 2, Ratisbonae: Pustet, 1903-1905.

Schmalzgrueber, Franciscus, *Jus Ecclesiasticum Universum*, 5 vols. in 12, Romae, 1843-1845.

Schmier, Franciscus, *Iurisprudentia Canonico-Civilis*, 3 vols., Salisburgi, 1716.

Sipos, Stephanus, *Enchiridion Iuris Canonici*, editio altera, Pécs, Hungary: Ex Typographia "Haladás R. T.," 1931.

Thomas Aquinas, St., *Summa Theologica*, 6 vols., Taurini: Marietti, 1937.

Timlin, Bartholomew T., *Conditional Matrimonial Consent*, The Catholic University of America Canon Law Studies, n. 89, Washington, D. C.: The Catholic University of America, 1934.

Tropper, Ioannes N., *Tractatus Duo in Quibus Impedimenta Matrimonii Contractum Impedientia et Dirimentia ex Theologiae et Iuris fontibus utriusque fori . . . explanantur*, Monachii, 1753.

Vermeersch, Arthurus, *What is Marriage? A Catechism according to the Encyclical "Casti Connubii" of Pope Pius XI*, New York: The America Press, 1932.

Vermeersch, A.-Creusen, J., *Epitome Iuris Canonici*, 3 vols., Vol. I, 6. ed., 1937; Vols. II et III, 5. ed., 1934-1936, Mechliniae-Romae: H. Dessain.

Vlaming, Th. M., *Praelectiones Iuris Matrimonii*, 3. ed., 2 vols., Bussum in Hollandia, 1919-1921.

Vromant, G., *Ius Missionariorum*, 7 vols., Louvain: Museum Lessianum, 1931.

Wanenmacher, Francis, *Canonical Evidence in Marriage Cases*, Philadelphia, Pa.: Dolphin Press, 1935.

Wernz, F.-Vidal, P., *Ius Canonicum*, 7 vols. in 9, Vol. V, *Ius Matrimoniale*, 2. ed., 1928; Vol. VI, *De Processibus*, 1927; Romae: Apud Aedes Universitatis Gregorianae.

Periodicals

Apollinaris, Romae, 1928—

Clergy Review, The, London, 1931—

Ecclesiastical Review, The (originally, *The American Ecclesiastical Review*), Philadelphia, 1889—; *The American Ecclesiastical Review*, Washington, D. C., 1944—

Ephemerides Theologicae Lovanienses, Brugis, 1924—

Irish Ecclesiastical Record, The, Dublin, 1864—

Jurist, The, Washington, D. C., 1941—

Ius Pontificium, Romae, 1921—

L'Ami du Clergé, Paris, 1878—

Periodica de Re Canonica et Morali, Brugis, 1905—; ab anno 1927: *Periodica de Re Canonica, Morali, Liturgica*, Brugis (1927-1936) et Romae (1937—).

Theologisch-praktische Quartalschrift, Linz, 1832—

Articles

Anonymous, "Un Nouveau Problème Morale,"—*L'Ami du Clergé*, LI (1934), 737-752.

Arend, G., "De genuina ratione impedimenti impotentiae,"—*Ephem. Theol. Lovan.*, IX (1932), 28-69.

Ayrinhac, H. A., "De quibusdam defectibus in consensu matrimoniali,"—*Ius Pontificium*, IX (1929), 25-33.

Bartoccetti, Victorius, "Circa inhabilitatem coniugum accusandi matrimonium," —*Apollinaris*, XI (1938), 201-214.

Browne, M. J., *The Irish Ecclesiastical Record*, XLIX (1937), 85-89.

Flieszer, Josef, "Ehewille und *bonum prolis*,"—*Quartalschrift*, XC (1937), 425-441.

Mancini, A., *Palaestro del Clero*, XIV (1935), 60-78.

Mahoney, E. J., "Matrimonial Consent and the 'Safe Period,' "—*The Clergy Review*, XIII (1937), 121-131, 412-413; XIV (1938), 184-185.

O'Donnell, M. J., "Matrimonial Consent in the New Code,"—*The Irish Ecclesiastical Record*, XII (1918), 274-290.

Oesterle, Gerardus, "Circa controversam validitatem matrimonii feminae recisae,"—*Ephem. Theol. Lovan.*, III (1926), 345-354.

Reh, Francis F., "Guilt of the Plaintiff in a Marriage Case,"—*The Jurist*, III (1943), 404-415.

Roberti, F., "Quaestiones quaedam de identificatione actionum ob vitia consensus in causis matrimonialibus,"—*Apollinaris*, VI (1933), 105-107.

Salsmans, I., "Sterilitas Facultativa Licita?"—*Ephem. Theol. Lovan.*, XI (1934), 562-570.

Vermeersch, Arthurus, "De prudenti ratione iudicandi sterilitatem physiologicam,"—*Periodica,* XXIII (1934), 238*-248*.

———, "De moralitate sic dictae abstinentiae periodicae in matrimonio,"—*Periodica,* XXIV (1935), 165*-170*.

———, "Aktuelle Fragen des Eherechts und der Ehemoral,"—*Quartalschrift,* LXXXIX (1936), 47-65.

Wanenmacher, Francis, "Some questions on vitiated marital consent,"—*The Ecclesiastical Review,* C (1939), 481-497; CI (1939), 131-149.

Zeiger, Ivo, "Nova matrimonii definitio?"—*Periodica,* XX (1931), 37*-59*.

ABBREVIATIONS

AAS—*Acta Apostolicae Sedis.*

Apos. Delegate's letter, 1938—Letter of the Apostolic Delegate on handling of marriage cases in the United States, Sept. 23, 1938.

ASS—*Acta Sanctae Sedis.*

C—Codex Justinianus.

CSEL—*Corpus Scriptorum Ecclesiasticorum Latinorum.*

Decisiones—*Sacrae Romanae Rotae Decisiones seu Sententiae.*

Denzinger—Denzinger-Bannwart-Umberg, *Enchiridion Symbolorum et Definitionum.*

Ephem. Theol. Lovan.—*Ephemerides Theologicae Lovanienses.*

Fontes—*Codicis Iuris Canonici Fontes.*

Instr., S. C. de Sacr., 1936—Matrimonial instruction of the Sacred Congregation of the Sacraments, Aug. 15, 1936.

Periodica—*Periodica de Re Canonica, Morali, Liturgica.*

Potthast—*Regesta Pontificum Romanorum.*

Quartalschrift—*Theologisch-praktische Quartalschrift.*

S.C.C.—Sacra Congregatio Concilii.

S.C. de Sacr.—Sacra Congregatio de Disciplina Sacramentorum.

S.C.S.Off.—Suprema Sacra Congregatio Sancti Officii.

S.R.R.—Sacra Romana Rota.

Thesaurus—*Thesaurus Resolutionum Sacrae Congregationis Concilii.*

ALPHABETICAL INDEX

BIOGRAPHICAL NOTE

Nicholas Orville Griese was born in Kewaunee, Wisconsin, on the fifth of December, 1915. After graduating from Holy Rosary Parochial School of that city in 1929, he spent six years under the guidance of the Fathers of the Divine Saviour (S.D.S.) at the Salvatorian Seminary, St. Nazianz, Wisconsin. From 1935 to 1937, he received his training in philosophy from the monks of St. Benedict at the St. Meinrad Major Seminary, St. Meinrad, Indiana. He was awarded the degree of Bachelor of Arts in 1937. He spent the first three years of theological studies at the *Grand Séminaire* of Quebec, Canada, and the final year at the Catholic University of America, Washington, D. C. He received the degree of Bachelor of Sacred Theology from the Faculty of Theology of Laval University, Quebec, Canada, in 1940, and the degree of Licentiate in Sacred Theology from the Catholic University of America, Washington, D. C., in 1941. After his ordination to the priesthood in Green Bay, Wisconsin, on the thirtieth of May, 1941, he returned to the Catholic University of America to complete the graduate studies required for the degree of Doctor of Sacred Theology. He received that degree in 1942. The following fall he entered the Graduate School of Canon Law of the same University, and received the degree of Bachelor of Canon Law in 1943, and the degree of Licentiate of Canon Law in 1944.

CANON LAW STUDIES *

1. Freriks, Rev. Celestine A., C.PP.S., J.C.D., Religious Congregations in Their External Relations, 121 pp., 1916.
2. Galliher, Rev. Daniel M., O.P., J.C.D., Canonical Elections, 117 pp., 1917.
3. Borkowski, Rev. Aurelius L., O.F.M., J.C.D., De Confraternitatibus Ecclesiasticis, 136 pp., 1918.
4. Castillo, Rev. Cayo, J.C.D., Disertacion Historico-Canonica sobre la Potestad del Cabildo en Sede Vacante o Impedida del Vicario Capitular, 99 pp., 1919 (1918).
5. Kubelbeck, Rev. William J., S.T.B., J.C.D., The Sacred Penitentiaria and Its Relation to Faculties of Ordinaries and Priests, 129 pp., 1918.
6. Petrovits, Rev. Joseph, J.C., S.T.D., J.C.D., The New Church Law on Matrimony, X-461 pp., 1919.
7. Hickey, Rev. John J., S.T.B., J.C.D., Irregularities and Simple Impediments in the New Code of Canon Law, 100 pp., 1920.
8. Klekotka, Rev. Peter J., S.T.B., J.C.D., Diocesan Consultors, 179 pp., 1920.
9. Wanenmacher, Rev. Francis, J.C.D., The Evidence in Ecclesiastical Procedure Affecting the Marriage Bond, 1920 (Printed 1935).
10. Golden, Rev. Henry Francis, J.C.D., Parochial Benefices in the New Code, IV-119 pp., 1921 (Printed 1925).
11. Koudelka, Rev. Charles J., J.C.D., Pastors, Their Rights and Duties According to the New Code of Canon Law, 211 pp., 1921.
12. Melo, Rev. Antonius, O.F.M., J.C.D., De Exemptione Regularium, X-188 pp., 1921.
13. Schaaf, Rev. Valentine Theodore, O.F.M., S.T.B., J.C.D., The Cloister, X-180 pp., 1921.
14. Burke, Rev. Thomas Joseph, S.T.D., J.C.D., Competence in Ecclesiastical Tribunals, IV-117 pp., 1922.
15. Leech, Rev. George Leo, J.C.D., A Comparative Study of the Constitution "Apostolicae Sedis" and the "Codex Juris Canonici," 179 pp., 1922.
16. Motry, Rev. Hubert Louis, S.T.D., J.C.D., Diocesan Faculties According to the Code of Canon Law, II-167 pp., 1922.
17. Murphy, Rev. George Lawrence, J.C.D., Delinquencies and Penalties in the Administration and the Reception of the Sacraments, IV-121 pp., 1923.
18. O'Reilly, Rev. John Anthony, S.T.B., J.C.D., Ecclesiastical Sepulture in the New Code of Canon Law, II-129 pp., 1923.

---

* From nn. 1-100 inclusive only nn. 25 and 57 are still obtainable.
From n. 101 onward all numbers are available except the following: nn. 101-118 inclusive, and also n. 122.

19. MICHALICKA, REV. WENCESLAS CYRILL, O.S.B., J.C.D., Judicial Procedure in Dismissal of Clerical Exempt Religious, 107 pp., 1923.
20. DARGIN, REV. EDWARD VINCENT, S.T.B., J.C.D., Reserved Cases According to the Code of Canon Law, IV-103 pp., 1924.
21. GODFREY, REV. JOHN A., S.T.B., J.C.D., The Right of Patronage According to the Code of Canon Law, 153 pp., 1924.
22. HAGEDORN, REV. FRANCIS EDWARD, J.C.D., General Legislation on Indulgences, II-154 pp., 1924.
23. KING, REV. JAMES IGNATIUS, J.C.D., The Administration of the Sacraments to Dying Non-Catholics, V-141 pp., 1924.
24. WINSLOW, REV. FRANCIS JOSEPH, O.F.M., J.C.D., Vicars and Prefects Apostolic, IV-149 pp., 1924.
25. CORREA, REV. JOSE SERVELION, S.T.L., J.C.D., La Potestad Legislativa de la Iglesia Catolica, IV-127 pp., 1925.
26. DUGAN, REV. HENRY FRANCIS, A.M., J.C.D., The Judiciary Department of the Diocesan Curia, 87 pp., 1925.
27. KELLER, REV. CHARLES FREDERICK, S.T.B., J.C.D., Mass Stipends, 167 pp., 1925.
28. PASCHANG, REV. JOHN LINUS, J.C.D., The Sacramentals According to the Code of Canon Law, 129 pp., 1925.
29. PIONTEK, REV. CYRILLUS, O.F.M., S.T.B., J.C.D., De Indulto Exclaustrationis necnon Saecularizationis, XIII-289 pp., 1925.
30. KEARNEY, REV. RICHARD JOSEPH, S.T.B., J.C.D., Sponsors at Baptism According to the Code of Canon Law, IV-127 pp., 1925.
31. BARTLETT, REV. CHESTER JOSEPH, A.M., LL.B., J.C.D., The Tenure of Parochial Property in the United States of America, V-108 pp., 1926.
32. KILKER, REV. ADRIAN JEROME, J.C.D., Extreme Unction, V-425 pp., 1926.
33. MCCORMICK, REV. ROBERT EMMETT, J.C.D., Confessors of Religious, VIII-266 pp., 1926.
34. MILLER, REV. NEWTON THOMAS, J.C.D., Founded Masses According to the Code of Canon Law, VII-93 pp., 1926.
35. ROELKER, REV. EDWARD G., S.T.D., J.C.D., Principles of Privilege According to the Code of Canon Law, XI-166 pp., 1926.
36. BAKALARCZYK, REV. RICHARDUS, M.I.C., J.U.D., De Novitiatu, VIII-208 pp., 1927.
37. PIZZUTI, REV. LAWRENCE, O.F.M., J.U.L., De Parochis Religiosis, 1927. (Not Printed.)
38. BLILEY, REV. NICHOLAS MARTIN, O.S.B., J.C.D., Altars According to the Code of Canon Law, XIX-132 pp., 1927.
39. BROWN, MR. BRENDAN FRANCIS, A.B., LL.M., J.U.D., The Canonical Juristic Personality with Special Reference to its Status in the United States of America, V-212 pp., 1927.
40. CAVANAUGH, REV. WILLIAM THOMAS, C.P., J.U.D., The Reservation of the Blessed Sacrament, VIII-101 pp., 1927.

41. DOHENY, REV. WILLIAM J., C.S.C., A.B., J.U.D., Church Property: Modes of Acquisition, X-118 pp., 1927.
42. FELDHAUS, REV. ALOYSIUS H., C.PP.S., J.C.D., Oratories, IX-141 pp., 1927.
43. KELLY, REV. JAMES PATRICK, A.B., J.C.D., The Jurisdiction of the Simple Confessor, X-208 pp., 1927.
44. NEUBERGER, REV. NICHOLAS J., J.C.D., Canon 6 or the Relation of the Codex Juris Canonici to the Preceding Legislation, V-95 pp., 1927.
45. O'KEEFE, REV. GERALD MICHAEL, J.C.D., Matrimonial Dispensations, Powers of Bishops, Priests, and Confessors, VIII-232 pp., 1927.
46. QUIGLEY, REV. JOSEPH A. M., A.B., J.C.D., Condemned Societies, 139 pp., 1927.
47. ZAPLOTNIK, REV. JOHANNES LEO, J.C.D., De Vicariis Foraneis, X-142 pp., 1927.
48. DUSKIE, REV. JOHN ALOYSIUS, A.B., J.C.D., The Canonical Status of the Orientals in the United States, VIII-196 pp., 1928.
49. HYLAND, REV. FRANCIS EDWARD, J.C.D., Excommunication, Its Nature, Historical Development and Effects, VIII-181 pp., 1928.
50. REINMANN, REV. GERALD JOSEPH, O.M.C., J.C.D., The Third Order Secular of Saint Francis, 201 pp., 1928.
51. SCHENK, REV. FRANCIS J., J.C.D., The Matrimonial Impediments of Mixed Religion and Disparity of Cult, XVI-318 pp., 1929.
52. COADY, REV. JOHN JOSEPH, S.T.D., J.U.D., A.M., The Appointment of Pastors, VIII-150 pp., 1929.
53. KAY, REV. THOMAS HENRY, J.C.D., Competence in Matrimonial Procedure, VIII-164 pp., 1929.
54. TURNER, REV. SIDNEY JOSEPH, C.P., J.U.D., The Vow of Poverty, XLIX-217 pp., 1929.
55. KEARNEY, REV. RAYMOND A., A.B., S.T.D., J.C.D., The Principles of Delegation, VII-149 pp., 1929.
56. CONRAN, REV. EDWARD JAMES, A.B., J.C.D., The Interdict, V-163 pp., 1930.
57. O'NEILL, REV. WILLIAM H., J.C.D., Papal Rescripts of Favor, VII-218 pp., 1930.
58. BASTNAGEL, REV. CLEMENT VINCENT, J.U.D., The Appointment of Parochial Adjutants and Assistants, XV-257 pp., 1930.
59. FERRY, REV. WILLIAM A., A.B., J.C.D., Stole Fees, V-136 pp., 1930.
60. COSTELLO, REV. JOHN MICHAEL, A.B., J.C.D., Domicile and Quasi-Domicile, VII-201 pp., 1930.
61. KREMER, REV. MICHAEL NICHOLAS, A.B., S.T.B., J.C.D., Church Support in the United States, VI-136 pp., 1930.
62. ANGULO, REV. LUIS, C.M., J.C.D., Legislation de la Iglesia sobre la intencion en la application de la Santa Misa, VII-104 pp., 1931.
63. FREY, REV. WOLFGANG NORBERT, O.S.B., A.B., J.C.D., The Act of Religious Profession, VIII-174 pp., 1931.

64. Roberts, Rev. James Brendan, A.B., J.C.D., The Banns of Marriage, XIV-140 pp., 1931.
65. Ryder, Rev. Raymond Aloysius, A.B., J.C.D., Simony, IX-151 pp., 1931.
66. Campagna, Rev. Angelo, Ph.D., J.U.D., Il Vicario Generale del Vescovo, VII-205 pp., 1931.
67. Cox, Rev. Joseph Godfrey, A.B., J.C.D., The Administration of Seminaries, VI-124 pp., 1931.
68. Gregory, Rev. Donald J., J.U.D., The Pauline Privilege, XV-165 pp., 1931.
69. Donohue, Rev. John F., J.C.D., The Impediment of Crime, VII-110 pp., 1931.
70. Dooley, Rev. Eugene A., O.M.I., J.C.D., Church Law on Sacred Relics, IX-143 pp., 1931.
71. Orth, Rev. Clement Raymond, O.M.C., J.C.D., The Approbation of Religious Institutes, 171 pp., 1931.
72. Pernicone, Rev. Joseph M., A.B., J.C.D., The Ecclesiastical Prohibition of Books, XII-267 pp., 1932.
73. Clinton, Rev. Connell, A.B., J.C.D., The Paschal Precept, IX-108 pp., 1932.
74. Donnelly, Rev. Francis B., A.M., S.T.L., J.C.D., The Diocesan Synod, VIII-125 pp., 1932.
75. Torrente, Rev. Camilo, C.M.F., J.C.D., Las Procesiones Sagradas, V-145 pp., 1932.
76. Murphy, Rev. Edwin J., C.PP.S., J.C.D., Suspension Ex Informata Conscientia, XI-122 pp., 1932.
77. MacKenzie, Rev. Eric F., A.M., S.T.L., J.C.D., The Delict of Heresy in its Commission, Penalization, Absolution, VII-124 pp., 1932.
78. Lyons, Rev. Avitus E., S.T.B., J.C.D., The Collegiate Tribunal of First Instance, XI-147 pp., 1932.
79. Connolly, Rev. Thomas A., J.C.D., Appeals, XI-195, pp., 1932.
80. Sangmeister, Rev. Joseph V., A.B., J.C.D., Force and Fear as Precluding Matrimonial Consent, V-211 pp., 1932.
81. Jaeger, Rev. Leo A., A.B., J.C.D., The Administration of Vacant and Quasi-Vacant Episcopal Sees in the United States, IX-229 pp., 1932.
82. Rimlinger, Rev. Herbert T., J.C.D., Error Invalidating Matrimonial Consent, VII-79 pp., 1932.
83. Barrett, Rev. John D. M., S.S., J.C.D., A Comparative Study of the Third Plenary Council of Baltimore and the Code, IX-221 pp., 1932.
84. Carberry, Rev. John J., Ph.D., S.T.D., J.C.D., The Juridical Form of Marriage, X-177 pp., 1934.
85. Dolan, Rev. John L., A.B., J.C.D., The Defensor Vinculi, XII-157 pp., 1934.
86. Hannan, Rev. Jerome D., A.M., S.T.D., LL.B., J.C.D., The Canon Law of Wills, IX-517 pp., 1934.

87. LEMIEUX, REV. DELISE A., A.M., J.C.D., The Sentence in Ecclesiastical Procedure, IX-131 pp., 1934.
88. O'ROURKE, REV. JAMES J., A.B., J.C.D., Parish Registers, VII-109 pp., 1934.
89. TIMLIN, REV. BARTHOLOMEW, O.F.M., A.M., J.C.D., Conditional Matrimonial Consent, X-381 pp., 1934.
90. WAHL, REV. FRANCIS X., A.B., J.C.D., The Matrimonial Impediments of Consanguinity and Affinity, VI-125 pp., 1934.
91. WHITE, REV. ROBERT J., A.B., LL.B., S.T.B., J.C.D., Canonical Ante-Nuptial Promises and the Civil Law, VI-152 pp., 1934.
92. HERRERA, REV. ANTONIO PARRA, O.C.D., J.C.D., Legislacion Ecclesiastica sobra el Ayuno y la Abstinencia, XI-191 pp., 1935.
93. KENNEDY, REV. EDWIN J., J.C.D., The Special Matrimonial Process in Cases of Evident Nullity, X-165 pp., 1935.
94. MANNING, REV. JOHN J., A.B., J.C.D., Presumption of Law in Matrimonial Procedure, XI-111 pp., 1935.
95. MOEDER, REV. JOHN M., J.C.D., The Proper Bishop for Ordination and Dismissorial Letters, VII-135 pp., 1935.
96. O'MARA, REV. WILLIAM A., A.B., J.C.D., Canonical Causes for Matrimonial Dispensations, IX-155 pp., 1935.
97. REILLY, REV. PETER, J.C.D., Residence of Pastors, IX-81 pp., 1935.
98. SMITH, REV. MARINER T., O.P., S.T.Lr., J.C.D., The Penal Law for Religious, VIII-169 pp., 1935.
99. WHALEN, REV. DONALD W., A.M., J.C.D., The Value of Testimonial Evidence in Matrimonial Procedure, XIII-297 pp., 1935.
100. CLEARY, REV. JOSEPH F., J.C.D., Canonical Limitations on the Alienation of Church Property, VIII-141 pp., 1936.
101. GLYNN, REV. JOHN C., J.C.D., The Promoter of Justice, XX-337 pp., 1936.
102. BRENNAN, REV. JAMES H., S.S., M.A., S.T.B., J.C.D., The Simple Convalidation of Marriage, VI-135 pp., 1937.
103. BRUNINI, REV. JOSEPH BERNARD, J.C.D., The Clerical Obligations of Canons 139 and 142, X-121 pp., 1937.
104. CONNOR, REV. MAURICE, A.B., J.C.D., The Administrative Removal of Pastors, VIII-159 pp., 1937.
105. GUILFOYLE, REV. MERLIN JOSEPH, J.C.D., Custom, XI-144 pp., 1937.
106. HUGHES, REV. JAMES AUSTIN, A.B., A.M., J.C.D., Witnesses in Criminal Trials of Clerics, IX-140 pp., 1937.
107. JANSEN, REV. RAYMOND J., A.B., S.T.L., J.C.D., Canonical Provisions for Catechetical Instruction, VII-153 pp., 1937.
108. KEALY, REV. JOHN JAMES, A.B., J.C.D., The Introductory Libellus in Church Court Procedure, XI-121 pp., 1937.
109. McMANUS, REV. JAMES EDWARD, C.SS.R., J.C.D., The Administration of Temporal Goods in Religious Institutes, XVI-196 pp., 1937.

110. Moriarty, Rev. Eugene James, J.C.D., Oaths in Ecclesiastical Courts, X-115 pp., 1937.
111. Rainer, Rev. Eligius George, C.SS.R., J.C.D., Suspension of Clerics, XVII-249 pp., 1937.
112. Reilly, Rev. Thomas F., C.SS.R., J.C.D., Visitation of Religious, VI-195 pp., 1938.
113. Moriarty, Rev. Francis E., C.SS.R., J.C.D., The Extraordinary Absolution from Censures, XV-334 pp., 1938.
114. Connolly, Rev. Nicholas P., J.C.D., The Canonical Erection of Parishes, X-132 pp., 1938.
115. Donovan, Rev. James Joseph, J.C.D., The Pastor's Obligation in Prenuptial Investigation, XII-322 pp., 1938.
116. Harrigan, Rev. Robert J., M.A., S.T.B., J.C.D., The Radical Sanation of Invalid Marriages, VIII-208 pp., 1938.
117. Boffa, Rev. Conrad Humbert, J.C.D., Canonical Provisions for Catholic Schools, VII-211 pp., 1939.
118. Parsons, Rev. Anscar John, O.M.Cap., J.C.D., Canonical Elections, XII-236 pp., 1939.
119. Reilly, Rev. Edward Michael, A.B., J.C.D., The General Norms of Dispensation, XII-156 pp., 1939.
120. Ryan, Rev. Gerald Aloysius, A.B., J.C.D., Principles of Episcopal Jurisdiction, XII-172 pp., 1939.
121. Burton, Rev. Francis James, C.S.C., A.B., J.C.D., A Commentary on Canon 1125, X-222 pp., 1940.
122. Miaskiewicz, Rev. Francis Sigismund, J.C.D., Supplied Jurisdiction According to Canon 209, XII-340 pp., 1940.
123. Rice, Rev. Patrick William, A.B., J.C.D., Proof of Death in Prenuptial Investigation, VIII-156 pp., 1940.
124. Anglin, Rev. Thomas Francis, M.S., J.C.D., The Eucharistic Fast, VIII-183 pp., 1941.
125. Coleman, Rev. John Jerome, J.C.D., The Minister of Confirmation, VI-153 pp., 1941.
126. Downs, Rev. John Emmanuel, A.B., J.C.D., The Concept of Clerical Immunity, XI-163 pp., 1941.
127. Esswein, Rev. Anthony Albert, J.C.D., Extrajudicial Penal Powers of Ecclesiastical Superiors, X-144 pp., 1941.
128. Farrell, Rev. Benjamin Francis, M.A., S.T.L., J.C.D., The Rights and Duties of the Local Ordinary Regarding Congregations of Women Religious of Pontifical Approval, V-195 pp., 1941.
129. Feeney, Rev. Thomas John, A.B., S.T.L., J.C.D., Restitutio in Integrum, VI-169 pp., 1941.
130. Findlay, Rev. Stephen William, O.S.B., A.B., J.C.D., Canonical Norms Governing the Deposition and Degradation of Clerics, XVII-279 pp., 1941.

131. GOODWINE, REV. JOHN, A.B., S.T.L., J.C.D., The Right of the Church to Acquire Property, VIII-119 pp., 1941.
132. HESTON, REV. EDWARD LOUIS, C.S.C., Ph.D., S.T.D., J.C.D., The Alienation of Church Property in the United States, XII-222 pp., 1941.
133. HOGAN, REV. JAMES JOHN, A.B., S.T.L., J.C.D., Judicial Advocates and Procurators, XIII-200 pp., 1941.
134. KEALY, REV. THOMAS M., A.B., Litt.B., J.C.D., Dowry of Women Religious, IX-152 pp., 1941.
135. KEENE, REV. MICHAEL JAMES, O.S.B., J.C.D., Religious Ordinaries and Canon 198, V-164 pp., 1942.
136. KERIN, REV. CHARLES A., S.S., M.A., S.T.B., J.C.D., The Privation of Christian Burial, XVI-279 pp., 1941.
137. LOUIS, REV. WILLIAM FRANCIS, M.A., J.C.D., Diocesan Archives, X-101 pp., 1941.
138. MCDEVITT, REV. GILBERT JOSEPH, A.B., J.C.D., Legitimacy and Legitimation, X-247 pp., 1941.
139. MCDONOUGH, REV. THOMAS JOSEPH, A.B., J.C.D., Apostolic Administrators, X-217 pp., 1941.
140. MEIER, REV. CARL ANTHONY, A.B., J.C.D., Penal Administrative Procedure Against Negligent Pastors, XI-240 pp., 1941.
141. SCHMIDT, REV. JOHN ROGG, A.B., J.C.D., The Principles of Authentic Interpretation in Canon 17 of the Code of Canon Law, XII-331 pp., 1941.
142. SLAFKOSKY, REV. ANDREW LEONARD, A.B., J.C.D., The Canonical Episcopal Visitation of the Diocese, X-197 pp., 1941.
143. SWOBODA, REV. INNOCENT ROBERT, O.F.M., J.C.D., Ignorance in Relation to the Imputability of Delicts, IX-271 pp., 1941.
144. DUBÉ, REV. ARTHUR JOSEPH, A.B., J.C.D., The General Principles for the Reckoning of Time in Canon Law, VIII-299 pp., 1941.
145. MCBRIDE, REV. JAMES T., A.B., J.C.D., Incardination and Excardination of Seculars, XX-585 pp., 1941.
146. KRÓL, REV. JOHN T., J.C.D., The Defendant in Ecclesiastical Trials, XII-207 pp., 1942.
147. COMYNS, REV. JOSEPH J., C.SS.R., A.B., J.C.D., Papal and Episcopal Administration of Church Property, XIV-155 pp., 1942.
148. BARRY, REV. GARRETT FRANCIS, O.M.I., J.C.D., Violation of the Cloister, XII-260 pp., 1942.
149. BOLDUC, REV. GATIEN, C.S.V., A.B., S.T.L., J.C.D., Les Études dans les Religions Cléricales, VIII-155 pp., 1942.
150. BOYLE, REV. DAVID JOHN, M.A., J.C.D., The Juridic Effects of Moral Certitude on Pre-Nuptial Guarantees, XII-188 pp., 1942.
151. CANAVAN, REV. WALTER JOSEPH, M.A., Litt.D., J.C.D., The Profession of Faith, XII-143 pp., 1942.
152. DESROCHERS, REV. BRUNO, A.B., Ph.L., S.T.B., J.C.D., Le Premier Concile Plénier de Québec et le Code de Droit Canonique, XIV-186 pp., 1942.

153. Dillon, Rev. Robert Edward, A.B., J.C.D., Common Law Marriage, X-148 pp., 1942.
154. Dodwell, Rev. Edward John, Ph.D., S.T.B., J.C.D., The Time and Place for the Celebration of Marriage, X-156 pp., 1942.
155. Donnellan, Rev. Thomas Andrew, A.B., J.C.D., The Obligation of the Missa pro Populo, VII-131 pp., 1942.
156. Eltz, Rev. Louis Anthony, A.B., J.C.D., Cooperation in Crime, XII-208 pp., 1942.
157. Gass, Rev. Sylvester Francis, M.A., J.C.D., Ecclesiastical Pensions, XI-206 pp., 1942.
158. Guiniven, Rev. John Joseph, C.SS.R., J.C.D., The Precept of Hearing Mass, XIV-188 pp., 1942.
159. Gulczynski, Rev. John Theophilus, J.C.D., The Desecration and Violation of Churches, X-126 pp., 1942.
160. Hammill, Rev. John Leo, M.A., J.C.D., The Obligations of the Traveler According to Canon 14, VIII-204 pp., 1942.
161. Haydt, Rev. John Joseph, A.B., J.C.D., Reserved Benefices, XI-148 pp., 1942.
162. Huser, Rev. Roger John, O.F.M., A.B., J.C.D., The Crime of Abortion in Canon Law, XII-187 pp., 1942.
163. Kearney, Rev. Francis Patrick, A.B., S.T.L., J.C.D., The Principles of Canon 1127, X-162 pp., 1942.
164. Linahen, Rev. Leo James, S.T.L., J.C.D., De Absolutione Complicis in Peccato Turpi, V-114 pp., 1942.
165. McCloskey, Rev. Joseph Aloysius, A.B., J.C.D., The Subject of Ecclesiastical Law According to Canon 12, XVII-246 pp., 1942.
166. O'Neill, Rev. Francis Joseph, C.SS.R., J.C.D., The Dismissal of Religious in Temporary Vows, XIII-220 pp., 1942.
167. Prince, Rev. John Edward, A.B., S.T.B., J.C.D., The Diocesan Chancellor, X-136 pp., 1942.
168. Riesner, Rev. Albert Joseph, C.SS.R., J.C.D., Apostates and Fugitives from Religious Institutes, IX-168 pp., 1942.
169. Stenger, Rev. Joseph Bernard, J.C.D., The Mortgaging of Church Property, 186 pp., 1942.
170. Waldron, Rev. Joseph Francis, A.B., J.C.D., The Minister of Baptism, XII-197 pp., 1942.
171. Willett, Rev. Robert Albert, J.C.D., The Probative Value of Documents in Ecclesiastical Trials, X-124 pp., 1942.
172. Woeber, Rev. Edward Martin, M.A., J.C.D., The Interpellations, XII-161 pp., 1942.
173. Benko, Rev. Matthew Aloysius, O.S.B., M.A., J.C.D., The Abbot *Nullius*, XVI-148 pp., 1943.
174. Christ, Rev. Joseph James, M.A., S.T.L., J.C.D., Dispensation from Vindicative Penalties, XIV-285 pp., 1943.

175. Clancy, Rev. Patrick M. J., O.P., A.B., S.T.Lr., J.C.D., The Local Religious Superior, X-229 pp., 1943.
176. Clarke, Rev. Thomas James, J.C.D., Parish Societies, XII-147 pp., 1943.
177. Connolly, Rev. John Patrick, S.T.L., J.C.D., Synodal Examiners and Parish Priest Consultors, X-223 pp., 1943.
178. Drumm, Rev. William Martin, A.B., J.C.D., Hospital Chaplains, XII-175 pp., 1943.
179. Flanagan, Rev. Bernard Joseph, A.B., S.T.L., J.C.D., The Canonical Erection of Religious Houses, X-147 pp., 1943.
180. Kelleher, Rev. Stephen Joseph, A.B., S.T.B., J.C.D., Discussions with Non-Catholics: Canonical Legislation, X-93 pp., 1943.
181. Lewis, Rev. Gordian, C.P., J.C.D., Chapters in Religious Institutes, XII-169 pp., 1943.
182. Marx, Rev. Adolph, J.C.D., The Declaration of Nullity of Marriages Contracted Outside the Church, X-151 pp., 1943.
183. Matulenas, Rev. Raymond Anthony, O.S.B., A.B., J.C.D., Communication, a Source of Privileges, XII-225 pp., 1943.
184. O'Leary, Rev. Charles Gerard, C.SS.R., J.C.D., Religious Dismissed After Perpetual Profession, X-213 pp., 1943.
185. Power, Rev. Cornelius Michael, J.C.D., The Blessing of Cemeteries, XII-231 pp., 1943.
186. Shuhler, Rev. Ralph Vincent, O.S.A., J.C.D., Privileges of Religious to Absolve and Dispense, XII-195 pp., 1943.
187. Ziolkowski, Rev. Thaddeus Stanislaus, A.B., J.C.D., The Consecration and Blessing of Churches, XII-151 pp., 1943.
188. Heneghan, Rev. John Joseph, S.T.D., J.C.D., The Marriages of Unworthy Catholics: Canons 1065 and 1066, XVI-213 pp., 1944.
189. Carroll, Rev. Coleman Francis, M.A., S.T.L., J.C.L., Charitable Institutions.
190. Ciesluk, Rev. Joseph Edward, Ph.B., S.T.L., J.C.L., National Parishes in the United States.
191. Coburn, Rev. Vincent Paul, A.B., J.C.D., Marriages of Conscience, XII-172 pp., 1944.
192. Connors, Rev. Charles Paul, C.S.Sp., A.B., J.C.D., Extra-Judicial Procurators in the Code of Canon Law, X-94 pp., 1944.
193. Coyle, Rev. Paul Raymond, A.B., J.C.D., Judicial Exceptions, X-142 pp., 1944.
194. Fair, Rev. Bartholomew Francis, A.B., S.T.L., J.C.L., The Impediment of Abduction.
195. Gallagher, Rev. Thomas Raphael, O.P., A.B., S.T.Lr., J.C.D., The Examination of the Qualities of the Ordinand, X-166 pp., 1944.
196. Gannon, Rev. John Mark, S.T.L., J.C.D., The Interstices Required for the Promotion to Orders, XII-100 pp., 1944.

197. Goldsmith, Rev. J. William, B.C.S., S.T.L., J.C.D., The Competence of Church and State Over Marriages—Disputed Points, X-128 pp., 1944.

198. Goodwine, Rev. Joseph Gerard, A.B., S.T.B., J.C.D., The Reception of Converts, XIV-326 pp., 1944.

199. Kowalski, Rev. Romuald Eugene, O.F.M., A.B., J.C.D., Sustenance of Religious Houses of Regulars, X-174 pp., 1944.

200. McCoy, Rev. Alan Edward, O.F.M., J.C.D., Force and Fear in Relation to Delictual Imputability and Penal Responsibility, XII-160 pp., 1944.

201. McDevitt, Rev. Vincent John, Ph.B., S.T.L., J.C.L., Perjury.

202. Martin, Rev. Thomas Owen, Ph.D., S.T.D., J.C.D., Adverse Possession, Prescription and Limitation of Actions: The Canonical "Praescriptio," XX-208 pp., 1944.

203. Miklosovic, Rev. Paul John, A.B., J.C.L., Attempted Marriages and Their Consequent Juridic Effects.

204. Mundy, Rev. Thomas Maurice, A.B., S.T.L., J.C.D., The Union of Parishes, X-164 pp., 1944.

205. O'Dea, Rev. John Coyle, A.B., J.C.D., The Matrimonial Impediment of Nonage, VIII-126 pp., 1944.

206. Olalia, Rev. Alexander Ayson, S.T.L., J.C.D., A Comparative Study of the Christian Constitution of States and the Constitution of the Philippine Commonwealth, XII-136 pp., 1944.

207. Poisson, Rev. Pierre-Marie, C.S.C., A.B., Ph.L., Th.L., J.C.L., Droits Patrimoniaux des Maisons et des Eglises Religieuses.

208. Stadalnikas, Rev. Casimir Joseph, M.I.C., J.C.D., Reservation of Censures, X-141 pp., 1944.

209. Sullivan, Rev. Eugene Henry, S.T.L., J.C.D., Proof of the Reception of the Sacraments, X-165 pp., 1944.

210. Vaughan, Rev. William Edward, J.C.D., Constitutions for Diocesan Courts, X-210 pp., 1944.

211. Paro, Rev. Gino, S.T.D., J.C.L., The Right of Apostolic Legation.

212. Balzer, Rev. Ralph Francis, C.P., J.C.L., The Computation of Time in a Canonical Novitiate.

213. Dougherty, Rev. John Whelan, A.B., S.T.L., J.C.L., De Inquisitione Speciali.

214. Dziob, Rev. Michael Walter, J.C.L., The Sacred Congregation for the Oriental Church.

215. Eidenschink, Rev. John Albert, O.S.B., B.A., J.C.L., The Election of Bishops in the Letters of Pope Gregory the Great.

216. Gill, Rev. Nicholas, C.P., J.C.L., The Spiritual Prefect in Clerical Religious Houses of Study.

217. Hynes, Rev. Harry Gerard, S.T.L., J.C.D., The Privileges of Cardinals, XII-183 pp., 1945.

218. McDevitt, Rev. Gerald Vincent, S.T.L., J.C.D., The Renunciation of an Ecclesiastical Office, XIV-179 pp., 1945.
219. Manning, Rev. Joseph Leroy, J.C.L., The Free Conferral of Offices.
220. Meyer, Rev. Louis G., O.S.B., A.B., S.T.B., J.C.D., Alms-gathering by Religious, XII-163 pp., 1945.
221. O'Donnell, Rev. Cletus Francis, M.A., J.C.L., The Marriage of Minors.
222. Prunskis, Rev. Joseph, J.C.D., Comparative Law, Ecclesiastical and Civil, in Lithuanian Concordat, X-161 pp., 1945.
223. Sweeney, Rev. Francis Patrick, C.SS.R., J.C.D., The Reduction of Clerics to the Lay State, X-199 pp., 1945.
224. Vogelpohl, Rev. Henry John, J.C.L., The Simple Impediments to Holy Orders.
225. Brockhaus, Rev. Thomas Aquinas, O.S.B., J.C.L., Religious who are known as *Conversi*.
226. Griese, Rev. Orville Nicholas, S.T.D., J.C.L., Marriage and the Procreation of Offspring.
227. Boudreaux, Rev. Warren Louis, J.C.L., The *"ab acatholicis nati"* of Canon 1099, § 2.
228. Bowe, Rev. Thomas Joseph, A.B., J.C.L., Religious Superioresses.
229. Diederichs, Rev. Michael Ferdinand, S.C.J., J.C.L., The Jurisdiction of the Latin Ordinaries over their Oriental Subjects.
230. Dingman, Rev. Maurice John, A.B., S.T.L., J.C.L., The Plaintiff in Contentious Trials.
231. Frison, Rev. Basil, C.M.F., M.Mus., J.C.L., The Retroactivity of Law.
232. Galvin, Rev. William Anthony, M.A., J.C.L., The Administrative Transfer of Pastors.
233. Goracy, Rev. Joseph C., J.C.L., The Diriment Matrimonial Impediment of Major Orders.
234. Hale, Rev. Joseph Francis, M.A., S.T.L., J.C.L., The Pastor of Burial.
235. Henry, Rev. Joseph Arthur, A.B., J.C.L., The Mass and Holy Communion: Interritual Law.
236. Linenberger, Rev. Herbert, C.PP.S., J.C.L., The False Denunciation of an Innocent Confessor.
237. Lowry, Rev. James Martin, A.B., J.C.L., Dispensation from Private Vows.
238. Lynch, Rev. George Edward, A.B., S.T.L., J.C.L., Coadjutors and Auxiliaries of Bishops.
239. Lynch, Rev. Timothy, M.S.SS.T., J.C.L., Contracts between Bishops and Religious Congregations.
240. McClunn, Rev. Justin David, A.B., S.T.L., J.C.L., Administrative Recourse.
241. McGarvey, Rev. Thomas Joseph, A.B., S.T.L., J.C.L., Bination.
242. McGrath, Rev. James, A.B., J.C.L., The Privilege of the Canon.
243. Marbach, Rev. Joseph Francis, A.B., J.C.L., Marriage Legislation for the Catholics of the Oriental Rites in the United States and Canada.

244. SHIMKUS, REV. BERNARD ALOYSIUS, A.B., J.C.L., The Determination and Transfer of Rite.
245. SMITH, REV. VINCENT MICHAEL, A.B., S.T.L., J.C.L., Ignorance Affecting Matrimonial Consent.
246. WACHTRLE, REV. PAUL ANTHONY, A.B., J.C.L., The Baptism of the Children of Non-Catholics.

www.ingramcontent.com/pod-product-compliance
Lightning Source LLC
LaVergne TN
LVHW050248080826
844660LV00012B/609

* 9 7 8 0 8 1 3 2 2 4 1 0 7 *